**Teacher's Edition**

# PUTTING ENGLISH TO WORK FOR WORK

RICHARD E. ROBERTS
English Department
Arlington High School
Pleasant Valley, New York

Consultant
James J. Farrell, Jr.
English Teacher, Mendham High School
Mendham, New Jersey

SILVER BURDETT COMPANY
Morristown, New Jersey
Glenview, Illinois · Palo Alto · Dallas · Atlanta

Printed in the United States of America.
Published simultaneously in Canada.



ISBN 0-382-29059-3
Library of Congress Catalog Card Number 80-54764

# CONTENTS

# A GUIDE FOR TEACHING THE PROGRAM

### *Purpose of the Program*

PUTTING ENGLISH TO WORK FOR WORK has a dual purpose. For the teacher of English it is a basic program that includes the blueprint, tools, and materials necessary for conducting a successful English course in career exploration and planning. For the students it is a textbook with a broad range of language arts activities that helps them focus on planning a career and on making an entry into the world of work.

The intent of this course is to offer students the opportunity to gain a perception of themselves and to examine their career goals. This is accomplished within the context of the program while developing the kinds of communication skills they will need and use in the working world. The program begins with the students' past experience and their present thoughts about career objectives. They are exposed to a variety of ideas and experiences both in literatures and in the real world. With this background, students are better equipped to make enlightened and realistic career decisions.

### *Scope of the Program*

Students perform best when the subject matter is of personal interest to them. In this program, the subject matter is the students themselves—their careers, their goals, their future. Once they realize that the work in this course helps them in making decisions important to them, the students are more determined to research thoroughly, write meticulously, and to examine carefully their career alternatives. They pay more attention to details that formerly had seemed to hold little relation to their future needs. The analysis of a poem for the thoughts hidden between the lines; the careful attention paid to sentence structure, punctuation, and capitalization in the writing of business letters; the patient painstaking research completed in the school library—all these skills come into full play in this course.

## Optional Assignments

Individual needs of students can be met by the optional assignments included in the program. Students with special interests have the opportunity for further exploration. For example, the teacher might have the entire class read Bill Sands's inspirational autobiography, *My Shadow Ran Fast,* and have only those students who express interest in a corporate career read the story of Watson and IBM in *Think.* The students may be required to read a magazine or newspaper profile of some prominent person whose career interests them, or perhaps they may choose to listen to a career tape about a specific job. An alternative for those motivated and equipped might be to prepare and present a photo essay describing a typical workday of someone whose career is in their field of interest.

## Organization of the Text

Effective career planning requires that students assemble and evaluate data in terms of themselves and in terms of conditions in the outside world. The first two units in the text lead students to discover basic information about themselves. This self-examination helps to determine the suitability of a career interest in the light of background, personality, capabilities, needs, and aspirations.

The third unit turns the direction of the search outward, and students take a look at opportunities in various career fields. In this unit students first begin to translate dreams into realities, and may even break away from their preliminary career objectives. The fourth unit concentrates on the procedures and strategies that help students in applying for specific jobs.

Unit Five alerts students to what they can and cannot expect once they are on the job. The sixth and last unit offers students the opportunity to appraise the data they have assembled about themselves and the career they intend to pursue.

## *Unit Organization*

Each unit, except for the sixth, has the same basic format. As an introduction, a quotation from a familiar source helps identify the theme of the unit. Below the unit number is a basic thematic statement for the unit. Next, classified as Useful Terms, are the words or expressions students should be familiar with either to understand the concepts introduced in the unit or to respond accurately and confidently to the problems presented in the report projects. Following these is a case history designed to personalize the problems and issues of the unit in a way a high school student can identify with.

The report projects comprise the most important part of the unit. Each report project is preceded by detailed notes and instructions establishing the purpose for each report and giving concise directions for completing it. Finally, the annotated list of reading selections may be utilized for a reading report requirement. These suggested readings have been thematically grouped in each unit.

## *Using the Program*

Before using this program, it should be understood that each teacher's approach ought to be unique and comfortably in accord with his or her own background, experience, temperament, and imagination. No attempt is made to impose a rigid methodology on all who teach this course. Indeed, experimentation may prove to be the key for the most successful approach. Class size and composition will certainly become a leading factor in how these materials are used. Therefore, the ideas presented here are merely suggestions based largely on the author's own classroom experience and observations in teaching this course.

## *Introducing the Unit*

Each unit begins with a famous quote and a thematic statement. Though short, both of these statements are related to the unit and can be used as the starting point for a lively class discussion. One way to launch such a discussion is to ask several of the students how they can relate the quote and thematic statement to their own background and experience.

This kind of activity will motivate students to begin thinking about their own personal life goals and about careers that may be of interest to them.

### *Using the Useful Terms*

Vocabulary exercises are an important part of this course. In Units 1–5, a section called Useful Terms introduces students to words that are associated with the ideas and concepts developed in the unit. For the most part, the words are ones commonly used in everyday employment situations.

If the words are unfamiliar to the students, they should be looked up in the Glossary and discussed. Once the definitions are familiar, students can proceed to the vocabulary exercise. Since the terms are words that working people should be aware of, it is important for students to study and know them. The vocabulary exercises found in the text can be a test to see if the students have learned the terms.

### *Assigning the Case Studies*

The case studies are short stories about young people involved in some phase of career planning. They are found in each unit and are geared to the theme of the unit.

The case studies should be assigned as homework for the students. Most students will be able to relate to these case studies, therefore useful class discussions should follow. At the end of each case study is a series of discussion questions that can be used to guide a class discussion.

### *Developing the Report Projects*

The report projects, being the backbone of the unit, require more extensive management. The teacher might wish to outline to the class the nature and scope of each of the projects for the unit. At this time the teacher might also wish to establish due dates for each report (see Appendix A) to help students plan their work more effectively. Initially, file baskets marked In and Return can be set up so that students can hand in and later claim their reports once they have been graded.

It should be mentioned that all students do not (and need not) progress at the same rate in the completion of their reports. Some students, for a variety of reasons, will take more time to complete reports than others. It is probably well to keep the deadline open for them, establishing absolute cutoff dates for submitting overdue reports only when grades must be turned in. As for the students who like to get their reports completed quickly, they can be assigned to look over the reading selections at the end of the unit. The teacher can assist these students in the choice of suitably challenging materials to be read and reported on.

Once the report projects for the unit are begun, the teacher can monitor the progress of individual students. The lead report for each unit is the Personal Essay. This is essentially a guided composition in which the student needs only to follow the outline given in the text and to provide the information called for. At the beginning of the course, the teacher should make it clear that each student must respond to every point of the outline in complete sentences. Also, the teacher might take this opportunity to help students determine how to group their sentences into paragraphs. Then, after the general instructions are given, the teacher needs to be on hand only to clarify a question or a point, to indicate where data have been left out, and to assist any student who needs help in the mechanics of writing.

Other report projects will vary in the type and amount of teacher supervision required. The method of writing letters, résumés, and job applications can be discussed with a student in a private conference to explain why certain things are better done one way than another. On the other hand, an extensive report such as the Career Monograph needs only to be checked to see if all the information called for is provided, and that it is up-to-date. The teacher may find it advisable to return a report to a student to correct or complete some portion of it before awarding a grade. There are several good reasons for doing this, not the least of which is giving the student the option of obtaining full credit.

## *The Importance of Literature*

While PUTTING ENGLISH TO WORK FOR WORK has been prepared mainly for a basic course in career exploration, the philosophy and psychology of work and careers are given a prominent place throughout the course. Many ideas and experiences are presented through the medium of literature. A short story or play is included in each of the first five units. The reading deals closely with the theme of the unit. In addition, suggested readings are given at the end of each unit. These readings are designed to further supplement the students' exposure to different experiences and ideas about the world of work.

The readings are offered only as suggestions and do not represent an exhaustive list of related literature. Most of the readings are readily available in paperback editions or are included in anthologies already on school bookshelves. The list has been annotated to help with the identification of themes and subject matter, and to stimulate the interest of students.

## *Using the Reading Report Form*

The last report for each unit is a reading report. Form B provides a model for a self-contained report form with instructions and spaces where the student can fill in answers. The report calls for identification of the selection, a paragraph that tells what is included in the reading, and finally a paragraph that describes how this selection influences the student's career plans. The books and periodicals for this reading requirement can be made available on shelves in the classroom. Each student can sign out the book or periodical of interest, read the selection, and complete a reading report. After evaluating the reports, the teacher may wish to hold conferences with certain students whose reports indicate more than a passing concern with the reading selection, or show difficulty in understanding the content.

### *Using Audiovisual Materials*

In using audiovisual materials, the teacher will be limited only by the budget allotment, the facilities in the school, and the demands of his or her time. Currently there is a huge variety of such materials available for career education programs. The best of these audiovisual materials deal with case histories involving choices and alternatives in carrer planning. During the course, the how-to films, filmstrips, or sound recordings can be used to advantage. These media presentations offer a change of pace from the standard routine of the classroom if used occasionally.

### *Scheduling Field Trips*

When dealing with career education, field trips are probably best arranged on an individual basis—except when an entire class might benefit from the experience. For example, a trip to show how a leading employer in the community is organized to process job applications or how to give new employees on-the-job training would be of value to the entire class. Since career interests are diversified, many individual visits or small group field trips would better suit the needs of the students in the class.

### *Evaluating Students*

It might be well to consider how the teacher is to evaluate student progress in a course of this kind. Career exploration is, by its very nature, a noncompetitive activity. While competition is very much a part of getting a job, one student does not compete with another at the developmental level of researching and planning a career. Logically, grading seems to have no bearing on what students learn or do not learn about themselves and the careers that interest them. The measure of this learning comes later. But respecting the need to comply with a more traditional aspect of schooling, the teacher will most likely be expected to record the student's progress.

One suggestion for evaluation is to award a standard grade of 95 or A to all assignments turned in and completed for each unit, grading down for details omitted or not covered fully.

A report not turned in at all earns a mark of zero. Grade reports are then based strictly on a simple numerical average. This grading system allows a teacher to adhere to a more objective approach as it is primarily based on the amount of work completed by the student.

Another approach to grading is to evaluate the student's communication skills. The teacher can adopt a two-grade system; one grade for thoroughness of content and the other for effectiveness of expression.

### *How the Program Evolved*

PUTTING ENGLISH TO WORK FOR WORK is the outgrowth of an earlier occupational research project introduced into the regular English curriculum in the early 1970s in a high school in New York State. By 1973 the course became a one-semester, twelfth-grade English elective. The course has continued from that time. Additions and deletions leading to the present text were derived from classroom experiences, systematic evaluations solicited from students, and information obtained from graduates, now either on the job or in continuing post-secondary educational programs.

The materials presented in this text have been used by the author in his high school for several years. Also for two years before publication, the program was field-tested in a high school in northern New Jersey. The results have been most gratifying; they clearly indicate that the text will fill a void that presently exists in the curriculum of most high schools.

The following pages contain sample forms that can be used for developing worksheets for students to use in completing some of the assignments in this course.

Form A Student's Record of Reports Completed (all units)

Form B Reading Report (all units)

Form C Employment Application (Unit 4)

Form D Cost-of-Living Report Assignments (Unit 5)

Form E Cost-of-Living Worksheets (Unit 5)

Form F Budget Report (Unit 5)

## Form A

Student's Record of Reports Completed

| Unit | Report Title | Due Date | In Date | Return Date | Grade | Comments |
|---|---|---|---|---|---|---|
| 1 | Personal Essay I | | | | | |
| | Introductory Talk | | | | | |
| | Experience Chart | | | | | |
| | Reading Report I | | | | | |
| 2 | Personal Essay II | | | | | |
| | Library Report | | | | | |
| | Taped Interview | | | | | |
| | Photo Essay | | | | | |
| | Reading Report II | | | | | |
| 3 | Personal Essay III | | | | | |
| | Work Experience Talk | | | | | |
| | [illegible] Letter | | | | | |
| | Career Monograph | | | | | |
| | Reading Report III | | | | | |
| 4 | Personal Essay IV | | | | | |
| | Résumé | | | | | |
| | Résumé Cover Letter | | | | | |
| | Job Market Survey | | | | | |
| | Job Application | | | | | |
| | Job Interview | | | | | |
| | Reading Report IV | | | | | |
| 5 | Personal Essay V | | | | | |
| | On-the-Job Clinic | | | | | |
| | Labor Laws Seminar | | | | | |
| | Educational Conference | | | | | |
| | Cost-of-Living Report | | | | | |
| | Reading Report V | | | | | |
| 6 | Personal Essay VI | | | | | |

Form B

Name:________________________________ Date:____________ Class Period ______

PUTTING ENGLISH TO WORK FOR WORK Reading Report Number ______________

## Reading Report

Directions You are required to read and report on five selections, one for each unit of the course. Supply the information called for in the spaces provided. If more space is needed, use the back of the page.

1. Class of literature (magazine article, novel, play, poem, short story, or other):

2. Author's name:

3. Title of book/title of article and publication:

4. Publisher's name:

5. Date of publication:

6. Summary of reading (brief description of the content of the selection):

7. How does the reading relate to your career development?

**Form C**

SILVER BURDETT COMPANY
250 JAMES STREET
MORRISTOWN, NEW JERSEY 07960

APPLICATION FOR EMPLOYMENT

NAME — LAST / FIRST / MIDDLE | TODAY'S DATE — MO / DAY / YR

PRESENT ADDRESS — NO. / STREET / CITY / STATE / ZIP | HOME TELEPHONE NO.

REFERRED TO SILVER BURDETT BY (PLEASE GIVE NAMES, DATES, ETC.)

Employment Agency ______________ Previously Employed ______________

Silver Burdett Employee ______________ Walk-in ______________

Advertisement ______________ Other ______________

SOCIAL SECURITY NO.

BIRTHDATE IF UNDER 18 OR OVER 65

HAVE YOU EVER BEEN EMPLOYED BY SILVER BURDETT BEFORE?

DO YOU HAVE OR HAVE YOU HAD ANY ILLNESSES, HEALTH PROBLEMS OR PHYSICAL DEFECTS THAT WOULD HINDER YOU IN THE PERFORMANCE OF YOUR DUTIES IN THE POSITION FOR WHICH YOU ARE APPLYING?

☐ NO ☐ YES (PLEASE GIVE DETAILS)

PERSON TO BE CONTACTED IN CASE OF EMERGENCY

NAME / NO. STREET / CITY / STATE / TELEPHONE NO.

POSITION OR TYPE OF WORK DESIRED | ☐ FULL TIME ☐ SUMMER ☐ PART TIME ☐ FREE LANCE | WEEKLY SALARY DESIRED | DATE YOU CAN START WORK

WHAT TYPE OF WORK DO YOU EVENTUALLY HOPE TO DO?

EDUCATION (INCLUDE SPECIALIZED AND VOCATIONAL COURSES)

| NAME OF SCHOOL | LOCATION (CITY & STATE) | TYPE OF DEGREE OR CERTIFICATE | MAJOR AND MINOR OR DESCRIPTION OF COURSE(S) | % OF EXPENSES EARNED |
|---|---|---|---|---|
| HIGH SCHOOL | | | | |
| COLLEGE/UNIVERSITY | | | | |
| COLLEGE/UNIVERSITY | | | | |
| GRADUATE SCHOOL | | | | |
| GRADUATE SCHOOL | | | | |
| OTHER | | | | |
| OTHER | | | | |

SKILLS

| TYPE? ☐ YES ☐ NO ______ W.P.M. | OFFICE, BUSINESS, EDP EQUIPMENT AND MACHINES THAT YOU CAN OPERATE | LANGUAGES, DEGREE OF PROFICIENCY (SPEAK, READ, WRITE) |
|---|---|---|
| SHORTHAND? ☐ YES ☐ NO ______ W.P.M. | | |

OTHER SKILLS, PROFESSIONAL DESIGNATIONS, LICENSES, ETC.

FORM 1073T

AN EQUAL OPPORTUNITY EMPLOYER M/F

(PLEASE TURN OVER)

## EXPERIENCE (INCLUDE ALL TEMPORARY, PART-TIME, SUMMER AND SELF EMPLOYMENT)

| NAME OF PRESENT OR LAST EMPLOYER | DATES EMPLOYED | | NAME AND TITLE OF IMMEDIATE SUPERVISOR |
|---|---|---|---|
| | STARTED | LEFT | POSITION AND DUTIES AND RESPONSIBILITIES |
| COMPLETE ADDRESS | WEEKLY SALARY | | |
| | START | FINAL | |
| TYPE OF BUSINESS | $ | $ | SPECIFIC REASON(S) FOR LEAVING |

| NAME OF NEXT PREVIOUS EMPLOYER | DATES EMPLOYED | | NAME AND TITLE OF IMMEDIATE SUPERVISOR |
|---|---|---|---|
| | STARTED | LEFT | POSITION AND DUTIES AND RESPONSIBILITIES |
| COMPLETE ADDRESS | WEEKLY SALARY | | |
| | START | FINAL | |
| TYPE OF BUSINESS | $ | $ | SPECIFIC REASON(S) FOR LEAVING |

| NAME OF NEXT PREVIOUS EMPLOYER | DATES EMPLOYED | | NAME AND TITLE OF IMMEDIATE SUPERVISOR |
|---|---|---|---|
| | STARTED | LEFT | POSITION AND DUTIES AND RESPONSIBILITIES |
| COMPLETE ADDRESS | WEEKLY SALARY | | |
| | START | FINAL | |
| TYPE OF BUSINESS | $ | $ | SPECIFIC REASON(S) FOR LEAVING |

## MILITARY

HAVE YOU EVER SERVED IN THE ARMED FORCES OF THE U.S.? NO / YES (DETAILS BELOW)

LIST DUTIES, SCHOOLS ATTENDED AND ANY SPECIAL TRAINING RECEIVED IN SERVICE

| BRANCH OF SERVICE | DATES | | RANK AT | |
|---|---|---|---|---|
| | FROM | TO | ENTRY | SEP. |
| | | | | |
| | | | | |

## PROFESSIONAL AND CHARACTER REFERENCES (DO NOT INCLUDE RELATIVES OR FORMER EMPLOYERS)

| NAME | HOME ADDRESS | TELEPHONE | OCCUPATION | NO. YEARS KNOWN |
|---|---|---|---|---|
| NAME | HOME ADDRESS | TELEPHONE | OCCUPATION | NO. YEARS KNOWN |
| NAME | HOME ADDRESS | TELEPHONE | OCCUPATION | NO. YEARS KNOWN |

## APPLICANT'S SIGNATURE

I certify that to the best of my knowledge, all statements made are complete and correct and I understand that any misrepresentations may result in loss of employment. I agree and understand that I must pass a physical examination and have all references cleared as a condition of employment.

SIGNATURE:

## FOR PERSONNEL DEPT. USE ONLY – DO NOT WRITE BELOW

| INTERVIEWED BY | COMMENTS | REFERRAL |
|---|---|---|
| | | |

*Form D*

Name:______________________________________ Date________________

PUTTING ENGLISH TO WORK FOR WORK Class Period ________

## Assignment Sheet for Cost-of-Living Reports

| Budget Item | Student Assigned |
|---|---|
| 1 Renting a room/apartment/house | ____________________ |
| 2 Buying a home | ____________________ |
| 3 Food tastes and expense | ____________________ |
| 4 Heating methods and costs | ____________________ |
| 5 Water usage and costs | ____________________ |
| 6 Electric usage and costs | ____________________ |
| 7 Telephone service and costs | ____________________ |
| 8 Sewer assessment | ____________________ |
| 9 Private transportation expenditures | ____________________ |
| 10 Public transportation expenditures | ____________________ |
| 11 Types of life insurance and costs | ____________________ |
| 12 Health insurance services and costs | ____________________ |
| 13 Auto insurance policies and costs | ____________________ |
| 14 Other insurance costs | ____________________ |
| 15 Clothing maintenance expenditures | ____________________ |
| 16 Laundering/cleaning/pressing costs | ____________________ |
| 17 Professional health care expenditures | ____________________ |
| 18 Personal health costs | ____________________ |
| 19 Eyeglasses expénses | ____________________ |
| 20 Dental care expenditures | ____________________ |

Name: ______________________________ 

Assignment Sheet for Cost-of-Living Reports

| Budget Item | Student Assigned |
| --- | --- |
| 21 Education costs | ______________ |
| 22 Types of recreation/entertainment costs | ______________ |
| 23 Personal grooming expenditures | ______________ |
| 24 Income tax | ______________ |
| 25 School and property tax | ______________ |
| 26 Sales tax | ______________ |
| 27 Auto and personal loans | ______________ |
| 28 Charge accounts | ______________ |
| 29 Magazines and newspapers expenses | ______________ |
| 30 Annual contributions and donations | ______________ |
| 31 Annual dues | ______________ |
| 32 Annual cost of pet care | ______________ |

**Form E**

Name:______________________________ Date______________

PUTTING ENGLISH TO WORK FOR WORK Class Period __________

## Cost-of-Living Worksheet

Directions These worksheets list the sixteen main budget items given in the text. Space has been provided under each heading for you to record the data that applies to your own expenditures. As you listen to each student presentation, write all the important information and figures you will need to complete your Budget Report.

Housing:

Food:

Utilities:

Transportation:

Name:____________________________________________

Cost-of-Living Worksheet

Insurance:

Clothing:

Health Care:

Continuing Education:

Entertainment/Recreation

Grooming and Toiletries:

Name:________________________________________ Page 3

Cost-of-Living Worksheet

Taxes:

Indebtedness:

Subscriptions:

Contributions and Donations:

Dues:

Pet Care:

Form F

Name:______________________________ Date:__________

PUTTING ENGLISH TO WORK FOR WORK Class Period:_____

## Budget Report

Directions Summarize your findings from the Cost-of-Living Worksheets on this paper and total your monthly and yearly budgetary expenditures.

| | Cost per month | Cost per year |
|---|---|---|
| Housing | ________ | ________ |
| Food | ________ | ________ |
| Utilities | ________ | ________ |
| Transportation | ________ | ________ |
| Insurance | ________ | ________ |
| Clothing | ________ | ________ |
| Health Care | ________ | ________ |
| Continuing Education | ________ | ________ |
| Entertainment/Recreation | ________ | ________ |
| Grooming and Toiletries | ________ | ________ |
| Taxes | ________ | ________ |
| Indebtedness | ________ | ________ |
| Subscriptions | ________ | ________ |
| Contributions and Donations | ________ | ________ |
| Dues | ________ | ________ |
| Pet Care | ________ | ________ |
| TOTALS | ________ | ________ |

## Additional Readings • Unit 1

## Additional Activities • Unit 1

## *Additional Readings • Unit 2*

## *Additional Activities • Unit 2*

## *Additional Readings · Unit 3*

## *Additional Activities · Unit 3*

## *Additional Readings • Unit 4*

## *Additional Activities • Unit 4*

## Additional Readings • Unit 5

## Additional Activities • Unit 5

## *Additional Readings • Unit 6*

## *Additional Activities • Unit 6*

# PUTTING ENGLISH TO WORK FOR WORK

**RICHARD E. ROBERTS**
**English Department**
**Arlington High School**
**Pleasant Valley, New York**

**Consultant**
**James J. Farrell, Jr.**
**English Teacher, Mendham High School**
**Mendham, New Jersey**

SILVER BURDETT COMPANY
Morristown, New Jersey
Glenview, Illinois · Palo Alto · Dallas · Atlanta

# PUTTING ENGLISH TO WORK FOR WORK

Printed in the United States of America.
Published simultaneously in Canada.



ISBN 0-382-29058-5

# ACKNOWLEDGMENTS

The author wishes to acknowledge the pioneering contributions, the suggestions, and the willing assistance provided by fellow teacher Jim Mara through all the stages of the preparation of this text; the critical comments provided by fellow teacher Jerry Weyant for the teacher's edition; the personal contribution of Tammy Wilcox Knutson; the materials and information donated by Cris Baldwin of the Dutchess County Cooperative Extension; the encouragement, backing, and cooperation of the Arlington Central School District; and finally, the supportive offerings of members of his own immediate family.

The publisher acknowledges the assistance of the Mendham School District, Mendham, New Jersey, Mr. James J. Farrell, Jr., and his students for their help in field-testing the materials in this book.

*Photo Credits*

Cover Photo: Silver Burdett
Photos: Silver Burdett

## A WORD TO THE STUDENT

If you are using this book, you are probably wondering what English has to do with working or getting a job. English, after all, is reading poems and stories and plowing through *A Tale of Two Cities*, *Les Miserables*, *Silas Marner*, *Ethan Fromo*, or *Hamlet* trying to understand what happens and why, and then writing about it. English is also writing "well-organized" compositions of so many words or paragraphs about some common problem or perhaps some experience you've had. English is learning the meanings of new words and the spellings of old ones. English is correcting mistakes in grammar and punctuation, and maybe giving an oral report or writing a research paper where you have to use the library. These things are not ordinarily connected with work, as any of you who are now working will quickly point out. But there *is* a connection, if you choose to look for it.

First, work is a big part of your life. It's what you do for a living. It involves making tough decisions and solving difficult problems. Pain and pleasure are associated with work. There are daily frustrations and daily satisfactions, and there are conflicts. So the problems that develop in a novel or a play or a short story are really not that different from the problems you encounter as you work from day to day or as you plan your education and your future career.

As for the language arts skills in a work setting, it often happens, you are asked to explain something or to make a report. In one instance you will be asked to "tell (us) something about yourself." This can take the written form of the résumé or the personal statement on a job application, or it can take the form of an oral presentation at a job or promotion interview. In either case you've got to tell your story knowledgeably and convincingly—and this requires organization, with as few language errors as possible.

Also, it is very much in your interest to do some research to learn more about a department, a job, or a career, or perhaps some company you think you'd like to work for. And, in the library, you can learn about the laws that protect you when you work, when you can't work, and when you don't work.

Thus this Guidebook is designed to make you think actively and creatively about yourself and your future, and about the work process. You'll be involved in the same language activities as you would be in any regular English class. The only difference is that here the reports and assignments you complete will count for more than just a grade. You'll be *using* English, making it work for you in laying the solid foundations for a more successful and happier working life.

# CONTENTS

UNIT 1

## WHO AM I? 1–26



UNIT 2

## WHAT DO I WANT OUT OF LIFE? 27–68

UNIT 3

## WHAT ARE MY CHOICES 69–114



UNIT 4

## HOW DO I GO ABOUT GETTING A JOB? 115–178

UNIT 6

## WHAT HAVE I LEARNED ABOUT MYSELF AND THE CAREER THAT INTERESTS ME? 223–230

# PUTTING ENGLISH TO WORK FOR WORK

# Who Am I? 1

Make it thy business to know thyself, which is the most difficult lesson in the world.

**Cervantes**

*What are the things I must know about myself as I begin thinking seriously about work and my future?*

**Note to the Teacher**

Before you assign any work in the text, survey your class to determine the students' perception of English as a subject and how it is used outside the classroom.

Discuss the following:

**1.** What is English? What English skills have the students learned in school? How have these skills helped the students?

**2.** How many students have work experience? (Take time to discuss some of the jobs your students have held.)

**3.** Have the students used certain English skills on the job? Which ones are most important?

**4.** Did they use these skills in getting their jobs? (You may want to question the students about the English skills they used in obtaining their jobs.)

**Unit I Introduction**

Discuss the Cervantes quote with the class. You may want to ask:

**1.** What does it mean to "know yourself"?

**2.** How many of you really know yourself? Do you think there are many people who know themselves? Why or why not?

**3.** Do you agree with Cervantes's statement that knowing yourself is "the most difficult business in the world"? Explain.

**Unit I Theme**

Learning to Know Yourself

# WORDS IN ACTION

**Words in Action**
Discuss the Useful Terms with your class. All unfamiliar words should be checked with the definitions found in the Glossary. When students are ready, assign the Vocabulary Exercise.

## USEFUL TERMS

1. aptitude
2. assets
3. compensated employment
4. commitment
5. disabilities
6. employability rating
7. employment risk
8. job security
9. résumé
10. vocational skill

**Vocabulary Exercise Answers**

| | |
|---|---|
| 1. aptitude | C |
| 2. assets | F |
| 3. compensated employment | I |
| 4. commitment | J |
| 5. disabilities | G |
| 6. employability rating | D |
| 7. employment risk | E |
| 8. job security | B |
| 9. résumé | A |
| 10. vocational skill | H |

**Correcting Mistakes**
Students should correct their mistakes by checking the terms and definitions in the Glossary.

## VOCABULARY EXERCISE

*On a separate sheet of paper list the terms above. Now read the selections below. Put the letter of each selection next to the term it describes. (You may use the Glossary at the back of the book if you need help.)*

**A.** The receptionist at the employment agency was not at the desk. Susan waited. She couldn't help but notice a single sheet of paper near the phone. It was neatly typed and looked like an advertisement. It had a name, address, and phone number centered at the top of the page. In the left margin were the titles "Education" and "Business Experience." To the right of these titles was a detailed record of personal accomplishments.

**B.** The job sounded as though it was made to order for Mike. He knew basic electrical circuitry, had some door-to-door sales experience, and enjoyed meeting new people. But one thing bothered him: he had seen this ad in the paper before. It appeared at regular intervals. Well, Mike needed a job. He was interviewed for this one and was hired with little difficulty.

It wasn't long before he discovered what the problem was. The life of a field representative was short—about 18 months.

**A.** résumé
**B.** job security

You either quit, were promoted, or were fired. Unless your performance was always right up there at the top, you were in trouble and sooner or later would be let go as "dead wood."

**C.** "You mean you've never really played together as a group before?" asked Jan in disbelief as the Rhythm Kings finished their last tune of the set and were strolling away from the stand.

"Well, no . . . not exactly," said Barbara. "We all know one another and how each of us plays. We also know the songs. That means we know what to expect. But mostly, we listen. Anybody who plays jazz must listen and hear what's going on."

**D.** Scott handed the want ad circled in the paper to his father. "This sounds pretty good," he said. "What do you think, Dad?"

Mr. Milano scanned the lines: " '$200 a week guaranteed start—in the fast-growing field of industrial maintenance chemicals—no experience necessary—hi comm'd. earnings and advancement—company benefits—immediate interviews—Flan Chem. Corp. . . .' How many kids your age do you think will be applying for this job?"

C. aptitude
D. employability rating
E. employment risk

"I don't know," said Scott. "Does that matter?"

"Think," said Mr. Milano. "You're competing for the job. Suppose you're the person that has to do the hiring. You have to fill the job today and you've got fifty people to interview. Now, ten applicants have no high school diplomas, ten people who applied don't know this is a sales job, ten never thought about what they would be doing, and ten don't know anything about this company. That leaves ten people who have a high school diploma or better, who have some sales experience, who have taken some chemistry in school, and who know a little about this company and what it does. Which ones would you consider seriously for the job?"

**E.** "Your application doesn't say you graduated from high school," said the interviewer. "Did you forget to fill that in?"

"No," replied Alan. "I quit. I wasn't doing much in school. I was absent a lot. I wasn't learning anything anyway, so I quit."

"I see . . ." the interviewer paused. "Alan, we like our employees to be high school graduates and there's a reason for that. We spend quite a bit of money to train our people before we put them on a permanent assignment. We think of it as a kind of investment, and I guess one way we can assure ourselves that we've hired a person who will be successful is to look at his track record—what he's been able to accomplish on his own. A measure of that, and practically the only measure for the trainee's job, is whether he has a high school diploma or not. I'm sure you understand. . . ."

**F.** "Did you bring any sketches with you?" Mary asked the girl in the next cubicle who was also filling out a job application. "They said on the phone to bring samples of some of the things you have done."

"Oh, no," replied the girl. "I'm here for the modeling job. All I've got to show is me!"

**G.** Toni was beginning to wonder if she had bitten off more than she could chew. She had gotten the job all right. It was fielding customer complaints and answering questions for Mid-Valley Gas & Electric. In the interview she didn't think about her hearing problem because she was face-to-face with the interviewer and could *see* what was being said. But later, when she thought about it, she wasn't so sure she could handle the problems over the phone. She was told that this would be about half her job.

F. assets
G. disabilities
H. vocational skill
I. compensated employment
J. commitment

**H.** Allison had her high school diploma with her and thought that this would be enough to get a steady, well-paying job—at least, that's what everyone had said. But each place she applied to asked her what she would like to do or what she could do. She found it hard to come up with answers. It soon became clear that most companies wanted people who were trained to perform specialized functions. They had to be able to type or take shorthand; or they had to know how to operate business machines of one sort or another.

**I.** Angelo joined the Eagles Marching Band two years ago as a sophomore in high school. He had participated in many competitions and the rehearsals had taken so much of his free time. Now as a senior, he wanted a job. He wanted to work so he could earn money during his free time.

**J.** Francine went into social work knowing she would never make much money. That wasn't the important thing for her. It was helping the young people—getting them involved in wholesome activities, giving them a sense of pride in personal accomplishment, and giving them a good start in life.

# A CASE STUDY

## SHARON'S DILEMMA

Sharon was basically satisfied with her life, but felt uncertain about her future. She was 17 now, a senior in high school, but what would she be doing with her life? After graduation she would go to college and then to work. It was that simple. Or was it?

Somewhere along the way she had thought about becoming a nurse. But people said the field was overcrowded. What was the sense of going to college for four years and then finding out that there were no jobs when you graduated? Besides, she wasn't really sure she wanted to be a nurse. It was a role that had appealed to her since childhood but all that she knew about nursing came from watching television. She hadn't thought much about the work involved in nursing, or about any other career that might be right for her.

As for committing herself to a long period of special training, perhaps it was just too big a risk. Maybe it would be better for her to go to a liberal arts college and take a lot of different courses to see what she would like.

Something would turn up that she'd be interested in. She would have to wait and see. It was too much for her to worry about right now.

Sharon sensed that going away to college would be a big jump for her, leaving the sheltered world she had come to take for granted. She had been used to having others help her make decisions—parents, teachers, and guidance counselors. Soon she would have to make them for herself. She would be responsible for herself at last. No one would tell her what to do anymore. That would be good.

Still Sharon was a little nervous, uneasy about moving into a world she knew little about.

But she could probably handle college. What nagged at her now more than anything else was that suddenly she

**Sharon's Dilemma**

The Case Study concerns the theme of this unit. "Sharon's Dilemma" portrays a 17-year-old girl who is uncertain about her future.

Before assigning the reading, discuss with the students their plans upon graduation. Ask why they have selected their particular goals. Discuss the people who may have influenced their plans, and how they have come to their decisions about their future.

realized she knew so little about herself and what she wanted to do with her life.

Sharon's thoughts drifted to the other people around her: her friends at school, her brother, and her sister. How did they manage? Everyone, even her mother and father, had had to make decisions about what they wanted to do with their lives.

She wondered if her father had always wanted to be the manager of a department store. Was that why he went to college? Funny, it had never occurred to her to ask.

And what about Aunt Grace, who had been a nurse for years? Sharon never thought to ask Aunt Grace about her job. Maybe Sharon should ask both her father and Aunt Grace how they got to be what they are today.

Well, one thing was certain—she had, at least for the moment, determined that her future belonged to her. She would learn to rely on herself more and to do what she thought was best for her no matter what anyone else thought. There was consolation in her newfound confidence.

The fact is, you really never know much about yourself and what you want to do with your life until you sit down and think seriously about it. Unfortunately, most of us never carry our thinking far enough—that is, until we have to. If we are to get any satisfaction out of our work and our lives, we must first find out who we are and decide what it is we want to do, and then go on from there.

Sharon is right about one thing—it is best to depend on yourself. The trouble is, it's easy to drift away from resolutions unless they are accompanied by purposeful actions.

Sharon can ask her Aunt Grace what a job as a nurse is like, what training is needed, and why she went into the profession. Sharon can also consider doing volunteer work in a hospital nearby as a candy-striper, or serve as a counselor at a muscular dystrophy camp.

She can plan her choice of college and program of study to explore her immediate interests to see how they might be furthered. Or she can, like so many of her friends, just wait to see what happens, figuring that things will somehow work out by themselves.

If you are only vaguely aware of some of the choices and decisions you will soon have to make for yourself, and if you are a little uneasy about your future, there is no substitute for sitting down and settling a few things. Now is the time.

Begin with an idea or an interest you have and put it into motion. Write out questions for yourself. Little by little, plan a course of action intended to test your idea or further explore your interest. Substitute actions for worries. Work with concrete things as opposed to the things you can't put your finger on. Work with facts, numbers, books, newspapers, people—definite things. Get absorbed in your plans. Discuss your thoughts with others to gain more objectivity.

## Thinking It Through

1. *Describe Sharon's dilemma. Do you think she has a serious problem? Why?*
2. *Does Sharon really know herself? How do you know?*
3. *What are some of the things Sharon can do to learn more about herself and her career goals?*
4. *What are your future plans? What factors are helping you to decide what you will do once you are out of school?*
5. *Write down the one thing you would rather do more than anything else in the world. Now list all the jobs you can think of that include the thing you would most like to do. Number the jobs in order of first choice, second choice, and so on.*
6. *Ask some members of your family how they got into the work they do. Have their jobs met with their expectations? Had they originally wanted to do this type of work? Find out how they got started in their work and what they could have done to prepare themselves better.*

**Discussion Questions**

In addition to the discussion questions in the section Thinking It Through, you may want to discuss the following:

1. Sharon raises the question of what is the point of going to college for four years and then finding out there are no jobs after graduation. Isn't this a risk faced by anyone who goes for training, whether it be college, a technical school, or an occupational training course?
2. Discuss with the students ways to minimize the risks of unemployment. Discuss the *Occupational Outlook Handbook* (U.S. Department of Labor, Bureau of Labor Statistics) and its uses. Also make students aware that all occupational training institutions keep records of student placement upon graduation and will gladly provide this information upon request.
3. The students will soon be facing the same decisions as Sharon. Discuss how their situation is the same or different.
4. Encourage students to talk to their parents about career decisions their parents have made. The students might be surprised to learn how often chance determines the choice of a career. Discuss in class what the students learn from their parents.

**Report Projects**

Provide students with manila folders that will become their career files. You may want to keep these folders in a file drawer accessible to students. Establish the procedure that all report work is to be kept in these career files where it will be available when needed later in the course.

Give each student a separate copy of the **Student's Record of Reports Completed** form *(found on page T14 of the teacher's edition)*. Establish the due dates for the reports, and then explain any alternate or extra report arrangement. Establish an "in" and "returned" file and explain that when a report is completed, it goes in the "in" file and is then checked on the Student's Record of Reports Completed form. When the report has been evaluated, the teacher places it in the "returned" file. The student finds it, enters the grade in the "returned" column of the Student's Record of Reports Completed form, and files the report in his or her career file.

It is also a good idea to post a master Student's Record of Reports Completed form with the due dates filled in on a classroom bulletin board.

# REPORT PROJECTS

Before beginning work on these report projects, it would be well for you to understand that you will be doing them primarily for yourself. The results will be directly related to the amount of effort you put into them. These projects will help you become more aware of your abilities and will build your confidence when applying for a job.

As you begin this course, it would be wise to start and maintain a career file. Into this file you should place all the reports and other assignments during the school year. It will be an important guide to help you to establish yourself in the world of work.

## PERSONAL ESSAY I

***Introduction*** You are now ready to begin a project that will teach you a great deal about yourself. The information you gather is personal and will be useful to you and no one else. It will help you to evaluate yourself.

***Directions*** On a separate sheet of paper write an essay following the outline below. You should write complete statements for all the questions in the outline.

State each fact directly and definitely. Cover each point briefly, but accurately. Make the appraisal of your conduct candid and honest. Concentrate on your **assets.**

**Personal Essay I**

Before students begin this assignment, remind them to respond to all points on the outline in complete sentences without using the outline letters or numbers.

Discuss the organization of

### Outline

**A.** Personal Data

1. Name and address (My name is __________, and I live at __________)
2. Age, place of birth, marital status, family
3. Height and weight

4. Background
   a. What are your personal interests, talents, or hobbies?
   b. Are you interested in sports? Which ones?
   c. Travel experience within the United States
   d. Foreign residence or travel abroad
   e. Foreign languages you speak, read, or write. How did you acquire this ability?

B. School Experiences
   1. What do you think of your school? How would you make your school a better place to learn?
   2. Which classes do you most enjoy? (Give subjects, teachers, and reason for liking them.)
   3. Which subject would you like to pursue as a hobby or as a career?
   4. Do your school experiences lead you to read other books in your free time? Name the titles of these books.
   5. What school committees or clubs have you been a member of? What did your group accomplish?
   6. How do you get along with other students? With your teachers? In what ways could you improve your relationship with others at school?
   7. How often were you late to school last year? How many days were you absent?
   8. Have you ever quit school? (Describe the circumstances and tell what made you return.)

C. Vocational Self-Appraisal
   1. What are your present career goals or interests? At what stage are you in the pursuit of these interests? (Thinking, investigating, taking related courses or training, working at a lower-level job)

the essay. Indicate that paragraphs, in general, should follow from the major points on the outline:

A. Personal Data is paragraph one.
B. School Experiences is paragraph two.
C. Vocational Self-Appraisal is paragraph three.

Allow the students to begin this report in class and complete it overnight for homework. The teacher should move from desk to desk to assist, correct, or encourage students. Let the students know immediately that you are on hand to assist them. This is essential to an English course of this kind.

2. In general, how do you see yourself as an **employment risk** at the present time? (Excellent, good, average, poor—explain your answer.)

3. What could you bring to an interview to show you could be an **asset** to an employer? (Samples of your skills, work, licenses, school records, letters recommendations, and so on)

4. What are some of the things you think you could do to improve your **employability rating** and become more competitive in today's job market? (For example, take courses, get job-related experience or training, learn what the employers' needs are and what they are looking for in an employee.) How would you accomplish these things?

**Introductory Talk**

The objectives for the Introductory Talk and its presentation are:

1. To acquaint students with each other quickly.
2. To show students that many factors influence career decisions.

While students are thinking about particular careers, many influences may affect their choice. It is of value to know the influences that can affect the choice of a career. Perhaps there are factors the students have not considered because they don't know about them. Through the Introductory Talks students will be exposed to many such factors that will broaden their thinking about the kind of work they may choose for themselves and why.

Students should be permitted class time to prepare their talks and should be told the day the talks will be given. Essentially, these are 30 to 45 second presentations. If students seem to feel uncomfortable presenting their talk from the front of the classroom, permit them to simply stand at their desks and informally address the class and then sit down.

## PLANNING AN INTRODUCTORY TALK

***Introduction*** In this activity you are trying to learn something about yourself and about others. You want to think about your career interests and the influences affecting these choices.

***Directions*** You may plan either to introduce yourself to the class, or to pair up with a classmate and introduce each other in turn. Present the following information about yourself or your partner.

### Outline

**A.** Name ("I'm Mary Wells," or "This is Bill Stone.")

**B.** Age ("I'm seventeen years old and a senior," or "He is seventeen. . . .")

**C.** Career Interests ("Right now I am considering a career in sales," or "Bill has been thinking about a career in public health.")

**D.** Reasons for Career Interests ("I like to meet new people and talk to them and then help influence their decisions," or "Bill spent last summer as a junior lab technician with the county board of health. He worked with a microscope taking bacteria counts.")

**E.** Other factors that might have influenced your or your partner's thinking:

1. **aptitude** or interest surveys
2. interesting courses in school
3. hobbies or activities
4. the promise of earning a lot of money
5. a place in the family business
6. an excellent future for career growth
7. financial security
8. desire to make a **commitment** or contribution to society
9. special feeling for the land or sea
10. satisfaction gained by creating beauty and enjoyment for others

## PREPARING A BACKGROUND AND EXPERIENCE CHART

***Introduction*** Perhaps there is no better way to learn about yourself than to write about your experiences and your goals in life. After all, who knows more about you than you do yourself? There are always a few landmarks in the past that offer suggestions as to your present whereabouts and good routes for you to follow in the future.

By beginning and maintaining a complete personal record of your activities from month to month and year to year, you can establish or verify the direction you are taking. Such a record will help you gain confidence and knowledge that you are on the right course.

This record becomes a valuable reference later on when you begin to write your **résumé.** The Background and Experience Chart will provide a thorough account of

**Background and Experience Chart**

This is the major report for Unit I. Explain that words and thoughts have a way of getting away from us unless we write them down. The students are asked to reconstruct their lives on paper beginning when they first entered school. They are to write about successful experiences, good grades, special mentions, and commendations or prizes that have left them with a feeling of accomplishment.

As the students record their experiences they will most likely point in some vocational direction. The purpose of this report is to find that direction.

You might want to draw the first part of the chart on the board. This will give the students more confidence when they begin to organize their information on paper. Point out that the dates in the first column represent periods in their lives when something was accomplished. The second column would specify the schools they attended. The third column names the principals and teachers of the school. The next column explains the programs of study or the activities enjoyed. The last column lists the achievements attained. It is this last column that is the all important one. The good experiences, accurately recorded, show us *where* the student excels, which is the primary objective of this report.

The English skills involved in this report are recording details and organizing them into a time sequence. Many students will require help and encouragement since these skills appear to be especially difficult for young adults. Even when it concerns themselves and their future, students are not aware of how much they tend to leave out. Incomplete or disorganized reports should be returned ungraded for completion.

The last point to mention to your students is the value of this assignment in assembling later reports. Because of the detailed information the Background and Experience Chart contains, it will be used later in the course to aid in writing résumés and to fill out job application forms. The completed chart becomes the topography of the individual, showing features that will be of interest to an employer.

your education and employment history. This kind of information is used when completing job application forms. You will never be at a loss to remember a set of dates, the name of an employer or teacher, or an address and phone number. You will have a complete history of your activities since entering school.

***Directions*** Before you begin to gather information for your Background and Experience Chart, study the form on page 13. Notice that the chart is divided into three major parts: Education, Interests/Activities, and Employment. Each of these sections is arranged into five columns with appropriate headings at the top. All of your personal information can be organized around the five headings and written in the columns of your chart.

After studying the form, examine the completed model on pages 14 and 15. The personal data is arranged in a concise style which makes it easy to use when writing resumes or filling out job application forms.

Now begin to construct your Background and Experience Chart. Remember to make it as complete as possible. Use the sample headings and entries provided in the model. Check your dates; leave no gaps; account for all your time including extended vacations or periods of unemployment. Be sure your information is accurate. Above all, *stress your achievements*. You will want to save this document as you will be able to refer to it often in the future.

| BACKGROUND AND EXPERIENCE CHART – EDUCATION | | | | |
|---|---|---|---|---|
| Dates | Schools Attended/ Addresses | Principals/ Teachers | Courses Taken/ Activities | Achievements: Grades/Awards/ Honors/Certificates |
| | Elementary: | | | |
| | Middle/Junior High: | | | |
| | Senior High: | | | |
| | Post Secondary: | | | |

| BACKGROUND AND EXPERIENCE CHART – INTERESTS/ACTIVITIES | | | | |
|---|---|---|---|---|
| Dates | Activities/ Hobbies/Sports/ Special Interests | Description | Person In Charge | Achievements: Successes/Awards/ Performance/Honors |
| | | | | |

| BACKGROUND AND EXPERIENCE CHART – EMPLOYMENT | | | | |
|---|---|---|---|---|
| Dates | Employers/ Addresses | Job Title/ Description/Salary | Supervisor | Achievements: Performance/Awards/ Successes/Promotions |
| | | | | |

| BACKGROUND AND EXPERIENCE CHART – EDUCATION | | | | |
|---|---|---|---|---|
| Dates | Schools Attended/ Addresses | Principals/ Teachers | Courses Taken/ Activities | Achievements: Grades/Awards/ Honors/Certificates |
| | Elementary: | | | |
| *9/68 to 6/75* | *Lincoln School Main Street Springfield, N.Y.* | *Mrs. J. Finch, Principal* | *Grade K-6* | *Art – 95 Reading – 85 Math – 80 Spelling Bee Champ (1975)* |
| | Middle/Junior High: | | | |
| *9/75 to 6/78* | *Arlington J.H.S. West Avenue Springfield, N.Y.* | *Mrs. M. Cahill* | *English 7* | *Report: "The House We Live In" – A+* |
| | | *Mr. H. Betts* | *Woodworking* | *Bookshelf Project -- 98 Shop Assistant (1977-78)* |
| | Senior High: | | | |
| *9/78 to 6/81* | *Arlington Senior High School East Avenue Springfield, N.Y.* | *Mr. L. Chang* | *Plane Geometry* | *94 (mathematics is easy for me)* |
| | | *Ms. T. Wein* | *Sculpture* | *85 (my favorite course)* |
| | | *Mr. J. Phillips* | *Architectural Drawing* | *Won 2nd place in Modern Home Design Competition (1981)* |
| | | *Mrs. F. Green* | *Journalism* | *80 (I enjoy writing) Yearbook staff writer and photographer – 2 years* |
| | | *Mrs. E. Brown, Coach* | *Golf* | *Golf Team – 3 years* |
| | Post Secondary: | | | |
| *9/81 to 6/82* | *South Hills Community College Main Street Chester, N.Y.* | *P. David M. Bourne C. Cook I. Santos* | *Drafting 1 Blueprint Reading Technical English College Algebra* | *Planning a program in drafting, but may want to go on to school to study architecture or engineering* |

| BACKGROUND AND EXPERIENCE CHART – INTERESTS/ACTIVITIES | | | | |
|---|---|---|---|---|
| Dates | Activities/ Hobbies/Sports/ Special Interests | Description | Person in Charge | Achievements: Successes/Awards/ Performance/Honors |
| *Aug. 1975* | *Camp Waldron Dutchess County, N.Y. Boy Scout Camp* | *Camping/hiking/ nature study/ woodcraft/ swimming* | *Harry Blum, Camp Counselor* | *Advanced to First Class Scout* |
| *Aug. 1976* | *Scout trip* | *10-day canoe trip to Canada* | *Mack Davis, Troop Leader* | *Patrol Leader on trip. Responsible for three scouts and equipment* |

| BACKGROUND AND EXPERIENCE CHART – EMPLOYMENT | | | | |
|---|---|---|---|---|
| Dates | Employers/ Addresses | Job Title/ Description/Salary | Supervisor | Achievements: Performance/Awards/ Successes/Promotions |
| *6/72 to 9/78* | The Evening News *East Main Street Springfield, N.Y.* | *Newspaper carrier* | *Juan Gomez* | *In 6 years increased the size of the route from 65 to 114 newspapers* |
| *10/78 to 7/81* | *Ever-Open Supermarket* | *Part-time shelf stocker and cashier* | *Edward Duke* | *Worked after school and Saturdays* |
| *8/81 to present* | *Max's Service Station* | *Gas station attendent* | *Max Stine* | *Learning to make minor auto repairs* |

# RELATED READING

**Related Reading**

Literature is an important part of every English course. In this course all the readings are related closely to the themes of the Units. In Unit I the theme is "Learning to Know Yourself."

"A Summer's Reading" is reprinted here in its entirety. It's the story of a high school dropout who can't find a job but who has tried to convince his family and a neighbor that he is reading a lot to improve himself. This pretense begins to catch up with the boy and he finally decides he had better do what he said he was doing.

Assign the Related Reading "A Summer's Reading" to the class as homework. Then use the questions at the end of the reading selection as a guide for class discussion.

## A SUMMER'S READING

*Bernard Malamud*

George Stoyonovich was a neighborhood boy who had quit high school on an impulse when he was sixteen, run out of patience, and though he was ashamed everytime he went looking for a job, when people asked him if he had finished and he had to say no, he never went back to school. This summer was a hard time for jobs and he had none. Having so much time on his hands, George thought of going to summer school, but the kids in his classes would be too young. He also considered registering in a night high school, only he didn't like the idea of the teachers always telling him what to do. He felt they had not respected him. The result was he stayed off the streets and in his room most of the day. He was close to twenty and had needs with the neighborhood girls, but no money to spend, and he couldn't get more than an occasional few cents because his father was poor, and his sister Sophie, who resembled George, a tall bony girl of twenty-three, earned very little and what she had she kept for herself. Their mother was dead, and Sophie had to take care of the house.

Very early in the morning George's father got up to go to work in a fish market. Sophie left at about eight for her long ride in the subway to a cafeteria in the Bronx. George had his coffee by himself, then hung around in the house. When the house, a five-room railroad flat above a butcher store, got on his nerves he cleaned it up — mopped the floors with a wet mop and put things away. But most of the time he sat in his room. In the afternoons he listened to the ball game. Otherwise he had a couple of old copies of the *World Almanac* he had bought long ago, and he liked to read in them and also the magazines and newspapers that Sophie brought home, that had been left on the tables in the cafeteria. They were mostly picture magazines about movie stars and sports figures, also usually the *News* and *Mirror*. Sophie herself read whatever fell into her hands, although she sometimes read good books.

She once asked George what he did in his room all day and he said he read a lot too.

"Of what besides what I bring home? Do you ever read any worthwhile books?"

"Some," George answered, although he really didn't. He had tried to read a book or two that Sophie had in the house but found he was in no mood for them. Lately he couldn't stand made-up stories, they got on his nerves. He wished he had some hobby to work at — as a kid he was good in carpentry, but where could he work at it? Sometimes during the day he went for walks, but mostly he did his walking after the hot sun had gone down and it was cooler in the streets.

In the evening after supper George left the house and wandered in the neighborhood. During the sultry days some of the storekeepers and their wives sat in chairs on the thick, broken sidewalks in front of their shops, fanning themselves, and George walked past them and the guys hanging out on the candy store corner. A couple of them he had known his whole life, but nobody recognized each other. He had no place special to go, but generally, saving it till the last, he left the neighborhood and walked for blocks until he came to a darkly lit little park with benches and trees and an iron railing, giving it a feeling of privacy. He sat on a bench here, watching the leafy trees and the flowers blooming on the inside of the railing, thinking of a better life for himself. He thought of the jobs he had had since he had quit school — delivery boy, stock clerk, runner, lately working in a factory — and he was dissatisfied with all of them. He felt he would someday like to have a good job and live in a private house with a porch, on a street with trees. He wanted to have some dough in his pocket to buy things with, and a girl to go with, so as not to be so lonely, especially on Saturday nights. He wanted people to like and respect him. He thought about these things often but mostly when he was alone at night. Around midnight he got up and drifted back to his hot and stony neighborhood.

One time while on his walk George met Mr. Cattanzara coming home very late from work. He wondered if he was drunk but then could tell he wasn't. Mr. Cattanzara, a stocky, bald-headed man who worked in a change booth on an IRT station, lived on the next block after George's, above a shoe repair store. Nights, during the hot weather, he sat on his stoop in an undershirt, reading the *New York Times* in the light of the shoemaker's window. He read it from the first page to the last, then went up to sleep. And all the time he was reading the paper, his wife, a fat woman with a white face, leaned out of the window, gazing into the street, her thick white arms folded under her loose breast, on the window ledge.

Once in a while Mr. Cattanzara came home drunk, but it was a quiet drunk. He never made any trouble, only walked stiffly up the street and slowly climbed the stairs to the hall. Though drunk, he looked the same as always, except for his tight walk, the quietness, and that his eyes were wet. George liked Mr. Cattanzara because he remembered him giving him nickels to buy lemon ice with when he was a squirt. Mr. Cattanzara was a different type than those in the neighborhood. He asked different questions than the others when he met you, and he seemed to know what went on in all the newspapers. He read them, as his fat sick wife watched from the window.

"What are you doing with yourself this summer, George?" Mr. Cattanzara asked. "I see you walkin' around at nights."

George felt embarrassed. "I like to walk."

"What are you doin' in the day now?"

"Nothing much just right now. I'm waiting for a job." Since it shamed him to admit he wasn't working, George said, "I'm staying home — but I'm reading a lot to pick up my education."

Mr. Cattanzara looked interested. He mopped his hot face with a red handkerchief.

"What are you readin'?"

George hesitated, then said, "I got a list of books in the library once, and now I'm gonna read them this summer." He felt strange and a little unhappy saying this, but he wanted Mr. Cattanzara to respect him.

"How many books are there on it?"

"I never counted them. Maybe around a hundred."

Mr. Cattanzara whistled through his teeth.

"I figure if I did that," George went on earnestly, "it would help me in my education. I don't mean the kind they give you in high school. I want to know different things than they learn there, if you know what I mean."

The change maker nodded. "Still and all, one hundred books is a pretty big load for one summer."

"It might take longer."

"After you're finished with some, maybe you and I can shoot the breeze about them?" said Mr. Cattanzara.

"When I'm finished," George answered.

Mr. Cattanzara went home and George continued on his walk. After that, though he had the urge to, George did nothing different from usual. He still took his walks at night, ending up in the little park. But one evening the shoemaker on the next block stopped George to say he was a good boy, and George figured that Mr. Cattanzara had told him all about the books he was reading. From the shoemaker it must have gone down the street, because George saw a couple of people smiling kindly at him, though nobody spoke to him personally. He felt a little better around the neighborhood and liked it more, though not so much he would want to live in it forever. He had never exactly disliked the people in it, yet he had never liked them very much either. It was the fault of the neighborhood. To his surprise, George found out that his father and Sophie knew about his reading too. His father was too busy to say anything about it — he was never much of a talker in his whole life — but Sophie was softer to George, and she showed him in other ways she was proud of him.

As the summer went on George felt in a good mood about things. He cleaned the house every day, as a favor to Sophie, and he enjoyed the ball games more. Sophie gave him a buck a week allowance, and though it still wasn't enough and he had to use it carefully, it was a helluva lot better than just having two bits now and then. What he bought with the money — cigarettes mostly, an occasional beer or movie ticket — he got a big kick out of. Life wasn't so bad if you knew how to appreciate it. Occasionally he bought a paperback book from the newsstand, but he never got around to reading it, though he was glad to have a couple of books in his room. But he read thoroughly Sophie's magazines and newspapers. And at night was the most enjoyable time, because when he passed the storekeepers sitting outside their stores, he could tell they regarded him highly. He walked erect, and though he did not say much to them, or they to him, he could feel approval on all sides. A couple of nights he felt so good that he skipped the park at the end of the evening. He just wandered in the neighborhood, where people had known him from the time he was a kid playing punchball whenever there was a game of it going; he wandered there, then came home and got undressed for bed, feeling fine.

For a few weeks he had talked only once with Mr. Cattanzara, and though the change maker had said nothing more about the books, asked no questions, his silence made George a little uneasy. For a while George didn't pass in front of Mr. Cattanzara's house anymore, until one night, forgetting himself, he approached it from a different direction than he usually did when he did. It was already past midnight. The street, except for one or two people, was deserted, and George was surprised when he saw Mr. Cattanzara still reading his newspaper by the light of the street lamp overhead. His impulse was to stop at the stoop and talk to him. He wasn't sure what he wanted to say, though he felt the words would come when he began to talk; but the more he thought about it, the more the idea scared him, and he decided he'd better not. He even considered beating it home by another street, but he was too near Mr. Cattanzara, and the change maker might see him as he ran and get annoyed. So George unobtrusively crossed the street, trying to make it seem as if he had to look in a store window on the other side, which he did, and then went on, uncomfortable at what he was doing. He feared Mr. Cattanzara would glance up from his paper and call him a dirty rat for walking on the other side of the street, but all he did was sit there, sweating through his undershirt, his bald head shining in the dim light as he read his *Times*, and upstairs his fat wife leaned out of the window, seeming to read the paper along with him. George thought she would spy him and yell out to Mr. Cattanzara, but she never moved her eyes off her husband.

George made up his mind to stay away from the change maker until he had got some of his softback books read, but when he started them and saw they were mostly story books, he lost his interest and didn't bother to finish them. He lost his interest in reading other things too. Sophie's magazines and newspapers went unread. She saw them piling up on a chair in his room and asked why he was no longer looking at them, and George told her it was because of all the other reading he had to do. Sophie said she had guessed that was it. So for most of the day, George had the radio on, turning to music when he was sick of the human voice. He kept the house fairly neat, and

Sophie said nothing on the days when he neglected it. She was still kind and gave him his extra buck, though things weren't so good for him as they had been before.

But they were good enough, considering. Also his night walks invariably picked him up, no matter how bad the day was. Then one night George saw Mr. Cattanzara coming down the street toward him. George was about to turn and run but he recognized from Mr. Cattanzara's walk that he was drunk, and if so, probably he would not even bother to notice him. So George kept on walking straight ahead until he came abreast of Mr. Cattanzara and though he felt wound up enough to pop into the sky, he was not surprised when Mr. Cattanzara passed him without a word, walking slowly, his face and body stiff. George drew a breath in relief at his narrow escape, when he heard his name called, and there stood Mr. Cattanzara at his elbow, smelling like the inside of a beer barrel. His eyes were sad as he gazed at George, and George felt so intensely uncomfortable he was tempted to shove the drunk aside and continue on his walk.

But he couldn't act that way to him, and, besides, Mr. Cattanzara took a nickel out of his pants pocket and handed it to him.

"Go buy yourself a lemon ice, Georgie."

"It's not that time anymore, Mr. Cattanzara," George said, "I am a big guy now."

"No, you ain't," said Mr. Cattanzara, to which George made no reply he could think of.

"How are all your books comin' along now?" Mr. Cattanzara asked. Though he tried to stand steady, he swayed a little.

"Fine, I guess," said George, feeling the red crawling up his face.

"You ain't sure?" The change maker smiled slyly, a way George had never seen him smile.

"Sure I'm sure. They're fine."

Though his head swayed in little arcs, Mr. Cattanzara's eyes were steady. He had small blue eyes which could hurt if you looked at them too long.

"George," he said, "name me one book on that list that you read this summer, and I will drink to your health."

"I don't want anybody drinking to me."

"Name me one so I can ask you a question on it. Who can tell, if it's a good book maybe I might wanna read it myself."

George knew he looked passable on the outside, but inside he was crumbling apart.

Unable to reply, he shut his eyes, but when — years later — he opened them, he saw that Mr. Cattanzara had, out of pity, gone away, but in his ears he still heard the words he had said when he left: "George, don't do what I did."

The next night he was afraid to leave his room, and though Sophie argued with him he wouldn't open the door.

"What are you doing in there?" she asked.

"Nothing."

"Aren't you reading?"

"No."

She was silent a minute then asked, "Where do you keep the books you read? I never see any in your room outside of a few cheap trashy ones."

He wouldn't tell her.

"In that case you're not worth a buck of my hard-earned money. Why should I break my back for you? Go on out, you bum, and get a job."

He stayed in his room for almost a week, except to sneak into the kitchen when nobody was home. Sophie railed at him, then begged him to come out, and his old father wept, but George wouldn't budge, though the weather was terrible and his small room stifling. He found it very hard to breathe, each breath was like drawing a flame into his lungs.

One night, unable to stand the heat anymore, he burst into the street at one A.M., a shadow of himself. He hoped to sneak to the park without being seen, but there were people all over the block, wilted and listless, waiting for a breeze. George lowered his eyes and walked, in disgrace, away from them, but before long he discovered they were still friendly to him. He figured Mr. Cattanzara hadn't told on him. Maybe when he woke up out of his drunk the next morning, he had forgotten all about meeting George. George felt his confidence slowly come back to him.

That same night a man on a street corner asked him if it was true that he had finished reading so many books, and George admitted he had. The man said it was a wonderful thing for a boy his age to read so much.

"Yeah," George said, but he felt relieved. He hoped nobody would mention the books anymore, and when after a couple of days, he accidentally met Mr. Cattanzara again, *he* didn't, though George had the idea he was the one who had started the rumor that he had finished all the books.

One evening in the fall, George ran out of his house to the library, where he hadn't been in years. There were books all over the place, wherever he looked, and though he was struggling to control an inward trembling, he easily counted off a hundred, then sat down at a table to read.

## Discussion Questions

1. *Does George know himself? What evidence from the story can you present that shows he does or doesn't?*
2. *Why doesn't George go back to school?*
3. *What are some things George wants out of life?*
4. *What makes George tell Mr. Cattanzara that he reads a lot? What new problems does this create for George?*
5. *What do you think it was that Mr. Cattanzara did that he doesn't want George to do?*
6. *Do you think that George was influenced by Mr. Cattanzara's interest in him? How is this shown in the story?*
7. *At the end of the story, why does George go to the library?*

# ADDITIONAL READINGS

Auden, H.W., ***"The Unknown Citizen"***

Is it possible to go through life without ever being noticed? Are we conditioned to perform in a certain way by the pressure of society? Some of us, like the Unknown Citizen of this wry little poem, yield unwittingly to the standards of "the Greater Community" without ever considering what we might be sacrificing. After reading the poem, you might want to compare your ideas about yourself with what society says they should be.

Sands, Bill, ***My Shadow Ran Fast***

Discover in this inspirational autobiography what one ex-convict learned about himself in the process of his rehabilitation. Read what he accomplished as a result of his own research and observations. See if you agree with his conclusions.

Emerson, Ralph Waldo, ***"Self-Reliance"***

The great 19th Century Concord minister, poet, and thinker warns that "Society everywhere is in conspiracy against the manhood of every one of its members." If you feel uneasy about the demands being placed on you, Emerson has words of comfort for you—as well as words of advice.

Cather, Willa, ***"Paul's Case"***

Written in 1905, this short story tells about a boy who cannot accept the realities of his life and tries to keep himself in an imaginary world of wealth and culture. At last, unable and unwilling to conceal his boredom anymore, he is expelled from school. Put to work, he takes some money from his employer one weekend and takes a night train to New York to lose himself in a round of pleasures normally denied to one of his years. It is winter, but the city is warm

**Suggested Readings**

In addition to the reading included in each unit, there is an annotated suggested reading list. You may want to assign an additional reading to each member of the class.

As you teach this course you may find additional readings to add to the present list.

Each time a student finishes a reading assignment it is suggested that a Reading Report Form be completed and turned in to the teacher.

**Reading Report I**

The Reading Report is divided into three parts:

1. Identification of the selection
2. Substance of the reading
3. Evaluation—how the students relate what they have read to their working future

When periodicals or chapters from books are used, the students should give the title and author of the selection.

It should be pointed out to the students that the readings listed are associated closely with the theme of the unit. A list of these and other available readings can be posted on the bulletin board. Students should choose one (or more) of the titles, read the selection, and report on it. Alternate selections can be offered to students with special interests.

Upon completion of a reading, students should fill out a Reading Report Form. (***A model of this form is found on page T15 in the teacher's edition.***)

with life and he has money to burn. But, of course, it all has to end.

As you consider the fate of Paul in light of your own experiences and feelings, see if you can't extract some common principle that would serve to guide you as you get ready to make your way in the world.

Robinson, Edwin Arlington, ***"Miniver Cheevy"***

Here is a poem about a man, "a child of scorn," who has been unable to come to terms with the world he lives in. The times are not right for Miniver, but what does he do about it? Read for yourself and then decide if Miniver's solution has any merit.

Hesse, Hermann, ***Demian***

This is an absorbing short novel about a young man's restless pursuit of a spiritual release that would draw him together with his fate, his dream, and with nature. The theme of the book is that we set the limits of what we are and what we can do too narrowly. We identify ourselves only by how we differ from others. We discover traits we recognize as individual and let it go at that. Instead, we should explore the depths of our souls for possibilities of what we can be or do since we are the recipients and the carriers of all that has ever been known to the soul of man. What we are is inside us waiting to be discovered.

O'Neill, Eugene, ***Ah, Wilderness!***

This comedy made its first appearance on Broadway in 1933, starring George M. Cohan, the original "Yankee Doodle Dandy," as the father. The play is set on one Fourth of July early in the century in a small southern New England coastal town. The focus is on young Dick Miller who attempts valiantly—and somewhat comically—to break away from his close-knit family. Though the play might seem sentimental to some today, its value here is as a testament to the struggle young people experience as they pit their youthful ideals against the reality of adult life.

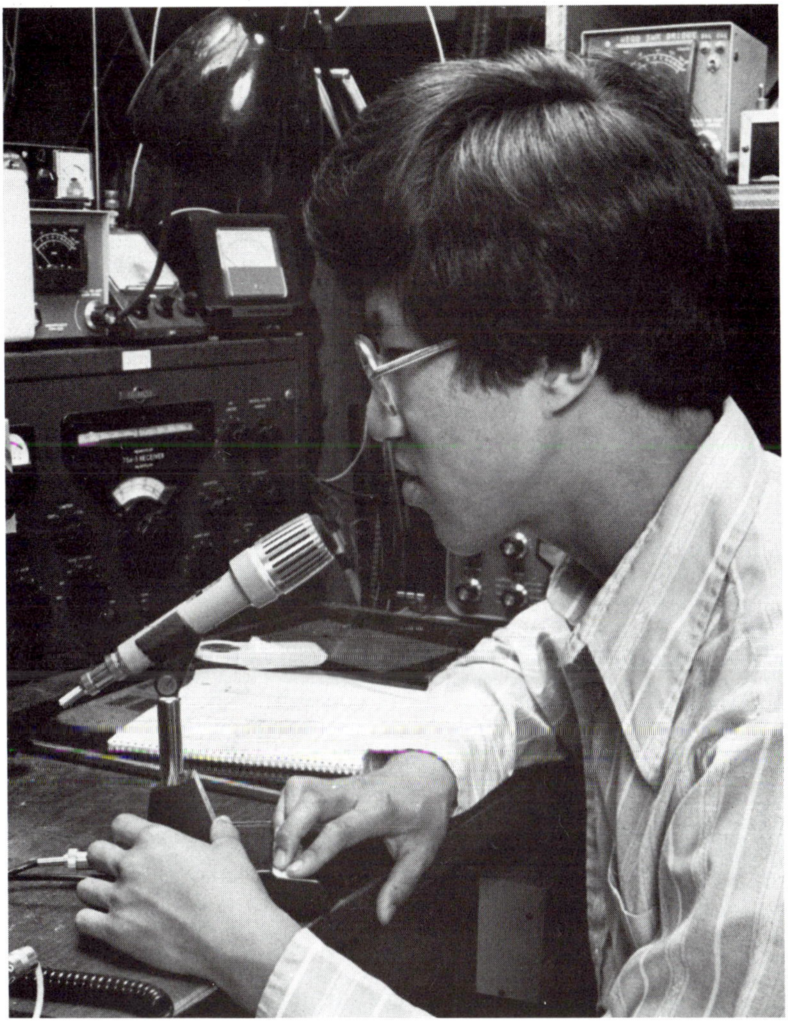

**Unit II Introduction**

Discuss the Thoreau quote with the class. You may want to ask:

1. Who was Henry David Thoreau?
2. What do you think he meant by the quote?
3. Should we try to plan or shape our own future or should we just let it happen? Why?

**Unit II Theme**

Learning About Life-styles and Careers

# What Do I Want Out of Life?

Let us consider the way in which we spend our lives.

**Henry David Thoreau**

*What are my desires, hopes, and dreams for the future?*

**Words in Action**

Discuss the Useful Terms with your class. All unfamiliar words should be checked with the definitions found in the Glossary. When students are ready, assign the Vocabulary Exercise.

# WORDS IN ACTION

## USEFUL TERMS

1. alternatives
2. avocation
3. continuing education
4. formal education
5. life-style
6. outbuildings
7. pecuniary gain
8. profile
9. relocate
10. rural
11. subsistence

**Vocabulary Exercise Answers**

| | |
|---|---|
| 1. alternatives | D |
| 2. avocation | G |
| 3. continuing education | I |
| 4. formal education | K |
| 5. life-style | A |
| 6. outbuildings | C |
| 7. pecuniary gain | J |
| 8. profile | F |
| 9. relocate | E |
| 10. rural | B |
| 11. subsistence | H |

**Correcting Mistakes**

Students should correct their mistakes by checking the terms and definitions in the Glossary.

## VOCABULARY EXERCISE

*On a separate sheet of paper list the terms above. Now read the selections below. Put the letter of each selection next to the term it describes. (You may use the Glossary at the back of the book if you need help.)*

A. life-style

**A.** Maria shivered as she waited for the bus that was to take her to Flushing on the first leg of her daily journey to her job in New York City. It was 6:30 in the morning and still dark and cold outside. The bus took her to the Main Street subway entrance where she bought a newspaper. After an uneventful forty-minute ride on the subway, she climbed into the new light of day and walked the four blocks to her office building. It was 7:45 as she squeezed out of the elevator at the fifteenth floor.

At 4:45, after a day of routine sorting and filing, two coffee breaks, and a tasteless lunch with the other girls in the company cafeteria, she elbowed her way back into the subway. The train emptied out at Main Street, and she found a place in the long bus line. Again it was cold and dark. After the jerky ride through the narrow back streets of College Point, she dropped once again to the pavement and crossed the street to number 14 in the long row of attached brick houses where she lived with her mother and three brothers. She helped her mother with the table, they ate and exchanged bits of news, and she then drifted off to her room to listen to records and to make a phone call.

Except for weekends and holidays, and the usual two-week vacation trip, this was the way it usually went for Maria—for some 245 days of the year.

**B.** Carrie grew up in the Bay Ridge section of Brooklyn. It wasn't until she was ten and spent the summer on her grandparents' farm in New Hampshire that she thought about living anywhere else.

The farm was settled into a notch between two long hills. There were sheep and cows and, best of all, horses that grazed on the slopes. Before dawn Carrie would help with the chores and then ride the sorrel to her favorite pond to watch the sun come up and listen to the birds. She decided then and there that the country was the place for her.

**C.** Hal was wondering where he was going to put the new garden tractor. The garage in the house, besides holding the family cars, was cluttered with ladders, tools, paint, and assorted junk. There was no room left. The only choice was to throw up a shed, probably near the fence at the far end of the yard.

**D.** "Your hitch is almost up, isn't it?" said Sergeant Knowles. "You'll be leaving the army soon. What are you going to do?"

"I don't know," said Al, buffing the stiff toe of his combat boot to a lustrous shine. "I haven't decided. I could take a civilian job with the Corps of Engineers. On the other hand, I might go back to school and get a degree in engineering. There's also the possibility I'll reenlist—if a promotion goes with it."

**E.** The promotion was a big one—too big to turn down. But it meant that Jennifer would have to move from Rockford to Chicago, leaving behind family and friends. The move would mean a whole new life for her.

**F.** The article appears in the trade publication *Gourmet Journal,* published by the Food Institute of America every three months. It is about an innkeeper from western Connecticut who runs one of the oldest inns in America. The article describes the

**B.** rural
**C.** outbuildings
**D.** alternatives
**E.** relocate
**F.** profile

inn and the work of its keeper. It tells how he got started in the hotel and restaurant business, and goes on to explain how the busy proprietor manages an active social life along with his thriving business.

**G.** Burt had just negotiated the loan with the bank to buy the truck and the equipment. He had worked for Andrews for two years as an exterminator, and now he was going into business for himself. But while his days were busy and filled with problems, his nights and weekends were filled with magic—literally. This is because he actually performed a popular magic act in neighborhood clubs and cabarets to earn extra money.

**H.** Anna opened the familiar envelope and threw the bill on the desk with the rest. Added now to the rent notice, the telephone bill, the electric bill, and the charge card payment was the auto insurance premium. She set the bills in order by due date and thought that even with the stamps she would find it hard to put food on the table for the rest of the month.

**G.** avocation
**H.** [illegible]
**I.** continuing education
**J.** pecuniary gain
**K.** formal education

**I.** Anita had her undergraduate degree in business and was now working as a junior analyst for a major brokerage firm in her town. She liked her job and made a good living but was beginning to feel that her life lacked something. One night she stopped off at the library for some books and saw the announcement on the bulletin board. An extension course in sewing was being offered at the junior high school. She decided on the spot to register. She hadn't taken any courses in home economics in school, and she felt she would like to learn about it now.

**J.** The idea was to make money. Arnie wasn't concerned about the quality of the merchandise, the goodwill of the customers, or whether he liked what he was doing. He wanted to get in and get out fast with as big a profit as he could make.

**K.** Biology was a 4-credit-hour course, anatomy was 3, and psychology was 2. At the end of the semester Fred would have earned 9 more credit hours that would count later when he applied for admission to medical school.

# A CASE STUDY

## PHIL'S WAY

From the time he could crawl, Phil was fascinated by electricity. He would study wall outlets, wondering what kind of magic came out of those little holes.

Soon he was interested in plugs. He collected them from his grandfather who had a huge assortment in a dusty old cigar box on a shelf in the back of the garage.

When he was nine years of age, insulators—glass ones of all shapes, sizes, and colors—became the objects of his attention. He could read now and could tell you about the Hemingray 19 from his catalog. (It was an insulator with an inner skirt or ring under the drip point circle; they were first made like that in the late 1920s.)

Then there was the model railroad. It was an N-gauge layout with the CTC panel alive with tiny lights that showed where the trains were as they passed key intersections. He designed it and built it himself. The circuit drawings were his. The relay switches once belonged to an electric company and were donated by a family friend.

By the time he reached seventh grade he wanted to know everything about antennas. Ground plane, center-loaded, whips; shortwave, long wave, VHF, UHF—Phil built them all out of wire coat hangers and taped them to the sheet-metal chimney shield on the roof of the house. He clamped them or fastened them with suction cups to the trunk lid and the roof of the car; or he fastened them to a stake and planted them at some high point in a nearby field. It wasn't long before he had worked out on a calculator a chart of dimensions for the lengths of the antenna elements from the formulas in his handbooks.

Phil, now in high school, is interested in CB radio. His "handle" is Antenna Swinger and he enjoys "shooting skip" when the atmospheric conditions are right. Also there is his multiband radio. It came in kit form. He bought it with money he earned as a part-time caretaker. In a

**Phil's Way**

The Case Study deals with the theme of the unit. It follows the interests and life-style of a boy who has been fascinated by electricity since he was a little boy.

Before assigning the reading, ask the students to write on a slip of paper the one thing each of them wants most to accomplish in life.

Collect the slips and appoint a student to read the goals aloud while you list them on the chalkboard, keeping track of identical or similar aspirations.

The list should provide the basis for a lively class discussion covering the wide range of goals people want to accomplish.

Next, with the help of the class, you might attempt to separate the goals into vocational and personal aspirations. Then ask about some of the ways in which vocational interests are related to personal interests or vice versa.

The object of this activity is to show that whatever it is we want out of life, or whatever life-style we favor for ourselves, will in some way depend on the vocation we choose.

couple of hours he assembled the kit, and now he is learning to decipher the CW transmissions he hears on the high frequencies.

He has fashioned a practice circuit with a telegrapher's key, and late into the night he taps out the hypnotic patterns of dots and dashes. He has found out that he has to know how to send and receive International Morse Code to qualify for his ham operator's license. That is what he wants to do right now, and his life revolves around it. He wants to build, own, and operate an amateur radio station.

■□■□■

Phil really isn't much different from other young people who want a lot out of life. His focus is maybe a little narrow now. It doesn't go much beyond tomorrow or the next day. This is not unusual or abnormal, and Phil will soon have other interests. There are girls, of course—later perhaps marriage and a family, a place to live, a certain way of life that agrees with him and allows him to develop his interests. There is also probably something that everybody is interested in at one time or another—the money that makes so many of these other things possible.

## Thinking It Through

1. *What do you think Phil will do when he graduates from high school? List several possibilities and tell why you chose them.*
2. *What is the difference between a vocation and an avocation?*
3. *Was Phil's interest in electricity leading him toward a vocation or an avocation? Why?*
4. *Can you think of any reasons why Phil developed such an intense interest in electricity? What evidence do you find in the story to support your reasons?*

**Thinking It Through**

In addition to the discussion questions in Thinking It Through, you may want to ask:

1. Have you ever had a hobby as involving as Phil's interest in electricity? What was it? How has your interest in this hobby changed with time?
2. Do most people change their interests throughout their lives? Why? How does this affect their life-style? How does their life-style affect their avocation? (You might discuss which has more influence, life-style over avocation or avocation over life-style; and how avocations sometimes lead to vocations.)

5. *What special interests or hobbies do you have that could lead to an avocation or a vocation?*
6. *How can a person's environment help influence his or her career choice?*
7. *What time do you usually get up in the morning? Would you get up at that time if you did not have to? What time would you get up? What time would you go to bed?*
8. *Prepare an ideal 24-hour schedule for yourself beginning with the time you would get up and ending with the time you would go to bed. Tell what you would do at various times during the day and in what places. Include such activities as eating, working, resting, traveling, shopping, recreational activities, school, studying, and so forth.*
9. *Do you think it is possible for someone to arrange his or her life according to a schedule like the one you just prepared for yourself? Why or why not?*
10. *What does the word* life-style *mean to you?*
11. *What kind of a life-style do you desire for yourself and what plans have you developed to obtain it?*

# REPORT PROJECTS

**Guide for Personal Essay II**

It is a good idea to make clear that choosing an environment in which to live and work, and setting up an agreeable life-style, goes hand in hand with choosing one's work. The life of a commercial jet pilot might seem glamorous and prestigious to some until it is understood that much time is spent checking in and out of hotels and waiting in airports. If an individual sets a premium on home and family life, this might not be a suitable vocation for that individual. Students should understand that in this essay they will be laying the groundwork for the kind of life they want for themselves, including but not depending on the kind of work they favor.

Before assigning this essay be sure students understand the meaning of the concept *life-style* as it relates to each of them. Also point out that the outline in the text is not all inclusive; that students should add or subtract items from the outline to help them write about their life-style.

## PERSONAL ESSAY II

***Introduction*** In this unit you will be considering the things that are important to you as you begin to plan for your future. By taking a look at the way others have ordered their lives and by laying out the requirements of a life-style that suits you, you will have a better idea of the kind of job situation to look for. You will want a job that offers you the best chance to lead a full life, a life where the present moment is cherished, the past is a record of progress, and the future is something to look forward to.

***Directions*** Write in essay form the answers to the following questions. Make direct and definite statements, answering all the questions. Use the capital letters of the outline for paragraph divisions, but do not actually write in the letters. You may wish to combine the answers to two or more questions in one paragraph.

### Outline

**A.** What kind of work appeals to you?

1. Be your own boss and fix your own work hours
2. Work from 9:00 to 5:00, five days a week, with paid vacations, holidays, and benefits
3. Work irregular hours, shifts, or nightwork
4. Work at a job that requires a lot of travel
5. Work indoors in an office or plant; work outdoors, doing seasonal work
6. Relocate within the United States or overseas
7. Maintain a daily routine or have variety in the working day

8. Work largely alone or with others
9. Deal directly with the public or work behind the scenes
10. Troubleshoot, or solve problems
11. Work with your hands
12. Persuade or influence people
13. Work out ideas, keep records, and arrange things
14. Work in a government job
15. Work at a skilled trade
16. Become a member of one of the professions

**B.** What do you want by way of a family?

1. Live alone or with parents
2. Get married and have children
3. Live in a communal setting

**C.** In what kind of an environment would you like to live?

1. Urban, suburban, rural
2. Mountains, shore, plains

**D.** In what kind of a dwelling would you like to live?

1. House, condominium, apartment
2. Style of architecture; split-level, colonial, ranch
3. Number and kinds of rooms, garages, barns, and other outbuildings

**E.** What kind of money do you want to be earning in ten years? In twenty years?

**F.** How would you like to spend your spare time?

1. Avocational interests
2. Travel
3. Special projects

4. Organizations
5. Sports

**G.** How much formal education do you want? Are there any academic or cultural courses you would like to take?

**H.** What special goals or objectives would you like to accomplish in your lifetime?

1. Learn to play the piano
2. Fly a plane
3. Visit a foreign country

**I.** What kind of life would you like to make possible for your children?

## LIBRARY REPORT

***Introduction*** For this report you will seek out and read the biography, profile, or obituary of a prominent figure who has worked in your field of interest. You will then write a brief report detailing the subject's life-style as it relates to his or her career.

***Directions*** Your report should include the information suggested below.

### Outline

**A.** Give the author's name, title, publisher's name, and copyright date if the report is on a book. If an article is used, give the author's name, title of the article, and the name and date of the magazine or journal.

**B.** Give the subject's name and occupational field.

**C.** Recount any important facts about the subject's background—place and date of birth, family life, schooling.

**Library Report**

This is a research report and will take the students into the school library. A class period might be spent as an indoctrination session in the use of library materials. A cooperative librarian can provide assistance in preselecting and setting aside books and magazines for the class, either on reserve shelves or on a cart that can be placed in the classroom.

Students should understand that this is *not just another book report*. A student interested in the work of a cosmetologist could certainly read a book like *Fire and Ice* by Andrew Tobias, which documents the life style of Charles Revson, founder of Revlon. The student would learn how one man in the cosmetics industry carved out an empire for himself. But much more could be learned about running a beauty salon by reading an article in a trade publication that describes how Doreen K., a successful beautician, runs her shop and manages her life. The student may be fascinated by Revson's story but will identify more with the problems of Doreen the shopkeeper and homemaker. Periodicals that specialize are most useful as good sources for these reports, and it is well to have close at hand a list of those subscribed to by the school library. Trade publications not available in the library can often be obtained by writing or visiting companies, local unions, or the county chamber of commerce.

**D.** Describe the daily life of the subject (how the subject combined work and private life).

**E.** Explain the steps the subject took to advance his or her career.

**F.** List the subject's major accomplishments.

## TAPE-RECORDED INTERVIEW

***Introduction*** For this report you will plan and conduct an interview with someone who is working at a job along the lines of your career interests to show how one's life-style is related to one's work. You may wish to share the results of your interview by playing it back to the class for an evaluation and a discussion of certain points.

***Equipment*** Cassette recorder (your own, or possibly one available for loan from your school) and cassettes.

***Directions*** Having located your subject through parents, friends, or other sources, contact the person to make an appointment for the interview. Identify yourself and explain that you are a high school student investigating careers as part of a course you are taking. You may want to tell the subject a little about the kinds of questions you will be asking.

Use the following questions as a basis for your interview, and write some questions of your own to find out more about the responsibilities and skills involved in the subject's work.

### Questions

**A.** What is your name?

**B.** What line of work are you in? How long have you been in that line of work?

**C.** What company are you currently working for? (name of company or organization, or type of self-employment)

**Tape-Recorded Interview**

This report can be substituted as an option to the Library Report, for double credit (two grades in place of one).

The procedure is outlined in detail in the text, and the suggested questions range from simple factual ones in the beginning to complex personal ones later in the interview. In explaining the report, it is advisable to mention that students electing this option are to play their interview to the class. This requirement adds an additional note of responsibility to the report.

When a sincere effort has been made to conduct a good interview, tapes are always well-received by the class, especially when the questions pertain to situations the students are or will be experiencing. It might also be a good idea not to hold too strictly to a due date for this report. The interview takes a certain amount of preparation and arranging, and its success depends on the cooperation of the interviewee.

Students should not be allowed to do the interview and record the answers on paper. This is an optional report and for that reason has special requirements—and benefits.

**D.** What is your job title?

**E.** Could you describe some of your duties? What are your hours? Do you ever have to work overtime?

**F.** Do you take work home? If so, what percentage of your work is done at home?

**G.** How far do you have to go to work each day? How long does it take you? Do you travel on the job? Where do you go? How often do you travel?

**H.** In general, would you say you like your work? What do you find interesting about it?

**I.** What size family do you have? (wife or husband, number of children, and any others residing at home)

**J.** Do you own or rent your home?

**K.** Do you moonlight at any part time job or run your own business in your spare hours? How can you do your regular job and still do this?

**L.** Are you involved with any civic or community organization? (child care center, chamber of commerce, rescue squad, or school board) Are you compensated in any way for your service?

**M.** What other organizations do you belong to?

**N.** What are some of your hobbies? Do you play at sports or do any physical exercise for relaxation?

**O.** What do you hope to accomplish in the future? Do you have some long-range project, goal, or dream?

**P.** Would you say you fit your life to your job, or your job to your life? How do you feel about this arrangement? Would you prefer it some other way?

**Q.** What would you do if you had your life to live over again?

*Note* You may substitute your own questions at any point or use a line of questioning that will serve your special interests.

## PHOTO ESSAY

*Introduction* In this assignment you will prepare a photo or slide essay of the life-style of someone in the field of work you are interested in. You might want to entitle your project "A Day in the Life of . . . (name, job title)" and share your experience in a class presentation.

*Equipment* Camera (your own, or possibly one loaned by arrangement with your school) and film.

*Directions* Phone and make an appointment to interview the subject. Identify yourself as a high school student doing a career investigation project for English class. Tell the subject you are considering a career along the line of work he or she is in and that you would like to conduct an interview. Ask if you may take some pictures of the subject at home and at work.

### Possible Shots

**A.** Subject getting ready to leave for work (morning coffee, on the way out the door with briefcase or tools)

**B.** Subject on the way to work (attention directed to mode of transportation—car, subway, or bus)

**C.** Outside view of the subject's place of work

**D.** Subject at work at various duties that are all a part of his or her job

**E.** Lunch with co-workers, clients

**F.** Subject leaving work

**G.** Subject returning home (various shots of subject around house and grounds—include members of family in typical settings)

**Photo Essay**

This report can also be substituted as an option to the Library Report for double credit (two grades in place of one).

The Photo Essay is for those who like to take pictures or who pursue photography as a hobby. The preparation and procedures are explained in detail in the text, but it is helpful to remind students who elect this option that the report has a unifying idea and a definite purpose. Photos should be presented in an order that makes it clear what the subject is doing and when. Interested students must also understand that they are to present their photo essay to the class and describe the work and the life-style shown by the pictures. Elaborate displays, albums, or captions are not necessary, but students must show a clear progression of the subject's life-style with relevant background information. Once the presentation has been made, the photos can be placed on display.

As for the taped interview, special arrangements must be made for this report. Since students must depend upon the cooperation of others, it might be well to leave the due date for the report open for as long as possible.

**H.** Subject and family at supper table

**I.** Subject engaged in leisure, avocational, or volunteer activity

***Presentation*** Don't hesitate to go in for close-ups to focus on details. Use the long shots for identification first, then go in for the close-ups.

Weave the story of your subject around the pictures giving the details as they present themselves around the clock. Be prepared to relate the story to the class as the pictures are shown.

If you are interested and equipped, you may wish to do this story on movie film. In any case, bear in mind that the filming need not be done in one day, even though the title suggests this. Shots can also be simulated—that is, set up out of the order in which the events actually occur. For example, background or family shots can be taken at any time.

# RELATED READING

## LAND

*Sinclair Lewis*

He was named Sidney, for the sake of elegance, just as his parents had for elegance in their Brooklyn parlor a golden-oak combination bookcase, desk, and shield-shaped mirror. But Sidney Dow was descended from generations of Georges and Johns, of Lorens and Lukes and Nathans.

He was little esteemed in the slick bustle of his city school. He seemed a loutish boy, tall and heavy and slow-spoken, and he was a worry to his father. For William Dow was an ambitious parent. Born on a Vermont farm, William felt joyously that he had done well in the great city of Brooklyn. He had, in 1885, when Sidney was born, a real bathroom with a fine tin tub, gas lights, and a handsome phaeton with red wheels, instead of the washtub in the kitchen for Saturday-night baths, the kerosene lamps, and the heavy old buggy which his father still used in Vermont. Instead of being up at 5:30, he could loll abed till a quarter of seven, and he almost never, he chuckled in gratification at his progress, was in his office before a quarter to eight.

But the luxury of a red-wheeled carriage and late lying did not indicate that William's Yankee shrewdness had been cozened by urban vice, or that he was any less solid and respectable than old George, his own father. He was a deacon in the Universalist church, he still said grace before meals, and he went to the theater only when Ben-Hur was appearing.

For his son, Sidney, William Dow had even larger ambitions. William himself had never gone to high

**Related Reading**

The story "**Land**" relates to the theme of the unit learning about life-styles and careers.

The reading is reprinted here in its entirety. It tells about a dentist whose lifelong goal was to farm the land, but he let himself be guided by his family's ambitions and never realized his dream.

Assign the story to the class as homework. Use the questions at the end of the reading selection as a guide for class discussion.

school, and his business was only a cautious real-estate and insurance agency, his home a squatting two-story brick house in a red, monotonous row. But Sidney—he should go to college, he should be a doctor or a preacher or a lawyer, he should travel in Europe, he should live in a three-story graystone house in the Forties in Manhattan, he should have a dress suit and wear it to respectable but expensive hops!

William had once worn dress clothes at an Odd Fellows' ball, but they had been rented.

To enable Sidney to attain all these graces, William toiled and sacrificed and prayed. American fathers have always been as extraordinary as Scotch fathers in their heroic ambitions for their sons—and sometimes as unscrupulous and as unwise. It bruised William and often it made him naggingly unkind to see that Sidney, the big slug, did not "appreciate how his parents were trying to do for him and give him every opportunity." When they had a celebrated Columbia Heights physician as guest for dinner, Sidney merely gawked at him and did not at all try to make an impression.

"Suffering cats! You might have been one of your uncles still puttering around with dirty pitchforks back on the farm! What are you going to do with yourself, anyway?" raged William.

"I guess maybe I'd like to be a truck driver," mumbled Sidney.

Yet, even so, William should not have whipped him. It only made him sulkier.

To Sidney Dow, at sixteen, his eagerest memories were of occasional weeks he had spent with his grandfather and uncles on the Vermont farm, and the last of these was seven years back now. He remembered Vermont as an enchanted place, with curious and amusing animals—cows, horses, turkeys. He wanted to return, but his father seemed to hate the place. Of Brooklyn, Sidney liked nothing save livery stables and occasional agreeable gang fights, with stones inside iced snowballs. He hated school, where he had to cramp his big knees under trifling desks, where irritable lady teachers tried to make him see the importance of A's going more rapidly than B to the town of X, a town in which he was even less interested than in Brooklyn—school where hour on hour he looked over the top of his geography and stolidly hated the whiskers of Longfellow, Lowell, and Whittier. He hated the stiff, clean collar and the itchy, clean winter underwear connected with Sunday school. He hated hot evenings smelling of tarry pavements, and cold evenings when the pavements were slippery.

But he didn't know that he hated any of these things. He knew only that his father must be right in saying that he was a bad, disobedient, ungrateful young whelp, and in his heart he was as humble as in his speech he was sullen.

Then, at sixteen, he came to life suddenly, on an early June morning, on his grandfather's farm. His father had sent him up to Vermont for the summer, had indeed exiled him, saying grimly, "I guess after you live in that tumble-down big old shack and work in the fields and have to get up early, instead of lying abed till your majesty is good and ready to have the girl wait on you—I guess that next fall you'll appreciate your nice home and school and church here, young man!" So sure of himself was his father that Sidney was convinced he was going to encounter hardship on the farm, and all the way up, in the smarting air of the smoker on the slow train, he wanted to howl. The train arrived at ten in the evening, and he was met by his uncle Rob, a man rugged as a pine trunk and about as articulate.

"Well! Come for the summer!" said Uncle Rob; and after they had driven three miles: "Got new calf—yeh, new calf"; and after a mile more: "Your pa all right?" And that was all the conversation of Uncle Rob.

Seven years it was since Sidney had been in any country wilder than Far Rockaway, and the silent hills of night intimidated him. It was a roaring silence, a silence full of stifled threats. The hills that cut the stars so high up on either side the road seemed walls that would topple and crush him, as a man would crush a mosquito between his two palms. And once he cried out when, in the milky light from the lantern swung beneath the wagon, he saw a porcupine lurch into the road before them. It was dark, chill, unfriendly and, to the boy, reared to the lights and cheery voices of the city, even though he hated them, it was appallingly lonely.

His grandfather's house was dark when they arrived. Uncle Rob drove into the barn, jerked his thumb at a ladder up to the haymow and muttered, "Y'sleep up there. Not allowed t' smoke. Take this lantern when we've unharnessed. Sure to put it out. No smoking in the barn. Too tired to help?"

Too tired? Sidney would have been glad to work till daylight if Uncle Rob would but stay with him. He was in a panic at the thought of being left in the ghostly barn where, behind the pawing of horses and the nibble of awakened cows, there were the sounds of anonymous wild animals—scratchings, squeaks, patterings overhead. He made the task as slow as possible, though actually he was handy with horses, for the livery stables of Brooklyn had been his favorite refuge and he had often been permitted to help the hostlers, quite free.

"Gee, Uncle Rob, I guess I'm kind of all thumbs about unharnessing and like that. Seven years since I been here on the farm."

"That so? G'night. Careful of that lantern now. And no smoking!"

The barn was blank as a blind face. The lantern was flickering, and in that witching light the stalls and the heap of sleighs, plows, old harness, at the back wall of the barn were immense and terrifying. The barn was larger than his whole house in Brooklyn, and ten times as large it seemed in the dimness. He could not see clear to the back wall, and he imagined abominable monsters lurking there. He dashed at the ladder up to the haymow, the lantern handle in his teeth and his imitation-leather satchel in one hand.

And the haymow, rising to the darkness of its hand-hewn rafters, seemed vaster and more intimidating than the space below. In one corner a space had been cleared of hay for a cot, with a blanket and a pea-green comforter, and for a chair and a hinged box. Sidney dashed at the cot and crawled into it, waiting only to take off his shoes and jacket. Till the lantern flame died down to a red rim of charred wick, he kept it alight. Then utter darkness leaped upon him.

A rooster crowed, and he startled. Past him things scampered and chittered. The darkness seemed to swing in swift eddies under the rafters, the smell of dry hay choked him—and he awoke to light slipping in silver darts through cracks in the roof, and to jubilant barn swallows diving and twittering.

"Gee, I must have fell asleep!" he thought. He went down the ladder, and now, first, he saw the barn.

Like many people slow of thought and doubtful of speech, Sidney Dow had moments of revelation as complete as those of a prophet, when he beheld a scene or a person or a problem in its entirety, with none of the confusing thoughts of glibber and more clever people with their minds forever running off on many tracks. He saw the barn—really saw it, instead of merely glancing at it, like a normal city boy. He saw that the beams, hand-hewn, gray with sixty years, were beautiful; that the sides of the stalls, polished with rubbing by the shoulders of cattle dead these fifty years, were beautiful; that the harrow, with its trim spikes kept sharp and rustless, was beautiful; that most beautiful of all were the animals—cows and horses, chickens that walked with bobbing heads through the straw, and a calf tethered to the wall. The calf capered with alarm as he approached it; then stood considering him with great eyes, letting him stroke its head and at last licking his hand. He slouched to the door of the barn and looked down the valley. More radiant in that early morning light than even the mountain tops covered with maples and hemlock were the upland clearings with white houses and red barns.

"Gosh, it looks nice! It's—it's sort of—it looks nice! I didn't hardly get it when I was here before. But gee"—with all the scorn of sixteen—"I was just a kid then!"

With Uncle Rob he drove the cows to pasture; with Uncle Ben he plowed; with his grandfather, sourly philanthropic behind his beard, he split wood. He found an even greater menagerie than in the barn—turkeys, geese, ducks, pigs and, in the woods and mowings, an exciting remnant of woodchucks, chipmunks, rabbits, and infrequent deer. With all of them—uncles and grandfather, beasts, wild or tame—he felt at home. They did not expect him to chatter and show off, as had his gang in Brooklyn; they accepted him. That, perhaps, more than any ancestral stoutness, more than the beauty of the land, made a farmer of him. He was a natural hermit, and here he could be a hermit without seeming queer.

And a good farmer he was—slow but tireless, patient, unannoyed by the endless work, happy to go to bed early and be up at dawn. For a few days his back felt as though he were burning at the stake, but after that he could lift all day in the hayfield or swing the scythe or drive the frisky young team. He was a good farmer, and he slept at night. The noises which on his first night had fretted his city-tortured nerves were soporific now, and when he heard the sound of a distant train, the barking of a dog on the next farm, he inarticulately told himself that they were lovely.

"You're pretty fair at working," said Uncle Rob, and that was praise almost hysterical.

Indeed, in one aspect of labor, Sidney was better than any of them, even the pine-carved Uncle Rob. He could endure wet dawns, wild winds, all-day drenching. It seems to be true that farmers are more upset by bad weather than most outdoor workers—sailors, postmen, carpenters, brakemen, teamsters. Perhaps it is because they are less subject to higher authority; except for chores and getting in the hay, they can more nearly do things in their own time, and they build up a habit of taking shelter on nasty days. Whether or no, it was true that just the city crises that had vexed Sidney, from icy pavements to sudden fire alarms, had given him the ability to stand discomforts and the unexpected, like a little Cockney surprisingly stolid in the trenches.

He learned the silent humor of the authentic Yankee. Evenings he sat with neighbors on the bench before the general store. To a passing stranger they seemed to be saying nothing, but when the stranger had passed, Uncle Rob would drawl, "Well, if I had fly nets on my hosses, guess I'd look stuck-up too!" and the others would chuckle with contempt at the alien.

This, thought Sidney, was good talk—not like the smart gabble of the city. It was all beautiful, and he knew it, though in his vocabulary there was no such word as "beautiful," and when he saw the most flamboyant sunset he said only, "Guess going to be clear tomorrow."

And so he went back to Brooklyn, not as to his home but as to prison, and as a prison corridor he saw the narrow street with little houses like little cells.

Five minutes after he had entered the house, his father laughed. "Well, did you get enough of farming? I guess you'll appreciate your school now! I won't rub it in, but I swear, how Rob and Ben can stand it——"

"I kind of liked it, Dad. I think I'll be a farmer. I—kind of liked it."

His father had black side whiskers, and between them he had thin cheeks that seemed, after Uncle Rob and Uncle Ben, pallid as the under side of a toadstool. They flushed now, and William shouted:

"You're an idiot! What have I done to have a son who is an idiot? The way I've striven and worked and economized to give you a chance to get ahead, to do something worth while, and then you want to slip right back and be ordinary, like your uncles! So you think you'd like it! You're a fool! Sure you like it in summer, but if you knew it like I do—rousted out to do the chores five o'clock of a January morning, twenty below zero, and maybe have to dig through two feet of snow to get to the barn! Have to tramp down to the store, snowstorm so thick you can't see five feet in front of you!"

"I don't guess I'd mind it much."

"Oh, you don't! Don't be a fool! And no nice company like here—go to bed with the chickens, a winter night, and no nice lodge meeting or church supper or lectures like there is here!"

"Don't care so much for those things. Everybody talking all the while. I like it quiet, like in the country."

"Well, you will care so much for those things, or I'll care you, my fine young man! I'm not going to let you slump back into being a rube like Ben, and don't you forget it! I'll make you work at your books! I'll make you learn to appreciate good society and dressing proper and getting ahead in the world and amounting to something! Yes, sir, amounting to something! Do you think for one moment that after the struggle I've gone through to give you a chance—the way I studied in a country school and earned my way through business college and went to work at five dollars a week in a real-estate office and studied and economized and worked late, so I could give you this nice house and advantages and opportunity——No, sir! You're going to be a lawyer or a doctor or somebody that amounts to something, and not a rube!"

It would have been too much to expect of Sidney's imagination that he should have seen anything fine and pathetic in William's fierce ambition. That did not move him, but rather fear. He could have broken his father in two, but the passion in this blenched filing-case of a man was such that it hypnotized him.

For days, miserably returned to high school, he longed for the farm. But his mother took him aside and begged: "You mustn't oppose your father so, dearie. He knows what's best for you, and it would just break his heart if he thought you were going to be a common person and not have something to show for all his efforts."

So Sidney came to feel that it was some wickedness in him that made him prefer trees and winds and meadows and the kind cattle to trolley cars and offices and people who made little, flat, worried jokes all day long.

He barely got through high school. His summer vacations he spent in warehouses, hoisting boxes. He failed to enter medical school, botched his examinations shockingly—feeling wicked at betraying his father's ambitions—and his father pushed him into a second-rate dental school with sketchy requirements, a school now blessedly out of existence.

"Maybe you'd be better as a dentist anyway. Requires a lot of manipulation, and I will say you're good with your hands," his father said, in relief that now Sidney was on the highway to fortune and respectability.

But Sidney's hands, deft with hammer and nails, with reins or hoe or spade, were too big, too awkward for the delicate operations of dentistry. And in school he hated the long-winded books with their queer names and shocking colored plates of man's inwards. The workings of a liver did not interest him. He had never seen a liver, save that of a slain chicken. He would turn from these mysteries to a catalogue of harvesting machinery or vegetable seed. So with difficulty he graduated from this doubtful school, and he was uneasy at the pit of his stomach, even when his father, much rejoicing now, bought for him a complete dental outfit, and rented an office, on the new frontier of the Bronx, in the back part of a three-story red-brick apartment house.

His father and mother invited their friends over from Brooklyn to admire the office, and served them coffee and cake. Not many of them came, which was well, for the office was not large. It was really a single room, divided by a curtain to make a reception hall. The operating room had pink-calcimined walls and, for adornment, Sidney's diploma and a calendar from a dental supply house which showed, with no apparent appropriateness, a view of Pike's Peak.

When they had all gone, mouthing congratulations, Sidney looked wistfully out on the old pasture land which, fifteen years later, was to be filled solidly with tall, cheap apartment houses and huge avenues with delicatessen shops and movie palaces. Already these pastures were doomed and abandoned. Cows no longer grazed there. Gaunt billboards lined the roads and behind their barricades were unkempt waste lands of ashes and sodden newspapers. But they were open grass, and they brought back the valleys and uplands of Vermont. His great arms were hungry for the strain of plowing, and he sighed and turned back to his shining new kit of tools.

The drill he picked up was absurd against his wide red palm. All at once he was certain that he knew no dentistry, and that he never would; that he would botch every case; that dreadful things would happen—suits for malpractice——

Actually, as a few and poorly paying neighborhood patients began to come in, the dreadful things didn't happen. Sidney was slow, but he was careful; if he did no ingenious dental jeweling, he did nothing wrong. He learned early what certain dentists and doctors never learn—that nature has not yet been entirely supplanted by the professions. It was not his patients who suffered; it was he.

All day long to have to remain indoors, to stand in one place, bent over gaping mouths, to fiddle with tiny instruments, to produce unctuous sounds of sympathy for cranks who complained of trivial aches, to try to give brisk and confident advice which was really selling talk—all this tortured him.

Then, within one single year, his mother died, his grandfather died on the Vermont farm, Uncle Rob and Uncle Ben moved West, and Sidney met the most wonderful girl in the world. The name of this particular most wonderful girl in the world, who unquestionably had more softness and enchantment and funny little ways of saying things than Helen of Troy, was Mabelle Ellen Pflugmann, and she was cultured; she loved the theater, but rarely attended it; loved also the piano, but hadn't time, she explained, to keep up her practice, because, her father's laundry being in a state of debility, for several years she had temporarily been cashier at the Kwiturwurry Lunch.

They furnished a four-room apartment and went to Vermont for their honeymoon. His grandfather's farm—Sidney wasn't quite sure just who had bought it—was rented out to what the neighborhood considered foreigners—that is, Vermonters from way over beyond the Ridge, fifteen miles away. They took in Sidney and Mabelle. She enjoyed it. She told how sick she had become of the smell and dish clatter of the ole lunch and the horrid customers who were always trying to make love to her. She squealed equally over mountains and ducklings, sunsets and wild strawberries, and as for certain inconveniences—washing with a pitcher and bowl, sleeping in a low room smelling of the chicken run, and having supper in the kitchen with the menfolks in shirt sleeves—she said it was just too darling for words—it was, in fact, sweet. But after ten days of the fortnight on which they had planned, she thought perhaps they had better get back to New York and make sure all the furniture had arrived.

They were happy in marriage. Mabelle saw him, and made him see himself, as a man strong and gallant but shy and blundering. He needed mothering, she said, and he got it and was convinced that he liked it.

He was less gruff with his patients, and he had many more of them, for Mabelle caused him to be known socially. Till marriage he had lived in a furnished room, and all evening he had prowled alone, or read dentistry journals and seed catalogues. Now Mabelle arranged jolly little parties—beer and Welsh rabbit and a game of five hundred. If at the Kwiturwurry Lunch she had met many light fellows, West Farms Lotharios, she had also met estimable but bohemian families of the neighborhood—big traveling men whose territory took them as far west as Denver, assistant buyers from the downtown department stores, and the office manager of a large insurance agency.

Mabelle, a chatelaine now, wanted to shine among them, and wanted Sidney to shine. And he, feeling a little cramped in a new double-breasted blue serge coat, solemnly served the beer, and sometimes a guest perceived that here was an honest and solid dentist upon whom to depend. And once they gave a theater party—six seats at a vaudeville house.

Yet Sidney was never, when he awoke mornings, excited about the adventure of standing with bent, aching shoulders over patients all this glorious coming day.

They had two children in three years and began to worry a little about the rent bill and the grocery bill, and Sidney was considerably less independent with grumbling patients than he had been. His broad shoulders had a small stoop, and he said quite humbly, "Well, I'll try my best to fix 'em to your satisfaction, Mrs. Smallberg," and sometimes his thick fingers tapped nervously on his chin as he talked. And he envied now, where once he had despised them, certain dental-school classmates who knew little of dentistry, but who were slick dressers and given to verbal chuckings under the chin, who had made money and opened three-room offices with chintz chairs in the waiting room. Sidney still had his old office, with no assistant, and the jerry-built tenement looked a little shabby now beside the six-story apartment houses of yellow brick trimmed with marble which had sprung up all about it.

Then their children, Rob and Willabette, were eight and six years old, and Mabelle began to nag Sidney over the children's lack of clothes as pretty as those of their lovely little friends at school.

And his dental engine—only a treadle affair at that—was worn out. And his elbows were always shiny. And in early autumn his father died.

His father died, muttering, "You've been a good boy, Sid, and done what I told you to. You can understand and appreciate now why I kept you from being just a farmer and gave you a chance to be a professional man. I don't think Mabelle comes from an awful good family, but she's a spunky little thing, and real bright, and she'll keep you up to snuff. Maybe some day your boy will be a great, rich banker or surgeon. Keep him away from his Vermont relations—no ambition, those folks. My chest feels so tight! Bless you, Sid!"

He was his father's sole heir. When the will was read in the shabby lawyer's office in Brooklyn, he was astonished to find that his father had still owned—that he himself now owned—the ancestral Vermont home. His slow-burning imagination lighted. He was touched by the belief that his father, for all his pretended hatred of the place, had cherished it and had wanted his son to own it. Not till afterward did he learn from Uncle Rob that William, when his own father had died, had, as eldest son, been given the choice of the farm or half the money in the estate, and had taken the farm to keep Sidney away from it. He had been afraid that if his brothers had it they would welcome Sidney as a partner before he became habituated as a dentist. But in his last days, apparently, William felt that Sidney was safely civilized now and caught. With the farm Sidney inherited some three thousand dollars—not more, for the Brooklyn home was mortgaged.

Instantly and ecstatically, while the lawyer droned

senseless advice, Sidney decided to go home. The tenant on his farm—his!—had only two months more on his lease. He'd take it over. The three thousand dollars would buy eight cows—well, say ten—with a cream separator, a tractor, a light truck, and serve to put the old buildings into condition adequate for a few years. He'd do the repairing himself! He arched his hands with longing for the feel of a hammer or a crowbar.

In the hall outside the lawyer's office, Mabelle crowed: "Isn't it—oh, Sid, you do know how sorry I am your father's passed on, but won't it be just lovely! The farm must be worth four thousand dollars. We'll be just as sensible as can be—not blow it all in, like lots of people would. We'll invest the seven thousand, and that ought to give us three hundred and fifty dollars a year—think of it, an extra dollar every day! You can get a dress suit now, and at last I'll have some decent dresses for the evening, and we'll get a new suit for Bob right away—how soon can you get the money? did he say?—and I saw some lovely little dresses for Willabette and the cutest slippers, and now we can get a decent bridge table instead of that rickety old thing, and——"

As she babbled, which she did, at length, on the stairs down from the office, Sidney realized wretchedly that it was going to take an eloquence far beyond him to convert her to farming and the joys of the land. He was afraid of her, as he had been of his father.

"There's a drug store over across. Let's go over and have an ice-cream soda," he said mildly. "Gosh, it's hot for September! Up on the farm now it would be cool, and the leaves are just beginning to turn. They're awful pretty—all red and yellow."

"Oh, you and your old farm!" But in her joy she was amiable.

They sat at the bright-colored little table in the drug store, with cheery colored drinks between them. But the scene should have been an ancient castle at midnight, terrible with wind and lightning, for suddenly they were not bright nor cheery, but black with tragedy.

There was no manner of use in trying to cajole her. She could never understand how he hated the confinement of his dental office; she would say, "Why, you get the chance of meeting all sorts of nice, interesting people, while I have to stay home," and not perceive that he did not want to meet nice, interesting people. He wanted silence and the smell of earth! And he was under her spell as he had been under his father's. Only violently could he break it. He spoke softly enough, looking at the giddy marble of the soda counter, but he spoke sternly:

"Look here, May. This is our chance. You bet your sweet life we're going to be sensible and not blow in our stake! And we're not going to blow it in on a lot of clothes and a lot of fool bridge parties for a lot of fool folks that don't care one red hoot about us except what they get out of us! For that matter, if we were going to stay on in New York——"

"Which we most certainly are, young man!"

"Will you listen to me? I inherited this dough, not you! Gee, I don't want to be mean, May, but you got to listen to reason, and as I'm saying, if we were going to stay in the city, the first thing I'd spend money for would be a new dental engine—an electric one.

"Need it like the mischief—lose patients when they see me pumping that old one and think I ain't up-to-date—which I ain't, but that's no skin off their nose!"

Even the volatile Mabelle was silent at the unprecedented length and vigor of his oration.

"But we're not going to stay. No, sir! We're going back to the old farm, and the kids will be brought up in the fresh air instead of a lot of alleys. Go back and farm it——"

She exploded then, and as she spoke she looked at him with eyes hot with hatred, the first hatred he had ever known in her:

"Are you crazy? Go back to that hole? Have my kids messing around a lot of manure and dirty animals and out working in the hayfield like a lot of cattle? And attend a little one-room school with a boob for a teacher? And play with a lot of nitwit brats? Not on your life they won't! I've got some ambition for 'em, even if you haven't!"

"Why, May, I thought you liked Vermont and the farm! You were crazy about it on our honeymoon, and you said——"

"I did not! I hated it even then. I just said I liked it to make you happy. That stifling little bedroom, and kerosene lamps, and bugs, and no bathroom, and those fools of farmers in their shirt sleeves—Oh, it was fierce! If you go, you go without the kids and me! I guess I can still earn a living! And I guess there's still plenty of other men would like to marry me when I divorce you! And I mean it!"

She did, and Sidney knew she did. He collapsed as helplessly as he had with his father.

"Well, of course, if you can't stand it——" he muttered.

"Well, I'm glad you're beginning to come to your senses! Honest, I think you were just crazy with the heat! But listen, here's what I'll do: I won't kick about your getting the electric dental doodingus if it don't cost too much. Now how do you go about selling the farm?"

There began for this silent man a secret life of plotting and of lies. Somehow—he could not see how—he must persuade her to go to the farm. Perhaps she would die——But he was shocked at this thought, for he loved her and believed her to be the best woman living, as conceivably she may have been. But he did not obey her and sell the farm. He lied. He told her that a Vermont real-estate dealer had written that just this autumn there was no market for farms, but next year would be excellent. And the next year he repeated the lie, and rented the farm to Uncle Rob, who had done well enough on Iowa cornland but was homesick for the hills and sugar groves and placid maples of Vermont. Himself, Sidney did not go to the farm. It was not permitted.

Mabelle was furious that he had not sold, that they had only the three thousand—which was never invested—for clothes and bridge prizes and payments on the car and, after a good deal of irritated talk, his electric dental engine.

If he had always been sullenly restless in his little office, now he was raging. He felt robbed. The little back room, the view—not even of waste land now, but of the center of a cheap block and the back of new tenements—the anguish of patients, which crucified his heavy, unspoken sympathy for them, and that horrible, unending series of wide-stretched mouths and bad molars and tongues—it was intolerable. He thought of meadows scattered with daisies and devil's-paintbrush, of dark, healing thundershowers pouring up the long valley. He must go home to the land!

From the landlord who owned his office he got, in the spring a year and a half after his father's death, the right to garden a tiny patch amid the litter and cement areaways in the center of the block. Mabelle laughed at him, but he stayed late every evening to cultivate each inch of his pocket paradise—a large man, with huge feet, setting them carefully down in a plot ten feet square.

The earth understood him, as it does such men, and before the Long Island market gardeners had anything to display, Sidney had a row of beautiful radish plants. A dozen radishes, wrapped in a tabloid newspaper, he took home one night, and he said vaingloriously to Mabelle, "You'll never get any radishes like these in the market! Right out of our own garden!"

She ate one absently. He braced himself to hear a jeering "You and your old garden!" What he did hear was, in its uncaring, still worse: "Yes, they're all right, I guess."

He'd show her! He'd make her see him as a great

farmer! And with that ambition he lost every scruple. He plotted. And this was the way of that plotting:

Early in July he said, and casually, "Well, now we got the darn car all paid for, we ought to use it. Maybe we might take the kids this summer and make a little tour for a couple weeks or so."

"Where?"

She sounded suspicious, and in his newborn guile he droned, "Oh, wherever you'd like. I hear it's nice up around Niagara Falls and the Great Lakes. Maybe come back by way of Pennsylvania, and see Valley Forge and all them famous historical sites."

"Well, yes, perhaps. The Golheims made a tour last summer and—they make me sick!—they never stop talking about it."

They went. And Mabelle enjoyed it. She was by no means always a nagger and an improver; she was so only when her interests or what she deemed the interests of her children were threatened. She made jokes about the towns through which they passed—any community of less than fifty thousand was to her New Yorkism a "hick hole"—and she even sang jazz and admired his driving, which was bad.

They had headed north, up the Hudson. At Glens Falls he took the highway to the right, instead of left toward the Great Lakes, and she, the city girl, the urban rustic, to whom the only directions that meant anything were East Side and West Side as applied to New York, did not notice, and she was still unsuspicious when he grumbled. "Looks to me like I'd taken the wrong road." Stopping at a filling station, he demanded, "How far is it to Lake George? We ought to be there now."

"Well stranger, way you're headed, it'll be about twenty-five thousand miles. You're going plumb in the wrong direction.

"I'll be darned! Where are we? Didn't notice the name of the last town we went through."

"You're about a mile from Fair Haven."

"Vermont?"

"Yep."

"Well, I'll be darned! Just think of that! Can't even be trusted to stay in one state and not skid across the border line!"

Mabelle was looking suspicious, and he said with desperate gayety, "Say, do you know what, May? We're only forty miles from our farm! Let's go have a look at it."

Mabelle made a sound of protest, but he turned to the children, in the back seat amid a mess of suitcases and tools and a jack and spare inner tubes, and gloated, "Wouldn't you kids like to see the farm where I worked as a kid—where your grandfather and great-grandfather were born? And see your Granduncle Rob? And see all the little chicks, and so on?"

"Oh, yes!" they shrilled together.

With that enthusiasm from her beloved young, with the smart and uniformed young filling-station attendant listening, Mabelle's talent for being righteous and indignant was gagged. Appearances! She said lightly to the filling-station man, "The doctor just doesn't seem to be able to keep the road at all, does he? Well, Doctor, shall we get started?"

Even when they had gone on and were alone and ready for a little sound domestic quarreling, she merely croaked, "Just the same, it seems mighty queer to me!" And after another mile of brooding, while Sidney drove silently and prayed: "Awfully queer!"

But he scarcely heard her. He was speculating, without in the least putting it into words, "I wonder if in the early summer evenings the fireflies still dart above the meadows? I wonder if the full moon, before it rises behind the hemlocks and sugar maples along the Ridge, still casts up a prophetic glory? I wonder if sleepy dogs still bark across the valley? I wonder if the night breeze slips through the mowing? I, who have for fortress and self-respect only a stuffy office room—I wonder if there are still valleys and stars and the quiet night? Or was that all only the dream of youth?"

They slept at Rutland, Sidney all impatient of the citified hotel bedroom. It was at ten in the morning—he drove in twenty minutes the distance which thirty years ago had taken Uncle Rob an hour and a half—that he drove up to the white house where, since 1800, the Dows had been born.

He could see Uncle Rob with the hayrake in the south mowing, sedately driving the old team and ignoring the visitors.

"I guess he prob'ly thinks we're bootleggers," chuckled Sidney. "Come on, you kids! Here's where your old daddy worked all one summer! Let's go! . . . Thirsty? Say, I'll give you a drink of real spring water—not none of this chlorinated city stuff! And we'll see the menagerie."

Before he had finished, Rob and Willabette had slipped over the rear doors of the car and were looking down into the valley with little sounds of excitement. Sidney whisked out almost as quickly as they, while Mabelle climbed down with the dignity suitable to a dweller in the Bronx. He ignored her. He clucked his children round the house to the spring-fed well and pumped a bucket of water.

"Oh, it's so cold, Daddy. It's swell!" said Rob.

"You bet your life it's cold and swell. Say! Don't use words like 'swell'! They're common. But hell with that! Come on, you brats! I'll show you something!"

There were kittens, and two old, grave, courteous cats. There was a calf—heaven knows by how many generations it was descended from the calf that on a June morning, when Sidney was sixteen, had licked his fingers. There were ducklings, and young turkeys with feathers grotesquely scattered over their skins like palm trees in a desert, and unexpected more kittens, and an old, brown-and-white, tail-wagging dog, and a pen of excited little pigs.

The children squealed over all of them until Mabelle caught up, puffing a little.

"Well," she said, "the kits are kind of cute, ain't they?" Then, darkly: "Now that you've got me here, Sid, with your plans and all!"

Uncle Rob crept up, snarling, "What you folks want? . . . By gracious, if it ain't Sid! This your wife and children? Well, sir!"

It was, Sidney felt, the climax of his plot, and he cried to his son, "Rob! This is your granduncle, that you were named for. How'd you like to stay here on the farm instead of in New York?"

"Hot dog! I'd love it! Them kittens and the li'l' ducks! Oh, they're the berries! You bet I'd like to stay!"

"Oh, I'd love it!" gurgled his sister.

"You would not!" snapped Mabelle. "With no bathroom?"

"We could put one in," growled Sidney.

"On what? On all the money you'd make growing orchids and bananas here, I guess! You kids—how'd you like to walk two miles to school, through the snow, in winter?"

"Oh, that would be slick! Maybe we could kill a deer," said young Rob.

"Yes, and maybe a field mouse could kill you, you dumbbell! Sure! Lovely! All evening with not a doggone thing to do after supper!"

"Why, we'd go to the movies! Do you go to the movies often, Granduncle Rob?"

"Well, afraid in winter you wouldn't get to go to the movies at all. Pretty far into town," hesitated Uncle Rob.

"Not—go—to—the—movies?" screamed the city children, incredulous. It was the most terrible thing they had ever heard of.

Rob, Jr., mourned, "Oh, gee, that wouldn't be so good! Say, how do the hicks learn anything if they don't go to the movies? But still, we could go in the summer, Ma, and in the winter it would be elegant, with sliding and hunting and everything. I'd love it!"

Mabelle cooked supper, banging the pans a good deal and emitting opinions of a house that had no porcelain sink, no water taps, no refrigerator, no gas or electricity. She was silent through supper, silent as Sidney, silent as Uncle Rob. But Sidney was exultant. With the children for allies, he would win. And the children themselves, they were hysterical. Until Mabelle screamed for annoyance; they leaped up from the table, to come back with the most unspeakable and un-Bronxian objects—a cat affectionately carried by his hind leg, but squealing with misunderstanding of the affection, a dead mole, an unwiped oil can, a muck-covered spade.

"But, Mother," they protested, "in the city you never find anything, except maybe a dead lemon."

She shooed them off to bed at eight; herself, sniffily, she disappeared at nine, muttering to Sidney, "I hope you and your boyfriend, Uncle Rob, chew the rag all night and get it out of your systems!"

He was startled, for indeed the next step of his plot did concern Uncle Rob and secret parleys.

For half an hour he walked the road, almost frightened by the intensity of stillness. He could fancy catamounts in the birch clumps. But between spasms of skittish city nerves he stretched out his arms, arched back his hands, breathed consciously. This was not just air, necessary meat for the lungs; it was a spirit that filled him.

He knew that he must not tarry after 9:30 for his intrigue with Uncle Rob. Uncle Rob was seventy-five, and in seventy-five times three hundred and sixty-five evenings he had doubtless stayed up later than 9:30 o'clock several times—dancing with the little French Canuck girls at Potsdam Forge as a young man, sitting up with a sick cow since then, or stuck in the mud on his way back from Sunday-evening meeting. But those few times were epochal. Uncle Rob did not hold with roistering and staying up till all hours just for the vanities of the flesh.

Sidney crept up the stairs to Uncle Rob's room.

Mabelle and Sidney had the best bedroom, on the ground floor; young Rob and Bette had Grampa's room, on the second; Uncle Rob lived in the attic.

City folks might have wondered why Uncle Rob, tenant and controller of the place, should have hidden in the attic, with three good bedrooms below him. It was simple. Uncle Rob had always lived there since he was a boy.

Up the narrow stairs, steep as a rock face, Sidney crept, and knocked.

"Who's there!" A sharp voice, a bit uneasy. How many years was it since Uncle Rob had heard anyone knock at his bedroom door?

"It's me, Rob—Sid."

"Oh, well—well, guess you can come in. Wait 'll I unlock the door."

Sidney entered his uncle's room for the first time in his life. The hill people, anywhere in the world, do not intrude or encourage intrusion.

Perhaps to fastidious and alien persons Uncle Rob's room would have seemed unlovely. It was lighted by a kerosene lamp, smoking a little, with the wick burned down on one side. There was, for furniture, only a camp cot, with a kitchen chair, a washstand and a bureau. But to make up for this paucity, the room was rather littered. On the washstand, beside a pitcher dry from long disuse, there were a mail-order catalogue, a few packets of seed, a lone overshoe, a ball of twine, a bottle of applejack, and a Spanish War veteran's medal. The walls and ceiling were of plaster so old that they showed in black lines the edges of every lath.

And Sidney liked it—liked the simplicity, liked the freedom from neatness and order and display, liked and envied the old-bach quality of it all.

Uncle Rob, lying on the bed, had prepared for

slumber by removing his shoes and outer clothing. He blinked at Sidney's amazing intrusion, but he said amiably enough, "Well, boy?"

"Uncle Rob, can't tell you how glad I am to be back at the old place!"

"H'm."

"Look, I——Golly, I feel skittish as a young colt! Hardly know the old doc, my patients wouldn't! Rob, you got to help me. Mabelle don't want to stay here and farm it—maybe me and you partners, eh? But the kids and I are crazy to. How I hate that ole city! So do the kids."

"Yeh?"

"Sure they do. Didn't you hear how they said they wouldn't mind tramping to school and not having any movies?"

"Sid, maybe you'll understand kids when you get to be a granddad. Kids will always agree with anything that sounds exciting. Rob thinks it would be dandy to hoff it two miles through the snow to school. He won't! Not once he's done it!" Uncle Rob thrust his hands behind his skinny, bark-brown old neck on the maculate pillow. He was making perhaps the longest oration of his life. The light flickered, and a spider moved indignantly in its web in a corner. "No," said Uncle Rob, "he won't like it. I never did. And the schoolmaster used to lick me. I hated it, crawling through that snow and then get licked because you're late. And jiminy—haven't thought of it for thirty years, I guess, maybe forty, but I remember how some big fellow would dare you to put your tongue to your lunch pail, and it was maybe thirty below, and your tongue stuck to it and it took the hide right off! No, I never liked any of it, especially chores."

"Rob, listen! I'm serious! The kids will maybe kind of find it hard at first, but they'll get to like it, and they'll grow up real folks and not city saps. It'll be all right with them. I'll see to that. It's Mabelle. Listen, Rob, I've got a swell idea about her, and I want you to help me. You get hold of the ladies of the township—

the Grange members and the Methodist ladies and like that. You tell 'em Mabelle is a swell city girl, and it would be dandy for the neighborhood if they could get her to stay here. She's grand, but she does kind of fall for flattery, and in the Bronx she ain't so important, and if these ladies came and told her they thought she was the cat's pajamas, maybe she'd fall for it, and then I guess maybe she might stay, if the ladies came—"

"They wouldn't!"

Uncle Rob had been rubbing his long and prickly chin and curling his toes in his gray socks.

"What do you mean?"

"Well, first place, the ladies round here would be onto your Mabelle. They ain't so backwoods as they was in your time. Take Mrs. Craig. Last three winters, her and her husband, Frank, have packed up the flivver and gone to Florida. But that ain't it. Fact is, Sid, I kind of sympathize with Mabelle."

"What do you mean?"

"Well, I never was strong for farming. Hard life, Sid. Always thought I'd like to keep store or something in the city. You forget how hard the work is here. You with your easy job, just filling a few teeth! No, I can't help you, Sid."

"I see. All right. Sorry for disturbing you."

As he crept downstairs in bewilderment, Sidney prayed—he who so rarely prayed—"O Lord, doesn't anybody but me love the land any more? What is going to happen to us? Why, all our life comes from the land!"

He knew that in the morning he would beg Mabelle to stay for a fortnight—and that she would not stay. It was his last night here. So all night long, slow and silent, he walked the country roads, looking at hemlock branches against the sky, solemnly shaking his head and wondering why he could never rid himself of this sinfulness of longing for the land; why he could never be grown-up and ambitious and worthy, like his father and Mabelle and Uncle Rob.

## Discussion Questions

1. *What made Uncle Rob think that Sidney's work as a dentist was easier than farm work? Do you think it actually was? Why do people often feel that the work of others is less demanding than their own?*
2. *Would Sidney have been happy as a farmer? What details in the story make you think he would or wouldn't?*
3. *What influence did Sidney's family have on him concerning his work?*
4. *Who arranged for Sidney's future? How?*
5. *Should parents have any say about the kind of work their children express an interest in? Explain.*
6. *To what extent do you feel parents should involve themselves in their children's futures?*
7. *Do you and your parents discuss your future plans? Explain.*

# ADDITIONAL READINGS

Thoreau, Henry David, ***"Life Without Principle"***

Is it **pecuniary gain** that you are interested in? Do you feel that hard work is reward enough in itself? Read this thought-provoking essay and you will learn how one New England observer viewed human endeavor and the institutions of the 1850s. Then you can decide for yourself whether basic attitudes toward work have changed, and if so, how.

Frost, Robert, ***"Two Tramps in Mud Time"***

Actually, why do we work? Is it just for pay? Or is it out of some other, hard-to-define special need? In this poem the poet reminds us that there really is such a thing as work for work's sake.

Sandburg, Carl, ***"Money"***

What money is and what it can and cannot buy is the subject of this poem. Sandburg may help you to understand more about what money is before you decide that that's all there is to life.

Nash, Ogden, ***"Kindly Unhitch That Star, Buddy"***

Even a humorous poem can provide us with insights into the byways of success. Here Ogden Nash plays with words for the fun of it, suggesting, indirectly that there are easier ways to become recognized.

Terkel, Studs, ***Working***

Is work just a "Monday through Friday sort of dying?" or is there more? This recent collection of interviews of working people catalogs the thoughts, feelings, and hopes of people in every walk of life as they go about their daily business. Their reflections on what they do for a living are often startling, especially for the uninitiated. (You may

**Additional Readings**

You may want to assign to each member of your class an additional reading from this list of readings concerning life-styles and careers.

Each time a student completes a reading assignment, it is suggested that a Reading Report Form be filled out and turned in to the teacher.

change your mind about wanting to become a model or a high-pressure business executive after reading these sections of this book.)

### Odets, Clifford, *"Waiting for Lefty"*

Do you feel as though the system or the establishment is stacked against you? This taut, one-act drama set in the Great Depression might tend to confirm your suspicions that you can't win. Are things today different than they were in the 1930s? Read the play and see if the people are right who say: "The more things change, the more they stay the same."

### Miller, Arthur, *Death of a Salesman*

This full-length play is an American tragedy of the mid-20th century. Willy Loman knows that it is very important to be well-liked. He realizes that he has to sell himself before he can sell anything else. But what happens when nobody buys him anymore?

### Updike, John, *Rabbit Run*

This disturbing novel of our times deals with a current and rather common problem—suddenly finding out that you are lost.

"Son, where do you want to go?" asks the garage attendant.

"Huh? I don't know exactly," answers Rabbit.

Harry (Rabbit) Angstrom is lost and running. He had been a star basketball player in high school. Now 26 years old, he is still running hard, but on a much bigger court.

"What are you afraid of, Harry?" asks his former coach. "Nobody cares what you do."

Are you a little like Rabbit? Running scared?

**Unit III Theme**
Making Decisions About Careers

**Unit III Introduction**
Discuss the de Tocqueville quote with the students. You may want to ask:
**1.** What does the first part of the quotation mean? "Chance is an element always present to the mind of those who live in the unstable conditions of a democracy. . . ."
**2.** What does the last part of the quotation mean? ". . . they come to love enterprises in which chance plays a part."

# What Are My Choices?

Chance is an element always present to the mind of those who live in the unstable conditions of a democracy, and in the end they come to love enterprises in which chance plays a part.

**de Tocqueville**

3. Ask the students if they believe the quote is true. Why or why not?

*What choices, priorities, and alternatives do I want to consider as I gather and evaluate information for my future?*

# WORDS IN ACTION

**Words in Action**

Discuss the Useful Terms with your class. All unfamiliar words should be checked with the definitions found in the Glossary. When students are ready, assign the Vocabulary Exercise.

## USEFUL TERMS

1. career source
2. fringe benefits
3. future demands
4. stop-gap job
5. work environment

**Vocabulary Exercise Answers**

| | |
|---|---|
| 1. career source | E |
| 2. fringe benefits | D |
| 3. future demands | B |
| 4. stop-gap job | C |
| 5. work environment | A |

**Correcting Mistakes**

Students should correct their mistakes by checking the terms and definitions in the Glossary.

## VOCABULARY EXERCISE

*On a separate sheet of paper list the terms above. Now read the selections below. Put the letter of each selection next to the term it describes. (You may use the Glossary at the back of the book if you need help.)*

**A.** Marcia surveyed with distaste the building she had been assigned to. The school was a well-preserved reminder of an earlier period in public education. From the outside, its massive red brick walls and stone arches, its iron fences and gates and caged rooftop made it look, for all the world, like a prison. But the interior, and particularly the classroom in which Marcia was to work, was warmed over by the years. There were well-worn wooden floorboards to which cast-iron and oak desks had been bolted. There were yellow oaken cabinets and bookshelves built right into the walls. There was a magical sliding-door which opened the oaken wardrobe; and inside, mounted on graduated oak strips, were cast-iron hooks, each one numbered perfectly with bold, black stenciled figures. Five great glass globes, suspended from chains, lit the room. Two metal-encased radiators spread out below the great windows that looked out on the dingy tenement across the street. This was Marcia's room now, the place where she would do her work. In an instant, she decided she liked it.

A. work environment

**B.** "But it's what I want to do!" exclaimed Jerry.

"O.K., O.K.," soothed his father. "Just remember you must put in four to six years before you're worth anything to anybody; first in school, then on the job. It's a tough racket. There are only a few openings now and not much call for this work any more. But if that's what you want, and you have the determination, maybe there will still be one or two openings left by the time you're ready."

**C.** It had been five months now since Mel graduated from college with a B.C.E. degree. His degree did not seem to be worth much in the job market as no one was hiring civil engineers these days. But he could not remain unemployed. When his friend Frankie told him of an opening in his company for a route salesman, Mel took the job. He was glad to be working, but he viewed this employment as temporary. He would work here only as long as it took him to find a job in his chosen field.

**D.** Cal knew he was starting at the bottom. The pay was low—minimum wage. But there were other compensations. It was a big company. Every employee had a comprehensive medical and dental plan, fully paid for by the company. Employees were given twelve sick days a year; the unused ones to be carried over each year of continuous employment. There was a generous expense allowance for business trips, and a country club for the exclusive use of employees. Cal felt these other compensations made up for his low rate of pay.

**E.** Jeannette thought for a moment. The best place to begin would be the guidance department of her school. Surely they would have some career information in the field of fashion merchandising. Then from a book or pamphlet she could get the name of a school or an agency to which she could write for additional career information.

**B.** future demands
**C.** stop-gap job
**D.** fringe benefits
**E.** career source

# A CASE STUDY

## DAVE'S CHOICE

**Dave's Choice**

The Case Study concerns the theme of the unit—making decisions about careers. "Dave's Choice" is a scenario about an eighteen-year-old boy who will graduate at the end of the school year. He is torn between two major but completely different career choices and he is having a difficult time making up his mind about which career to follow.

Assign the Case Study for homework. After students have read the scenario, use the section Thinking It Through to guide classroom discussion.

Questions 1–4 can be used for a group discussion of the case study.

Questions 5–9 may be assigned to students for homework. Answers to these questions should focus on the student's own background.

Question 10 could be a homework assignment to be collected at the next class period, or it could be a group activity involving the entire class. In this case the factors suggested by the students should be listed on the chalkboard.

Dave was clearly worried about the future—especially his future. He would be graduating from high school in June, and he had to make a decision about what he was going to do. He felt strongly that today's high school students couldn't look forward to doing something they wanted to do. "I think we're all going to have to look to see where the money is," said Dave, "because we're going to be sorry for it later if we don't. That's how I feel. I want to go into something that is going to have some kind of future in it."

He accepted the idea that schooling or training was necessary, but it had to be a program that wouldn't take too much of his time. The job situation could be worse next year. He wanted a good job with a future, and he didn't want to waste any time getting it.

As things stood now, Dave was considering two distinctly different career possibilities. Neither of these careers seemed to offer any solid assurance of a good job after he had completed the necessary schooling.

One of the fields that interested him was architecture. But the training period was long. The schoolwork was intense and demanding, and the cost was beyond his present means, even with a government loan. And what if there were no jobs when he graduated?

His other career interest was the culinary field. But he was not too sure about the kind of job he would get if he decided on this choice. To be sure, the school he had in mind was close, and he could live at home and save money. The training period was shorter, the courses more practical—not too much homework and studying. The tuition would be much less than at a university. And, they could guarantee him a job when he graduated. But would it be the kind of job he wanted?

Dave began to review the factors that led him to his

present state of uneasiness. He had a part-time job now as a kitchen helper in a nursing home. They offered him full-time work when he graduated from high school, with a flexible schedule that would permit him to attend the institute. He liked what he did there and thought he'd like to go further with it, to train to be a chef.

As a senior in high school, he was taking independent study in the architectural drafting program. The average of his past grades in Mechanical Drawing I and II was 97. Construction drawing had always been his hobby. He liked to work out plans for things that were to be built. He was also interested in the construction trades and knew a little about building materials. Certainly there was enough here to warrant serious consideration of a future in some branch of the architectural field.

He thought about his personal goals, about what he wanted for himself. He wanted his own home—first an apartment, then later a house he would design and build himself. Eventually he wanted to settle down—to get married and raise a family, two or three kids he figured. Above all, he wanted interesting work and the assurance of a steady job with a future. And that, of course, meant advanced training of one sort or another.

He recalled what some people had said about the careers he was considering. If he went into the culinary field and became a chef, he probably would be guaranteed a job when he graduated from the institute. But it would be a long time before he could command a solid position that paid well.

It occurred to him that while he could work in this or that restaurant and accumulate a well-rounded background as a second chef, the opportunities for advancement beyond this point might be limited. The positions of head chefs in the better restaurants and hotels usually went to chefs from Europe or the Orient where gastronomy is an accepted tradition as well as an art. As a career chef he would be facing stiff competition for these top positions.

Of course, the culinary field also included the catering business, fast-food services, even restaurant management—but he had no interest in these aspects of the business. They were not what had originally attracted him to the field.

Architecture was something of a different story. The

field was broad, and there was a lot of latitude especially where his interests and talents were concerned. Once cultivated, his skills would be marketable.

True, five years at a university was an expensive investment that would call for a lot of sacrifice if he expected to go into business for himself, designing and building homes or office buildings. But the extensive background and training he would receive would also equip him for many other related jobs: architectural drafting, building contracting, landscape development. There were no limits as far as his interests were concerned. He decided he would have to find out more before he could make up his mind.

Dave learned from his guidance counselor at school that he could enroll in his local community college and take the two-year program in architectural technology leading to an associate degree in applied science. Living at home and working part-time, possibly even full-time at the nursing home, he could manage the tuition fees.

He would be furthering his knowledge, skills, and interests in the field of architecture—and eating. He would also learn about new developments in the field. He would meet people with similar interests. And he could take his time investigating universities that offered bachelor's degree programs. He might even find summer or part-time work that would tie in with what he was learning.

It was an exciting prospect, and a workable idea. Of course, there were no guarantees of a good job on graduation, but Dave felt he would have the necessary training to make a career for himself with unlimited opportunity.

Dave's situation is not unique. Just about everyone at some point in life faces a career decision that determines the course of his or her future life. It is a momentous decision to make! The best choices stem from sound information based on what we know about ourselves and what we know about the jobs or careers we are interested in.

Take a look at what you're doing right now—at your work in school and at any part-time job you may have. What can you learn about yourself from these experiences? How can you use them to help you make decisions? Find out about the options open to you, and consult with people to learn about opportunities in the career fields that interest you most. You can then begin to weigh the factors of a career decision with more knowledge and with more confidence.

It was Dave's part-time job that got him thinking about his future. He learned something about himself from his work. He began to learn more about himself when he took a look at what he was doing and what he had done in school. He sorted out the pros and cons of both careers. It then became obvious to him that he needed additional information that would bring him closer to making a good decision for himself. Getting a few facts put everything into perspective, and Dave was on his way.

There are three things to consider when thinking about your future career:

(1) The talents and abilities you could use in earning a living

(2) The possibilities for school and training which are practical for you now

(3) Your goals for the future—what you can do to grow and further your career interest

## Thinking It Through

1. *What careers interested Dave?*
2. *Why was Dave having such a difficult time deciding upon which career to choose?*
3. *What were the advantages in the two careers Dave was considering? What disadvantages were there?*
4. *Which career choice do you think Dave finally made? Explain your answer.*
5. *Make a list of the jobs or careers that interest you the most.*
6. *Write down at least five conditions you consider as either essential or important in any future career or job you undertake. Number these conditions in order of importance, using number 1 for the most important, 2 for the*

*second most important, and so on. Be specific in defining each condition whenever possible. You may want to include such conditions as good pay with opportunities for growth, personal satisfaction with the job, or increasing responsibility as skills improve.*

7. *In preparing for a career, how important do you consider education? Explain your answer.*

8. *Make a list of all the kinds of schools, institutes, programs, or courses you can think of that serve to prepare people for jobs or careers.*

9. *What alternative is there to schooling in preparing for work? Record any advantages or disadvantages you can think of for the alternative you have given.*

10. *Schooling not only takes time but also is often very expensive. Is it wise to enroll in a lengthy program of studies before giving some thought as to where it might lead? List some factors you should think about when selecting a post-secondary educational program.*

# REPORT PROJECTS

## PERSONAL ESSAY III

***Introduction*** In this essay you will be asked to describe the part-time or seasonal jobs you have held and to evaluate your experiences in relation to what you might like to do in the future. It is important for you to be specific, accurate, and complete in your descriptions (not just, "I stock shelves and stamp prices," but rather, "It is my job to keep the shelves in the soap and detergent aisles fully stocked; to maintain a running inventory; to see that these products are clearly stamped with current prices; and to help customers find what they are looking for in my department or direct them to other store locations"). Your comparisons should stress the similarities of your jobs. Your evaluations should tell what it was you liked or disliked about your work on each job with a view to your future work plans.

***Directions*** The questions of Personal Essay III are written in outline form. Use the letter and numerals of the outline as guides to plan your paragraph topics, but do not use them in your essay.

The main topics headed by the letters A, B, C, D, E, F, should each be answered by a separate paragraph. You may wish to refer to your Background and Experience Chart as an additional guide to your essay.

### Outline

**A.** Job description

1. What is your present job?
2. When did you start work on this job?
3. Give your job title and describe your duties in detail.

**Personal Essay III**

Sections A and B of the outline are self-explanatory. However, caution the students to include all the necessary information. Points a and b of Section A-3 are most important and students should give considerable thought to their explanations of what duties they found enjoyable and what parts of their job they disliked.

Section C in the outline calls for the student to compare employment experiences, not jobs or duties. What is called for are the things common to the student's total employment experience: reporting to work on time, taking orders, handling merchandise or money, keeping records, working with others, dealing with customers, and so on.

Students should be directed to look for the common strands in their employment experiences, for example, "made mistakes keeping track of money," "got along well with both bosses," "disliked being interrupted all the time by people coming into the office while I was trying to get my work done," "liked it when I was told what to do and then left alone to do it."

The object is to extract behavior patterns and useful ideas that suggest parameters for future employment, not specific duties, skills, or operations. This objective is pursued in point D-2 as a realistic consideration in career planning.

Students with no previous work experience should be directed to proceed to sections D, E, and F of the outline when writing their essays.

a. Which of your duties do you find most enjoyable? Explain.

b. Which of your duties do you dislike the most? Explain.

**B.** Previous jobs

Give the same details for each job you have held in the past.

**C.** Comparison of work experiences

1. What qualities have your jobs had in common?

2. What insights do these job similarities give you about yourself and the way you relate to the world of work?

**D.** Plans for the future

1. What are your work plans for the immediate future?

2. What do you feel are your chances for success in this work, based on your past employment experiences, background, training, or interests?

3. Do you see this job interest as a stepping-stone to some future career objective, or simply as the job you'd like to have now?

**E.** Long-range goals

1. What job, or career field are you planning to enter?

2. Based on your work experience, present training, and what you have learned about yourself and the job that interests you, what do you think your chances of success are?

3. Do you feel you know enough about the field to make a realistic career decision at this time? List some of the things you would still like to know about your career interests.

**F.** Alternative plans

1. Have you considered any alternatives to the goals you have described in paragraph E above? Explain.

2. Do you have any strong feelings about settling for second best? What are they?

3. What conditions would seem to offer you the best chance of job satisfaction?

## PLANNING A WORK EXPERIENCE TALK

***Introduction*** Anyone who works probably can tell many stories about everyday experiences on the job. These job-related anecdotes offer valuable insights into the work process in general, but more to the point, they tell much about how people view their role in these situations. Depending upon how we react, we are reflecting basic attitudes that are useful in making future job or career decisions. If we make a conscious effort to cast these clues into a vocational perspective, we arrive at a better understanding of the type of work that will prove most rewarding to us.

***Directions*** Using the outline below, prepare a brief talk to be given to the class recounting one or two personal experiences you have had on the job or in any job-related situation. Then tell what you think these experiences mean as you consider future work for yourself.

### Outline

A. Tell briefly what you are doing now or what you have done in the past and for whom. (Refer to A or B of Personal Essay III.)

B. Tell about one or two work experiences you have had on the job that stand out in your mind.

C. Tell what these experiences suggest to you about yourself in relation to your choice of a career. (Refer to section E of Personal Essay III.)

**Work Experience Talk**

This oral report is the vocalized extension of the employment experience data called for in Personal Essay III. Here the student should provide the specifics of job experiences in the form of anecdotes to illustrate the conclusions of the essay. For this reason, it is important that the student be restricted to telling what actually happened in each incident, without generalizing or straying from the facts.

At the end of the oral report, the teacher can help the student zero in on the crux of the matter by asking such questions as: "Would you say, based on what you just told us, that you prefer working with things rather than dealing with people?" "Do you find it a challenge to try to calm down irate customers?" "Would you prefer to work in a neat, clean place?" "You aren't willing to put in long hours on the job?" The teacher, in effect, should help the students see what their attitudes are toward work and their work environment.

Students who have not held any job can tell about experiences in helping friends or family members with an enterprise, or about services they have performed for neighbors or family.

**Letter to a Career Information Source**

The object of this project is to have each student compose and mail a business letter requesting information from an agency whose function it is to promote an industry, trade, or profession. The expectation is that the students will receive career information of a general kind that will give them some background or perspective for the career of their choice.

Students should understand that they are not applying for work. While they should want to learn about opportunities for employment in one or more branches of the field, they should not expect job offers. The model letter suggests content and form. Of course, it is expected that the students will adapt it to their own needs and interests.

For this project it is a good idea for the teacher to provide a file of sources where students can write for information. It is suggested, therefore, that the teacher begin with a basic file of ten or twenty cards providing addresses of agencies for the vocations the students are most interested in. This file can grow over the years.

Two reference books which are helpful in generating sources are the *Encyclopedia of Business Information Sources* and the *Occupational Outlook Handbook*. Of course, students should also be encouraged to seek out their own sources.

Lastly, it is advisable that the teacher approve a handwritten first draft of the letter that will eventually be typed and mailed.

The teacher should also express an interest in seeing what sort of response the students receive.

# WRITING A LETTER TO A CAREER INFORMATION SOURCE

***Introduction*** There are many ways to get information about careers. One that is sometimes overlooked is to write to some central agency that promotes its profession or industry, such as the American Medical Association or the International Ladies Garment Workers Union. These organizations are operated by people who either work or have worked in the fields they represent. They know many people in these occupations and are usually willing to provide general information about their career field to anyone interested.

***Directions*** A model letter to a career information source is shown on the next page. Using the *Occupational Outlook Handbook* as a source, select a career agency to write to for information. Write or type your own letter to the agency. Keep a copy for your career file.

***Note*** Remember that you are writing a business letter and that your purpose for writing is to obtain career information that is of interest to you. State your purpose for the letter and make your request for information in the first paragraph.

In writing this or any other business letter, there are a few guidelines to follow. Check to make sure your letter is

1. short and to the point
2. specifically worded (not vague or ambiguous)
3. free of overused phrases and slang expressions
4. written with good sentence structure
5. positive in approach
6. courteous in tone
7. written in an appropriate business-letter form
8. neatly written or typed

## Model Letter

1026 Traver Road
Pleasant Valley, New York 12569
June 30, 1981

American Association of Advertising
200 Park Avenue
New York, New York 10017

Dear Sir or Madam:

I am presently a senior in high school and am thinking about pursuing a career in advertising. I would like to learn more about the careers in this field, and about the training required for these jobs.

I would be very grateful to receive any information you think might be helpful to me.

Very truly yours,

Andrea Stone

Andrea Stone

**Career Monograph**

This is the major report project of Unit III. The outline can be reproduced leaving spaces for students to fill in the information, or students can simply use the outline headings as they write their report on notebook paper.

Since this is an extensive research report, it is advisable to line up the resources available ahead of time. The first place to consider is the school library. Many school libraries maintain career shelves for students as well as career files, cards, or folders, which offer information under common job titles. Two government publications that are basic to all research of this sort are the *Dictionary of Occupational Titles* (DOT) and the *Occupational Outlook Handbook*. If the school library does not carry them, it might be well to arrange with a local college library, a public library, or a government facility to borrow them for the duration of the research project.

Another resource possibility is the school guidance center. A career room might contain books, catalogs, career files, A-V materials, and possibly even a computer terminal that prints out information on occupations as well as on schools and colleges.

Beyond the school library and guidance center is the community itself. The state employment service; community vocational programs; colleges; public libraries; newspapers; chambers of commerce; the armed forces recruiting stations; post offices; county, state, and federal office buildings; unions; farm and home

# COMPLETING A CAREER MONOGRAPH

***Introduction*** The Career Monograph is both an extensive and on-going project, like the Background and Experience Chart of Unit 1. In this case the information being sought and assembled refers to a job. For this report you will be required to learn all you can about the job (or jobs) you are interested in and to write down the details under appropriate headings. Times change, and so do job classes and descriptions. Therefore, if your Career Monograph is to be of value, it must be kept up to date with as much current information as possible.

The research involves consulting many sources:

1. Government publications like the *Dictionary of Occupational Titles* (DOT) and the latest edition of the *Occupational Outlook Handbook*.
2. Computer-based systems that offer general and specific career information.
3. People now working at or still in touch with the job who can give you inside information.

This report can be put together in logical steps. Broad definitions, specifications, and statistics can be obtained from government publications and career guide files of one sort or another. Then, as this background is sketched in, more detailed description and up-to-date information can be added. Later informational sources might well include college or trade school bulletins, school guidance counselors, state employment service workers, private employment agencies, personnel officers of large firms, interviews with business agents of union locals, news from the business and finance pages of your newspaper, or people working at the job or in the field that you can arrange to talk with. First get what you can from the books and computer resources, if they are available. Become as familiar as possible with the job market before venturing forth into the field. You will then know what specific questions to ask of busy people, and you are more liable to get specific answers. In the end this will simplify your task measurably.

***Direction*** On a separate piece of paper fill in each of the headings below with information about the career or job you are interested in. (If you are thinking about more than one job, you may wish to prepare two or more monographs.) At the end of your report under the heading Sources, make a complete list of the persons, publications, or computer system you consulted, giving the dates the information was obtained.

## Outline

**A.** Name ________________ Date report completed _____

**B.** Job title ______________ DOT code number ________

**C.** Duties (describe)

**D.** Work environment (required to work outdoors in all weather, around machines, in an office)

**E.** Location of job (geographical center)

**F.** Earnings and hours table

| Entry-level income | Top-level income | Time it takes to reach top-level income | Average weekly hours |
|---|---|---|---|
| | | | |

**G.** Fringe benefits

**H.** Future demand (need for this kind of work expected to increase or decrease)

**I.** Advancement opportunities

**J.** Disadvantages of the job

cooperative extensions—all these are potentially valuable sources for the information required in the Career Monograph.

One particular problem to anticipate as this report is introduced will be guiding and monitoring those students who claim they have no idea of what they want to do and do not know how to begin the Career Monograph. The problem might be helped by looking into vocational aptitude and interest survey tests. Often administered directly by the school's guidance department, these tests are helpful in establishing and defining personal characteristics for certain careers. And, if the school is equipped with a computer facility with an occupational search file, the student can have his or her personal characteristics analyzed and sorted for specific occupations that qualify.

Since this report could require extensive preparation before any valid information is forthcoming and can be recorded by the student, it is well to be quite flexible on the due date. Actually, laying the proper foundation will put a heavier demand on the teacher's time than evaluating the final report, which is simply to verify that all the information called for has been properly cataloged and presented. The teacher should be certain that the student has cited *all* the sources used in the report.

**K.** Aptitudes required (How will you be expected to perform on this job?)

**L.** Interests and temperaments most suitable for the job

**M.** Physical requirements, if important to the work

**N.** Education or training required

**O.** Schools that offer programs, training, or courses in the career field

**P.** Period of schooling, unit cost of education, and entrance requirements

**Q.** Locally administered on-the-job training programs

**R.** Related fields of occupations

**S.** Local employers who hire for this job or for this kind of work

| LIST OF SOURCES | |
|---|---|
| Publications/Agencies/ Persons Consulted/ Job-site Visited | Dates Accomplished |
| | |

# RELATED READING

## A STUDENT IN ECONOMICS

*George Milburn*

All of the boys on the third floor of Mrs. Gooch's approved rooms for men had been posted to get Charlie Wingate up that afternoon. He had to go to see the Dean. Two or three of them forgot about it and two or three of them had other things to do, but Eddie Barbour liked waking people up. Eddie stuck his weasel face in at Charlie's door just as the alarm clock was giving one last feeble tap. The clock stood on the bottom of a tin washpan that was set upside-down on a wooden chair beside the bed. The alarm had made a terrific din. Eddie had heard it far down the hall. The hands showed two o'clock. Pale needles from a December sun were piercing the limp green window shade in a hundred places.

Eddie Barbour yelled, "Aw right, Charlie! Snap out of it!" He came into the chilly room and stood for a moment staring vaguely at the ridge of quilts on the sagged iron bed. The only sound was the long, regular sough of Charlie Wingate's breathing. He hadn't heard a thing. Eddie made a sudden grab for the top of the covers, stripped them back and began jouncing the sleeper by the shoulders. Charlie grunted every time the bed springs creaked, but he nuzzled his pillow and went on sleeping. Eddie went over to the study table where a large, white-enameled water pitcher stood and he came back to the bed with the water, breathing giggles. He tipped the water pitcher a little and a few drops fell on the back of Charlie's neck without waking him. Eddie sloshed the icy water up over the pitcher's mouth. A whole cupful splashed

**Related Reading**

The Related Reading for Unit III is "A Student in Economics," which is reprinted here in its entirety.

This is the story of a student, Charlie Wingate, who tries to work and attend college at the same time. He is in danger of flunking out of college for a variety of reasons and circumstances. In the end it comes to the point where Charlie has to pass his economics course or leave school.

Assign the reading to the class as homework. Then use the Discussion Questions at the end of the reading as a guide for class discussion.

Question 10 could be a homework assignment to be collected at the next class period, or it could be a group activity involving the entire class with the answers recorded on the chalkboard.

on Charlie's head. Charlie sat up quickly, batting his arms about, and Eddie Barbour whinnied with laughter.

"Arise, my lord, for the day is here," he said, going across and ceremoniously raising the crooked window shade. Charlie sat straight up among the rumpled quilts with his head cocked on one side, staring dully. He had slept with his clothes on. He sat up in bed all dressed, in a soldier's brown uniform, all but his shoes and roll puttees.

"You got army today?" Eddie asked, putting the pitcher down.

Charlie looked at him for a moment and blinked. Then he said in a voice stuffy with sleep, "Naw. I had army yesterday. I got army make-up today." He worked his mouth, making clopping noises.

"What time you got army make-up, Charlie? When you come in from class you said get you up because you had to go see the Dean at two-thirty."

"Yeah, I do have to go see the Dean at two-thirty. But I got army make-up too. I got to make up drill cuts from three till six." All at once he flopped back down on the bed, sound asleep again.

"Hey!" Eddie cried, jumping forward. "Come out of that! Wake up there, Charlie! You can't sleep no more if you got to see the Dean at two-thirty. You just about got time to make it." He jerked him back up in bed.

"Forget the Dean," Charlie said; "two hours' sleep ain't enough."

"Is two hours all the sleep you got last night?"

"Where you get the 'last night'? I worked all night last night. I had classes till noon. Two hours' sleep was all I got today. And darn little more yesterday or the day before. When is Sunday? Sunday's the first day I'm due to get any real sleep. Two hours' sleep is not enough sleep for a man to get."

He plumped his stockinged feet onto the cold floor and got up stiffly. He went over to the washstand, where he picked up his tooth brush and tooth paste and a bar of soap and slowly took his face towel down from beside the warped looking-glass. He came back to where his shoes lay and stood looking at the toilet articles in his hands as if he had forgotten what he meant to do with them. He dumped them on the bed, took the pan with the alarm clock on it and set it on the floor. Then he sat down on the chair and picked up one of the heavy army shoes, held it and felt it and studied it carefully before he put it on. He put on the other shoe with equal deliberation and stood up without lacing either of them. He took his things up from the bed and started off for the bathroom, his loose shoes clogging. Eddie Barbour followed him down the drafty hall.

The creosote disinfectant that Mrs. Gooch used in her bathrooms gave off a strong odor. "Dag gum bathroom smells just like a hen coop," Charlie said thickly as he stood in front of the white-specked mirror twisting his face. He wouldn't need a shave for another day. He had a fairly good-looking face, tan and thin, with ringlets of black hair tumbling down over his forehead. His large ears stuck straight out. He looked at his image with dark eyes made narrow by two purplish puffs under them, and he yawned widely.

Eddie Barbour stood leaning against the jamb of the bathroom door. He said, "You ought to try and get more sleep, Charlie."

"Are you telling *me*?" Charlie said, running water in the face bowl. Eddie Barbour was a freshman too.

## II

Charlie Wingate came walking along University Boulevard toward campus, hunched up in his army overcoat. The raw December wind whipped his face and made him feel wide awake. He passed a bunch of fraternity men pitching horseshoes in the drive beside the K.A. house. Two or three, sprucely dressed, gave him impersonal glances as he passed. They did not speak, and he walked past self-consciously, seeing them without looking toward them.

When he reached the business section opposite the campus he turned in at the white-tiled front of The Wigwam. The noon rush was over and Nick was not at the cash register. A few noon "dates" were still sitting in the booths along the wall. Charlie walked straight back along the white-tile counter and sat down on the end stool. Red Hibbert was standing by the coffee urns reading the sports section. When Charlie sat down Red folded his newspaper slowly and came over to wait on him. Charlie sat with his cheeks resting on the heels of his hands.

"How's it, Chollie, old boy, old boy?" Red Hibbert said.

"Not bad. Give me a cup of javy without and a couple of them Grandma's oatmeal cookies over there, Red. Where's Nick?"

Red scooted the plate with the cookies on it down the glassy white counter top and came along with the cup of black coffee. "This is Nick's day for Kiwanis," he said. "It looks to me like you'd stay home and get some sleep once in a while. You're dyin' on your feet."

"I am going to get some sleep Sunday, don't you never worry. I have to go see the Dean this afternoon. And I got make-up drill at three o'clock. I've got to make up some drill cuts."

"What you got to go see the Dean about?"

"I don't know what about; here's all it said." Charlie reached in his overcoat pocket and pulled out a jagged window envelope and a mimeographed postal card. He pushed the envelope across the counter along with the postal card. "I got that other in the morning mail too."

Red took the printed form from the Dean of Men's office out of the envelope and glanced at it. Then he picked up the postal card. It was headed,

FOURTH AND FINAL NOTICE

You are hereby summoned to appear before the chairman of the Student Senate Committee on Freshman Activities, Rm 204 Student Union Bldg., not later than 4 P.M., Friday afternoon. It will be to your advantage not to ignore this summons as you have three previous ones. This is positively the last opportunity you will be given to rectify your delinquency. Should you fail to appear this time, steps will be taken to bring you.

*(signed) Aubrey H. Carson, Chrmn*
*Com. on Frshmn Actvts.*

Red waggled the postal card. "What you going to do about this?"

"Tear it up like I did the others, I guess. I know what they want. They want to try and make me buy one of them damn' freshman caps."

"Take a tip from me, Charlie: I'd go see them. It won't hurt nothing, and it might be a lot easier on you in the long run."

"Hell, what can they do?"

"Plenty. They could sick the Black Hoods onto you."

"Ah! The Black Hoods, that bunch of amateur ku kluckers!"

"Call 'em amateurs if you want to, Charlie, but it wasn't only but last Friday night they took Sol Lewis out of the rooming house where I stay. It look to me like they did a pretty professional job on him. They used the buckle-end of a belt on him. They claim he was a stool pigeon for the University."

"Stool pigeon! Ah, you know that guy wasn't a stool pigeon, Red."

"We-ell, I'm not saying one way or the other. Anyhow, that's what you're up against when you take to fooling with that Student Committee on Freshman Activities, Charlie."

"Prexy claimed in his opening address at the first of school that he had put a stop to these masked frats and all this hazing."

“Yeah, he said he had; but how’s he going to put a stop to the Black Hoods? He can’t kick out all the biggest shots in the University, can he? All the big shots on the campus are Black Hoods. Football stars and fellas like that. You won’t see the President kicking guys like that out of the University.”

“Maybe not, but—why, hell, that freshman cap business is nothing but a racket. That’s all it is. Damn’ if I let ’em scare me into paying a dollar for a little old sleazy green cloth cap!”

“O.K., Charlie; I guess you know what you want to do.”

“Anyway, how could I get around to see that committee before four o’clock this afternoon, and see the Dean at two-thirty, and go to make-up drill from three till six? I’ll be late to drill and get bawled out by the captain again. The captain’s already about to flunk me for cuts. That’s what’s getting me down—Military. It’s this Military that’s getting me down.”

“Gosh, I don’t know, Charlie; seems like I get a bigger kick out of army than I do any other course I got. They sure learn you more in army than they do in anything else *in* this University.”

“Yeow, you learn plenty in army, all right. But what I don’t like is the compulsory part. I don’t think they ought to be allowed to make it compulsory for freshmen and sophomores. That’s just like they had it over in Germany before they got rid of the Kaiser.”

The red-haired boy gave him a startled look. He frowned heavily. “Charlie,” he exclaimed, “where are you getting all these radical ideas you been spouting around here lately?” Charlie peered at him. Red’s face was set in earnestness.

“Why, that’s not a radical idea,” Charlie said, pushing back his empty coffee cup. “That’s just a plain historical fact, that’s all that is. I don’t see where they got any right to make Military Training compulsory. This is supposed to be a *free* country. That compulsory stuff is what Mussle-leany and birds like that pull.”

"But, Charlie, it's all for your own benefit. The University is just looking out after your own interests."

"How do you figure they're looking out for *my* interests?"

"Well, for one thing, when the next war comes we'll all be officers, us fellas that got this training in college. We'll go right into the regular army as officers. There's where we'll have the edge on guys that never did take advantage of a college education. Person'ly, when the next war comes along, I'm not hankerin' after any front-line trenches. And you know darn' well they're not going to stick their college-trained officers into front-line trenches to get shot. So there's where I figure us guys in R.O.T.C. will have a big advantage."

"Yeah, you might be right, at that, Red. But I'm not kicking about R.O.T.C. It's just the compulsory part I'm kicking against."

Red perked his head and scowled impatiently. "Charlie, they *got* to make it compulsory. If it wasn't compulsory, how many of the fellas would enroll in it? They have to make Military compulsory in order to give the fullest benefits. What good could they do if only a few of the fellas was taking it?"

"Anyway, I know some it's not compulsory for," Charlie said stubbornly. "Last night there was a Phi Gam pledge in here bragging about how he got out of Military. He told them at the first of school he didn't want to take Military. They told him he *had* to take it—required of all able-bodied freshmen. Couldn't get his degree without it. So he had to go buy his army shoes. Well, he got the shoe store to send the bill to his old man. His old man is one of these they call 'em pacifists. When his old man gets the bill for his kid's army shoes, maybe you think he don't get the President of this University on long distance and tell him where to head in it. And this kid didn't have to take Military, neither. His old man's a big shot lawyer in the City."

"Yeah, but you got to have pull to get away with that, Charlie."

"That's what I mean, Red. You can get away with plenty in this University if you got the pull."

## III

Charlie Wingate loped up the steps of the Administration Building, hurried through the revolving doors, and walked past hissing steam radiators down the long hall to the Dean of Men's office. He was ten minutes late. Before he opened the frosted-glass door he took out a pair of amber-colored spectacles and put them on. Then he went in and handed his summons to the secretary.

"The Dean will see you in a moment," she said. "Please take a chair."

Charlie sat down and gave an amber-hued glance about the outer office. Three dejected freshmen, holding their green caps, were waiting with him. He recognized none of them, so he picked up a week-old copy of the *Christian Science Monitor* and started to read it. But the room was warm and he immediately went to sleep. He had his head propped back against the wall. The newspaper slipped down into his lap. His amber-colored glasses hid his eyes and no one could see that they were closed. He was awakened by the secretary shaking him. She was smiling and the freshmen were all snickering.

"Wake up and pay for your bed, fella!" one of the freshmen called, and everyone laughed heartily.

"I sort of drowsed off. It's so nice and warm in here," Charlie said, apologizing to the pretty secretary.

The Dean of Men got up as he entered and, with his eyes on the slip bearing Charlie's name, said, "Ah, this is Charles Wingate, isn't it?" He grasped Charlie's hand as if it were an honor and pressed a button under the edge of his desk with his other hand. The secretary appeared at the door. "Miss Dunn, will you bring in Wingate's folder—Charles W-i-n-g-a-t-e. How do you like college by now, Wingate? Eyes troubling you?"

"Pretty well, sir. Yes, sir, a little. I wear these glasses."

The secretary came back with the folder and the Dean looked through it briefly. "Well, Wingate, I suppose you're anxious to know why I sent for you. The unpleasant truth is, Wingate, you don't seem to be doing so well in your college work. Your freshman adviser conferred with you twice about this, and this week he turned your case over to me. My purpose, of course, is to help you. Now, to be quite frank, Wingate, you're on the verge of flunking out. Less than a third of the semester remains, and you have a failing grade in English 101, conditional grades in Psychology 51 and Military Training; three hours of F and four hours of D, almost half your total number of hours. On the other hand, you have an A average in Spanish 1 and a B in Economics 150. Wingate, how do you account for your failing English when you are an A student in Spanish?"

"To tell you the truth, sir, I got behind on my written work in English, and I've never been able to catch up. And I don't really have to study Spanish. My father is a railway section foreman in my home town, and he's always had a gang of Mexicans working for him. I've been speaking Mexican ever since I was a kid. It's not the pure, what they call Castilian, Spanish, but I probably know almost as much Spanish as my professor."

"How about this B in Economics? That's a fairly high grade."

"Yes, sir. Doctor Kenshaw—he's my Ec professor—doesn't give exams. Instead he gives everyone a B until he calls for our term papers. We don't recite in his class. We just listen to him lecture. And the grade you get on your term paper is your semester grade."

"Ah! What you students term a pipe course, eh, Wingate?"

"Not exactly, sir. We have to do a lot of outside reading for the term paper. But I'm counting on keeping that B in Ec."

"That's fine, Wingate. But it appears to me that it's high time you were getting busy on some of these other grades, too. Why can't you dig in and pull these D's up to B's, and this F up to at least a C? You've got it in you. You made an unusually high grade on your entrance exams, your record shows. Graduated from high school with honors. What's the trouble, Wingate? Tell me!"

"I don't know, sir, except I work at night and—"

"Oh, I see it here on your enrollment card now. Where do you work?"

"I work nights for Nick Pappas, down at The Wigwam."

"How many hours a night do you work?"

"Ten hours, sir. From nine till seven. The Wigwam stays open all night. I eat and go to eight o'clock class when I get off."

"Very interesting, Wingate. But don't you suppose that it would be advisable to cut down a bit on this outside work and attend a little more closely to your college work? After all, that's what you're here for, primarily—to go to college, not work in a café."

"I couldn't work fewer hours and stay in school, sir. I just barely get by as it is. I get my board at The Wigwam, and I pay my room rent, and I've been paying out on a suit of clothes. That leaves only about a dollar a week for all the other things I have to have."

"Wingate, shouldn't you earn more than that, working ten hours?"

"I get the regular, first-year-man rate, sir. Twenty cents an hour. It's set by the University. Nick takes out a dollar a day for board. Pays me five dollars a week in cash."

"Can't you arrange for a little financial support from home?"

"No, sir, I'm afraid I couldn't. I have two brothers and two sisters at home younger than I am. It wouldn't be right for me to ask my father to send money out of what he makes."

"But surely you could get out and land something a little more lucrative than this all-night restaurant job, Wingate."

"No, sir. Twenty cents an hour is standard rate for working students, and I haven't found anything better. Nick says he has at least thirty men on the waiting list for this job I have."

"Well, there's this about it, Wingate. The University is here, supported by the taxpayers of this State, for the purpose of giving the young men and women of this State educational opportunities. The University is not here for the purpose of training young men to be waiters in all-night restaurants. And, so far as I can see, that's about all you are deriving from your University career. So it occurs to me that you should make a choice: either find some way to devote more attention to your college work or drop out of school altogether. We are very loathe to encourage students who are *entirely* self-supporting. And yet, I will admit that I know any number of first-rate students who are entirely self-supporting. There's Aubrey Carson, for example. Quarterback on the football team, delegate to the Olympics, president of the Student Senate, and he's a straight A student. Aubrey Carson was telling me only last week that he hasn't had any financial assistance from home since he enrolled as a freshman. Aubrey is a fine example of the working student."

"Yes, sir; but look at the job Carson has. He works for a big tobacco company, and all he has to do is hand out Treasure Trove cigarettes to other students. The tobacco company pays him a good salary for passing out samples of their cigarettes."

"Why, Wingate, you surely must be mistaken about that. I don't believe Aubrey Carson smokes. In fact, I know he doesn't smoke. He's one of the finest all-'round athletes in this country."

"No, sir; I don't say he smokes either. But that's the straight stuff about his job with the cigarette company.

They figure it's a good advertisement to have a popular guy like Aubrey Carson passing out Treasure Troves. Sort of an endorsement."

"All the same, Wingate, it doesn't reflect a very good attitude on your part, criticizing the way one of your fellow students earns his college expenses."

"Oh, I didn't mean to criticize him, sir. I was only saying—"

"Yes, yes, I know; but all this is beside the point. We're here to discuss the state of your grades, Wingate. The fact is, you are on probation right now. As you must know, any student who is passing in less than half his work is automatically suspended from the University and must return to his home. Now one F more and out you'll go, Wingate. That's just being frank with you."

"I'd hate to have to go back home like that, sir."

"Well, you'd have to. If you flunk out, the University authorities are obliged to see that you return to your home immediately."

"I'd hate that, sir. I'd hate to go back home and have to live off my family, and that's probably what I'd have to do. I had a letter from mother yesterday, and she says that nearly all the boys who graduated from high school with me are still there, loafing on the streets and living off their old folks. I don't like that idea. Mother's proud of me because I'm working my way through college. You know there are not many jobs to be had nowadays, sir, and I'd hate to have to go back home and loaf."

"It *is* a problem, I'll confess, Wingate. But what's the point in your coming to the University and working all night in a café and then flunking your class work? Moreover, your freshman adviser reports that you make a practice of sleeping in class. Is that true?"

"Well, yes, sir. I suppose I do drop off sometimes."

"Pretty impossible situation, isn't it, Wingate? Well, I've given you the best advice I can. Unless you can alter your circumstances I suggest that you withdraw from the University at once. We have six thousand other students here who need our attention, and the University has to be impartial and impersonal in dealing with these problems. Unless you can find some means to avoid flunking out I suggest withdrawing beforehand."

"Withdrawal would be a disgrace to me, sir. If I withdrew and went back home now, everyone at home would say that I had been expelled. You know how small towns are."

"Ah, now, Wingate, when you begin dealing with small-town gossip, I fear you're really getting outside my province. But I should think you'd prefer honorable withdrawal to flunking out."

"I believe I'll try to stick it through, sir. I'll try to remove the conditional grades, and maybe I can luck through on my finals."

"I hope you can, Wingate. As long as you feel that way about it, good luck to you." The Dean of Men stood up. Charlie stood up too. The Dean put out his hand and showed his teeth in a jovial smile and bore down hard on Charlie's knuckles. "I'm counting on you strong, old man," he said, encircling Charlie's shoulders with his left arm. "I know you have the stuff and that you'll come through with flying colors one of these days."

"Thank you, sir," Charlie said, grinning tearfully while the Dean gave his shoulder little pats. He edged toward the door as soon as the Dean released him, but when he reached it he hesitated and pulled the postal card out of his pocket. "Oh, pardon me, sir, but there's something I forgot to ask you. I got this in the mail today. I've been a little bothered about what to do about it."

The Dean of Men took the mimeographed card and read it quickly. "Why, I should say that you ought to go see what they want, Wingate. You shouldn't ignore things of this sort, you know. It's all a part of the normal activities of college life. No reason for antagonizing your fellow-students by ignoring a request of this kind."

"All right, sir; I'll go see them."

"Why, to be sure, go see them! Always keep in mind that the University is a social as well as an educational institution, Wingate."

## IV

Room 204, Student Union Building, was a newly finished, rather barren office that smelled dankly of lime in the fresh plaster. It was fitted with a metal desk painted to imitate painted walnut, a large brass spittoon, a square metal wastepaper basket, a green metal filing cabinet, a large bank calendar, a huge pasteboard shipping case, and Aubrey H. Carson, who had the freshman cap concession.

Charlie Wingate hesitantly opened the door and saw Aubrey H. Carson tilted back in a chair, his feet on the metal walnut desk, reading a copy of *Ballyhoo*.

"Co-ome in! Co-ome in!" Aubrey Carson called loudly without putting down his magazine. "All right, old timer. What's on your mind?"

Charlie held out the mimeographed card. Carson held his magazine a moment longer before accepting the card. He shoved his hat down over one eye, turning the card, looking first at the back, then at the name on the front. "Um-m-m," he grunted. He reached over to a drawer in the filing cabinet without taking his feet down and flipped through the cards. He looked at the name on the postal card again, pulled a card out of the file, and drew his thick lips up into a rosette. He looked at the file card in silence.

"Wingate," he said at last in a severe tone, "you have been dilatory. Indeed, Wingate, I might even go so far as to say you have been remiss. At the beginning of this semester you applied for and received a refund on your student ticket fee. That signifies that you have not attended a single football game this season, and that you have no intention of honoring any of the University's athletic spectacles with your presence this season. Also, the record discloses that you did not register at the Y.M.C.A. freshman mixer. Neither did you respond to polite solicitation for a trifling monetary pledge to the Memorial Stadium Fund. And, most heinous offense of all, Wingate, we find that you have yet to pay in one dollar for your freshman cap, prescribed by your seniors and purveyed to you on a non-profit basis by the Student Committee on Freshman Activities. And yet, Wingate, I find you duly enrolled and attending classes in this here now University. Wingate, what possible excuse do you have for such gross neglect of University tradition? Speak up!"

Charlie said meekly, "Well, I work nights and it's hard for me to get here in the daytime, and I can't afford to buy a cap."

"What's this!" Carson exclaimed, jerking his legs down from the desk top and banging the desk with two flat hands. "Why, boy, this is treason! You mean you can't afford *not* to buy a freshman cap."

"No, I just came to tell you that a dollar has to go a long way with me and that I need every cent I earn to stay in school. So I wish you'd please excuse me from buying a freshman cap."

Carson's lean, florid face suddenly became rigid and he stuck his jaw out with his lower teeth showing and, in spite of his marcelled taffy pompadour and his creased tailored suit, he again looked very much as he did in all the sporting section photographs. "See here, Wingate," he said, hard-lipped, "You're still a freshman at this University. You'll have to wait another year before you can start saying what you will do and won't do, see? Now we've been patient with you. You've been in school here three months without putting on a freshman cap. Do you realize that over eighty-five percent of the freshman class came in here and bought their caps before the first week of school ended? Now who do you think *you* are, Wingate—Mr. God? You're going to get you a cap, and you're going to wear it. See? No ifs, ands, or buts about it. And if you don't leave this office with a green cap on your head then I don't mind telling you that we've got ways of getting one on you before another day passes."

"Well, if I buy one it's going to put me in a bad hole. All the money I've got is what I saved out to pay my room rent this week."

"Listen, fella, if we let horsefeathers like that go here, half the freshman class wouldn't be wearing freshman caps right now. Now I've said all I'm going to to you. Do you want your green cap now or will you wait till later? That's all I want to know. I don't aim to give you any high-pressure sales talk on something that's already been decided for you. Take it or leave it."

Carson reached over into the large pasteboard box, groped far down in it, and brought forth a small green monkey cap. He tossed it on the desk. Charlie Wingate stuck his forefinger in his watch pocket and pulled out a small pad of three carefully folded dollar bills. He unfolded them and laid one on the desk and picked up the cap. Carson put the dollar in his pocket and stood up.

Charlie stood holding his cap. He scuffed the cement floor with his shoe toe and began doggedly, "The only thing is—"

"Aw, that's O.K., Wingate, old man," Carson said suavely, "No hard feelings whatsover." He held out a freshly opened pack of cigarettes. "Here, have a Treasure Trove on me before you go."

## V

That night all the stools along the counter at The Wigwam were filled when Charlie Wingate came in, still dusty from the drill field. He got himself a set-up back of the counter and went into the kitchen. He moved about the steam-table, dishing up his dinner. He dragged a stool over to a zinc-covered kitchen table and sat down to eat. The kitchen was warm and steamy and the air was thick with the odors of sour chili grease and yellow soap melting in hot dishwater.

Charlie's fork slipped through his fingers, and he began nodding over his plate.

Fat Kruger, the night dishwasher and short-order cook, yelled, "Hey, there, wake up and pay for your bed!" Charlie jerked his head up and looked at the ponderous, good-humored cook with half-lidded eyes. "Why'n't you try sleeping in bed once in a while, Charlie?" Fat said in a friendly tone. "You're going to kill yourself if you don't watch out, trying to go without sleep."

"Don't worry, Fat. I can take it," Charlie said.

Almost two hours had to pass before it would be the hour for him to come on, but not time enough for him to walk back to his room and catch a nap, so he took the book on which he had to make an outside reading report in Economics 150 and went up to the last booth to study until nine o'clock. He fell asleep and he did not wake up until Red Hibbert, going off, shook him and told him that it was almost time for him to come on. He closed his book and went back to the washroom. The acrid stench of the mothballs that Nick used to deodorize the latrine cleared his head. He took down his apron and tied it on over his army breeches. Then he slipped into a white coat.

The usual black-coffee addicts came dribbling in. When the telephone rang, Charlie answered it, jotting down short orders to go. The delivery boy came in and went out and banged off on his motorcycle with paper bags full of "red hots" and nickel hamburgers and coffee in paper cylinders. The Wigwam's white tile shone under the inverted alabaster urns. There was a pale pink reflection in the plate-glass window as the Neon sign outside spelled and re-spelled "Wigwam Eats. Open All Night." A party of drunken Betas came in at ten-thirty and seated themselves noisily in the last booth. They tossed Charlie's economics book out into the aisle with a whoop, and he came and picked it up and took their orders in silence while they kidded him about his flap ears and the grease on his white coat. At eleven o'clock the last whistle at the University power house blew for the closing hour, and a couple of lingering "dates" scurried out. Finally the drunks left, after one had been sick in a corner of the booth. The delivery boy came coasting up at midnight and checked in and roared away again on his motorcycle. The long small hours began inching past.

At one o'clock Charlie finished cleaning up the drunk's mess and he had cleared off the last of the tables. The Wigwam was empty, so he opened the book he must read for Ec 150. He had read a few lines when a bunch of girls from the Theta house down the street came charging in, giggling and talking in gasps and screams, their fur coats clutched over their sleeping pajamas. It was long after the closing hour, and they told Charlie to keep an eye out for the University night watchman. They took up the two back booths and they consulted The Wigwam's printed menu card without failing to read aloud the lines "Nick (Pericles) Pappas," "We Employ Student Help Exclusively," and "Please Do Not Tip. A Smile Is Our Reward" with the customary shrieks. Nearly all ordered filet mignon and French fries, which were not on the menu, but two or three ordered pecan waffles and coffee, which were. When he had served their orders Charlie went back to his book again, but the low buzz of their talk and their sudden spurts of laughter disturbed him and he could not read. At a quarter of two they began peering round corners of their booths. They asked Charlie in stage-whispers if the coast were clear.

Charlie went to the door and looked out on the street and beckoned widely with his arm. They trooped out with their fur coats pulled tight, their fur-trimmed silken mules slapping their bare heels. Charlie went on back to clear away their dishes. They had left about thirty cents as a tip, all in cents and nickels. The coins were carefully imbedded in the cold steak grease and gluey syrup and putty-colored cigarette leavings on their plates. Charlie began stacking the plates without touching the money. He carried the dirty dishes back and set them through the opening in the kitchen wall. Fat Kruger came to the opening and Charlie went back to his book.

Fat called, "Hey, Charlie, you leavin' this tip again?"

"You're damn' right, I'm leaving it!" Charlie said. "I can get along without their tips. They leave it that way every time. I guess they think I'll grabble on their filthy plates to get a lousy thirty cents. It takes a woman to think up something like that."

"Charlie, you're too proud. I don't see where you can afford to be so proud. The way I figure it, thirty cents is thirty cents."

"Hell, I'm not proud, Fat. I just try to keep my self-respect. When those sorority sows come in and plant their tips in the dirt and grease of their plates, damn' if I'll lower myself to grub it out."

He sat down on a counter stool with the economics book before him, trying to fix his mind on it. He read a page. The print became thin blurred parallels of black on the page. His eyelids kept drooping shut and he propped the muscles with his palms at his temples, trying to keep his eyes open. His head jerked forward and he caught it and began reading again. Soon his face lowered slowly through his hands and came to rest on the open book.

Fat Kruger came through the kitchen swinging door and tiptoed up front. Fat stood grinning, watching Charlie sleep. Cramped over with his head on the counter, Charlie snored softly. Fat gave his head a gentle shove, and Charlie started up to catch his balance.

"For God sakes, guy, you're *dead*!" Fat howled. "Don't you never get no sleep except like that?"

"What time is it?" Charlie said, yawning and arching his back.

"Half-past two."

"Jees, is that all?"

"Charlie, go back there and lay down on the kitchen table. I'll watch the front for you. Nobody'll be coming in for a while."

As he was talking old Uncle Jim Hudson ambled in, a bundle of sweaters, overcoats, and grizzled dewlaps, his black timeclock slung over one shoulder by a leather lanyard. Uncle Jim laid his long, nickled flashlight carefully on the counter and eased himself onto a stool. He ordered a cup of black coffee and in a lecherous wheeze began telling dirty stories selected from his twenty years' experience as a campus night-watchman. Fat Kruger nickered loudly after each telling, and Charlie jerked his eyes open and smiled sleepily. It was three-thirty when Uncle Jim left. Charlie opened his book again.

"Charlie, I wouldn't put my eyes out over that damn' book if I was you, when you're dyin' for sleep," Fat said.

"I've got to get it read, Fat. It's my outside reading in Economics and the whole semester grade depends on it. It's the hardest book to keep your mind on you ever saw. I've been reading on it for over a month and I'm only half through, and he's going to call for these reports any day now. If I flunk Ec I flunk out of school."

"Why mess with reading it? I know a guy over at the Masonic Dorm who'll read it and write your report for two bucks. He writes all my English themes for me, and I'm making a straight A in English. He only charges fifty cents for short themes and two bucks for term papers. You ought to try him."

"Hell, Fat, you get five dollars a week from home. Where am I going to get two dollars for hiring a guy to read this book?"

"Charlie, I just can't figure you out. You never do get any real sleep. You sure must want a college education bad. It don't look to me like you would figure it's worth it."

"Oh, it's worth it! It's a big satisfaction to my folks to have me in college. And where can a man without a college degree get nowadays? But I'll tell you the truth, I didn't know it was going to be like this when I came down here last Fall. I used to read *College Humor* in high school, and when fellows came home from University for the holidays, all dressed up in snappy clothes, talking about dates and football and dances, and using college slang—well, I had a notion I'd be like that when I got down here. The University publicity department sent me a little booklet showing how it was easy to work your way through college. So here I am. I haven't had a date or been to a dance or seen a football game since I enrolled. And there are plenty of others just like me. I guess I'm getting a college education, all right—but the only collegiate thing I've been able to do is go to sleep in class."

"How you get by with sleeping in class, Charlie?"

"I wear those colored spectacles and prop myself, and the profs can't see I've got my eyes closed."

Fat waggled his heavy face mournfully. "Boy, it sure is tough when a man don't get his sleep."

"Yeah, it is," Charlie said, looking down at his book again. "I'll get a break pretty soon, though. I'd rather chop off a hand thanto flunk out of University before I'd even finished one semester."

## VI

The tardiest of the hundred students enrolled in Dr. Sylvester C. O. Kenshaw's Economics 150 straggled into the lecture room and made their ways to alphabetically-assigned chairs with much scuffling and trampling of toes and mumbled apologies. Ec 150, renowned as a pipe course, was always crowded. Doctor Kenshaw was the celebrated author of seven textbooks on economics, five of which his students were required to buy each semester. Doctor Kenshaw's national reputation as an economist permitted him to be erratic about meeting his classes, but fame had never dimmed his fondness for student flattery. The only students who ever flunked Ec 150 were those who gave affront to Doctor Kenshaw by neglecting to buy his textbooks or by not laughing at his wit or by being outrageously inattentive to his lectures.

Doctor Kenshaw was late that morning. Charlie Wingate sat in his chair on the back row in an agony of waiting. He had on his amber glasses and he could fall asleep as soon as Doctor Kenshaw opened his lecture. But he had to stay awake until then. There was a slow ache in the small of his back. The rest of his body was numb. He had not taken off his army shoes for twenty hours, and his feet were moist and swollen. Every time he shifted position his arms and legs were bathed in prickling fire. He kept his eyes open behind the amber lenses, watching the clock. Small noises of the classroom came to him as a low, far-off humming.

When the clock on the front wall showed nine after eleven the seated class began stirring as if it were mounted on some eccentric amusement-park device. Excited whispers eddied out on the warm air of the steam heated lecture room. "He's giving us another cut!" "He's not meeting this class today!" "He's got one more minute to make it!" "Naw; six more! You have to wait fifteen minutes on department heads."

There was a seething argument on this point, but when the clock showed fourteen minutes after eleven a bold leader sprang up and said, "Come on, everybody!" All but five or six especially conscientious students rose and milled after him toward the door. Charlie Wingate followed, thoroughly awakened by the chance of getting to bed so soon. The leader yanked the door open and Doctor Kenshaw stumbled in, all out of breath, his eyeglasses steamed, his pointed gray beard quivering, a vain little man in a greenish-black overcoat.

"Go back to your seats!" Doctor Kenshaw commanded sternly as soon as he could get his breath. He marched over to his lecture table and planked down his leather brief case. He took off his overcoat and began wiping the steam from his eyeglasses while the students hurried back to their chairs. "It does seem to me," he said, his voice quavering with anger, "that it would be no more than courteous for this class to await my arrival on those rare occasions when I am delayed. Day after day you come lagging into my classes, and I have always been extremely lenient in giving credit for attendance, no matter how tardy your arrival. Certainly it is no more than my privilege to ask that you wait for me occasionally."

A few students exchanged meaning glances. They meant, "Now we're in for it. The old boy has on one of his famous mads."

"Today, I believe I shall forego delivering my prepared lecture," Doctor Kenshaw went on in a more even voice, but with elaborate sarcasm, "and let *you* do the talking. Perhaps it would be meet to hear a few outside reading reports this morning. All of you doubtless are aware that these reports were due last week, although I had not expected to call for them at once. I trust that I have impressed you sufficiently with the importance of these reports. They represent to me the final result of your semester's work in this course. The grades you receive on these reports will be your grades for the semester. Let us begin forthwith. When your name is called, you will rise and read your report to the class." He opened his roll book.

"Mr. Abbott!" he called. Mr. Abbott stammered an excuse. Doctor Kenshaw passed coldly on to Miss Adams, making no comment. All through the A's it was the same. But with the B's an ashen, spectacled Miss Ballentyne stood up and began reading in a droning voice her report on *The Economic Consequences of the Peace*. Obviously Doctor Kenshaw was not listening to her. His hard little eyes under craggy brows were moving up one row and down the other, eager for a victim. On the back row, Charlie Wingate's propped legs had given way and he had slipped far down into his seat, fast asleep. When Doctor Kenshaw's preying eyes reached Charlie they stopped moving. Someone tittered nervously and then was silent as Doctor Kenshaw jerked his head round in the direction of the noise. Miss Ballentyne droned on.

When she had finished, Doctor Kenshaw said dryly, "Very good, Miss Ballentyne, very good, indeed. Er—ah—would someone be kind enough to arouse the recumbent young gentleman in the last row?"

There was a murmur of laughter while everyone turned to look at Milton Weismann nudging Charlie Wingate. Doctor Kenshaw was running down the list of names in his small record book. Milton Weismann gave Charlie another stiff poke in the ribs, and Charlie sprang up quickly. Everyone laughed loudly at that.

"Mr.—ah—Wingate, isn't it? Mr. Wingate, your report."

"Pardon me, sir?"

"Mr. Wingate, what was the title of the book assigned to you for report in this class?"

"*Theory of the Leisure Class* by Veblen, sir."

"Ah, then, that's the explanation. So you were assiduously engaged in evolving your own theory of the leisure class. Is that right, Mr. Wingate? You have evidently concluded that Economics 150 is the leisure class."

The class rocked with laughter. Doctor Kenshaw, pleased with his pun and flattered by the response to it, found it hard to keep his face straight. Suddenly he was back in good humor. "Mr. Wingate's theory is quite apparently one to which the majority of this class subscribes. Now I try to be lenient with students in this class. Surely no one could describe me as a hard taskmaster. But I resent your implication that I have been too easy-going. Now these reading reports were assigned to you last September, and you have had ample time to prepare them. I'll not call for any more of them today, but at the next session of this class I expect every one of these papers in. As for you, Mr. Wingate, if you'll see me directly after class, I'll be glad to hear any explanation or apology that you may wish to make. I want most of all to be fair. I have always given every student the benefit of the doubt until a student deliberately flouts me with his indifference. But I am capable of being quite ruthless, I assure you."

"Thank you, sir," Charlie mumbled. He suffered a slow torture, trying to keep awake until the class bell rang. He rolled his hot, red-veined eyes up with drunken precision to see the clock. Fifteen minutes had to pass before the bell would ring.

When the bell rang the class arose quickly and began clumping out. Several co-eds and men, politickers and apple-polishers wangling for A's, crowded about the lecture table. Doctor Kenshaw always remained behind after each class to accept their homage. But today he looked up over the heads of the eager group. He silenced their inane questions and flagrant compliments by placing his right forefinger against his thin, unsmiling lips. "Sh-h-h!" he said. The apple-polishers turned their heads in the direction of his gaze and then, giggling softly, tiptoed away. When the last had gone out, Doctor Kenshaw unscrewed his fountain pen and opened his roll book. He ran his finger down the list until he came to "Wingate, C." and in the space opposite under "Smstr Grd" he marked a precise little F.

A whiffling snore escaped Charlie Wingate in the back of the room. Doctor Kenshaw looked back across the varnished chair rows with a frown of annoyance. He took his overcoat from its hanger, slipped into it, and strapped up his brief case. He jammed on his hat and strode out of the lecture room, slamming the door. The noise made a hollow echo in the empty room, but it did not disturb Charlie Wingate. He slept on behind his amber glasses.

## Discussion Questions

1. *A dilemma is briefly defined as "an awkward situation." What is Charlie Wingate's dilemma?*
2. *What choice does the Dean of Men at the university offer Charlie? Does this choice seem fair to you? Explain.*

3. *Is the Dean justified in his example of Aubery Carson as being a model self-supporting student? Explain.*
4. *What incident in the story shows that Charlie Wingate has at least some measure of self-respect?*
5. *In view of his economic stress, do you think it is wise for Charlie to be "proud"? Explain.*
6. *Charlie says it is very important for him to keep from flunking out of the university. What reasons does he give for wanting to stay? Do you consider these good reasons? Why or why not?*
7. *What determines whether Charlie will stay in school or flunk out?*
8. *What has been Charlie's major problem right along? Does he flunk out finally because of this?*
9. *On a sheet of paper make two columns: one headed, Condition; the other, Charlie's Reaction. In the first column, list each external condition you can find that had a direct impact on Charlie's life at the university. In the second column, match each condition with Charlie's reaction.*
10. *On the basis of your notes and your evaluation of the situation, would you regard Charlie as a victim of circumstances? Explain.*

# ADDITIONAL READINGS

Thurber, James, ***"The Secret Life of Walter Mitty"***

Daydreaming is the subject matter of this humorous short story. Walter Mitty can become, in his imagination, the greatest anything-in-the-world at the slightest suggestion. As young children, we imagined ourselves in a variety of roles—invincible lawman, fearless race driver, nerveless surgeon—and we were always the best in any field. As young adults, we are more hesitant and often a little worried about our future. We are less secure about our status. Being the best is not the main concern; just getting a start is. Daydreams may be useful, however, in pointing the way.

Roethke, Theodore, ***"Dolor"***

The author of this short poem reflects sadly on the monotony of office work. Does it add up only, as he says, to "Endless duplication of lives and objects"? Do we allow ourselves to become colorless copies of each other in a system that ignores our individuality?

Harrington, Michael, ***"The Poverty of the Bowery"***

Two kinds of choices are presented in this essay: the man who chooses as his work ministering to the needs of those less fortunate than he, and the men he serves who have committed themselves to alcohol, "their working lives . . . ruined by their drinking." Compassion, caring about others—these are noble sentiments. But what happens when those you are trying to help cannot understand why you would want to waste your time on them?

**Additional Readings**

In addition to the reading included in this unit, there is an annotated suggested reading list. You may want to assign one of these readings to each member of the class.

Each time a student finishes a reading assignment it is suggested that a Reading Report Form be completed and submitted to the teacher.

**Reference Books**

The following books will be of great value and assistance to your students for this unit:

1. ***Encyclopedia of Associations, Volume I, National Organizations of the United States,*** Gale Research Co., Detroit, Michigan.
2. ***Encyclopedia of Business Information Sources,*** Paul Wasserman, et al., Gale Research Co., Detroit, Michigan.
3. ***Dictionary of Occupational Titles (DOT).*** U.S. Department of Labor, Superintendent of Documents, U.S. Government Printing Office, Washington, D.C.
4. ***Occupational Outlook Handbook.*** U.S. Department of Labor, Bureau of Labor Statistics, Superintendent of Documents, U.S. Government Printing Office, Washington, D.C.

Your librarian and guidance counselor should have most of these reference materials.

Robinson, Edwin Arlington, ***"Cassandra"***

An unheeded prophecy is the subject of this poem. The author, echoing Cassandra, the prophetess of Greek mythology, lashes out at the nation's young, who do not consider the lessons of history in planning their enterprises. While it is true that most of us tend to shun or scoff at prophets of doom, there are stinging accusations here that are hard to ignore, warning all those who are wise enough to listen.

Galsworthy, John, ***"Quality"***

The code by which a man lives may not always be in harmony with the times. Mr. Gessler, the subject of this short story, is a boot-maker. He is a master craftsman of the old school who either refuses or simply does not know how to relax his standards while others of his trade sacrifice quality to satisfy the demand for mass production.

Markham, Edwin, ***"The Man with the Hoe"***

Something less than human, something to be feared should he ever rise up against those who have kept him and his toiling brothers in bondage over the centuries—this is the stooped figure of Markham's poem, the perennial slave to the lords and masters of the land.

Rice, Elmer, ***The Adding Machine***

One drama critic called this unconventional play of 1923 "a merciless satire of the white-collar worker, a slave to his job and the victim of the very system he supports through his labor." Mr. Zero could well be the twentieth-century version of Edwin Markham's "The Man with the Hoe," defused and reduced to the ultimate waste product of modern civilization. The play has little to say for the system that keeps the "Zeros" in constant check. ("You can't change the rules—nobody can—they've got it all fixed. It's a rotten system. . . .") There is one optimistic note however: Those who run the system don't like it either!

## Brown, Claude, ***Manchild in the Promised Land***

In the matter of making choices, this autobiography is unique. It is difficult enough to escape from familiar, comfortable surroundings that threaten to engulf you. But when you're black, and your surroundings are the streets of Harlem, an extra dimension is added. A minister explains it this way to nineteen-year-old Claude: "All youngsters in Harlem are confused in their thinking. Their thinking is influenced by their environment and external values—not their own, but the values of the community, the people around them." Claude recalls his experience as a morbid fear that "became so intense that it would just swallow you. . . . I was afraid of what Harlem could bring out in a person. When I decided to move, I was trying to get away from the fear." Others remain convinced they are destined to live out their lives in the streets or in the jails. Claude learns that no one is destined for anything. They have simply made that decision—and he has made his.

## Rodgers, William, ***Think: A Biography of the Watsons & IBM***

This book tells the story of the IBM empire from its humble beginnings in 1911 to its present status as one of the world's most dynamic, admired, hated, feared, and influential corporate power. It is the story of the super company that computerized the world, and of the man who served as its guiding light from the beginning, Thomas J. Watson. For those who may be thinking about a corporate career, this would be a good book to read.

## O'Neill, Eugene, ***Beyond the Horizon***

Some of us are clearly fitted by nature to perform a certain role or to follow some special calling in life. (The Latin base *voca* in the word *vocation* means "call.") It is not unusual, however, that something gets in the way. In this tragic play, one brother of a farming family was clearly meant to work the land; the other, to roam the seas in search of adventure and romance. Because of their love and regard for one another, they reverse these roles rather than let a woman come between them. The double sacrifice proves to be unworkable, and three lives are tragically altered.

### Lewis, Sinclair, ***Babbitt***

Though written in 1922, this novel remains the "major documentation in the literature of American business culture in general." George F. Babbitt slipped comfortably into an existence that left no escape route. A partner in his father-in-law's real estate firm, one of a growing order of up-and-coming business enterprises in the bustling midwestern city of Zenith, Babbitt became a joiner and a booster. He was successful within his own circle, yet vaguely aware that he was trapped. What was it that prevented him from being anything but the Babbitt his family, friends, and business associates had come to expect? He wasn't sure, but his final words to his son are revealing.

# How Do I Go About Getting a Job?

What is a man worth?
What can he do?
What is his value?
On the one hand those who buy labor,
On the other hand those who have nothing to sell but their labor.
And when the buyers of labor tell the sellers, "Nothing doing today, not a chance!"—then what?

**Carl Sandburg**

**Unit IV Introduction**

Discuss Sandburg's poem with the class. You may want to ask:

1. Who was Carl Sandburg?
2. What did he mean by "those who buy labor," and "those who have nothing to sell but their labor"?
3. What do the last three lines of the poem suggest is happening?

*What tools and strategies can I employ that will open the doors to a job and to a career of my choice?*

**Unit IV Theme**

Finding work: approaches, systems, and strategies.

**Words in Action**

Discuss the Useful Terms with your class. All unfamiliar words should be checked with the definitions found in the Glossary. When students are ready, assign the Vocabulary Exercise.

**Vocabulary Exercise Answers**

| | |
|---|---|
| 1. affiliation | K |
| 2. commitment | O |
| 3. dependents | A |
| 4. disability | N |
| 5. employment experience | D |
| 6. extracurricular activity | I |
| 7. immediate supervisor | F |
| 8. marital status | J |
| 9. personal references | H |
| 10. previous addresses | M |
| 11. referral | P |
| 12. relevant | S |
| 13. rotational work schedule | Q |
| 14. security data | C |
| 15. shift work | L |
| 16. significant | G |
| 17. spouse | E |
| 18. surname | B |
| 19. vocational-technical school | R |

**Correcting Mistakes**

Students should correct their mistakes by checking the terms and definitions in the Glossary.

A. dependents
B. surname
C. security data

# WORDS IN ACTION

## USEFUL TERMS

1. affiliation
2. commitment
3. dependents
4. disability
5. employment experience
6. extracurricular activity
7. immediate supervisor
8. marital status
9. personal references
10. previous addresses
11. referral
12. relevant
13. rotational work schedule
14. security data
15. shift work
16. significant
17. spouse
18. surname
19. vocational-technical school

## VOCABULARY EXERCISE

*On a separate sheet of paper list the terms above. Read the responses below, which are taken from an employee's job application form. Put the letter of each response next to the term it best describes. (You may use the Glossary at the back of the book if you need help.)*

A. Karen L., age 5; Kris L., age 2

B. Heinemann

C. Arrested April 1979 on a trespassing violation. Arraigned before Justice W. Simmons in Lincoln, New York, June 1979. Entered plea of guilty. Fined $15, sentence suspended.

**D.** September 1979–June 1980

Part-time dishwasher in diner, Pop's Place, 10 Main St., Maywood, N.J. Salary: $3.10/hr. Supervisor: Hal Duffy, Manager. Left to take full-time employment.

June–August 1979

Water Safety Counselor & Lifeguard at Camp Ramapo, Arden, N.Y. Instructed swimming, lifesaving, and boating. Salary: $400/season. Supervisor: Arthur Keough, Camp Director. Returned to school at close of camp season.

**E.** Mary Spencer Heinemann, wife

**F.** Carter Chapman, Group Foreman

**G.** Speak German fluently

**H.** Dr. Anthony Baston, 1265 Broadway, Yonkers, N.Y.
Rev. Michael Walsh, Holy Trinity Church, Mt. Vernon, N.Y.
Mr. & Mrs. Erich Bach, 79 Creek Rd., Bogota, N.J.

**I.** Volunteer, Hackensack Rescue Squad; high school band; German Club; baseball team (varsity letter)

**J.** Married

**K.** Local 987, International Brotherhood of Aircraft Mechanics; Lions Club

**L.** ☒ yes (8 A.M. to 4 P.M., or 4 P.M. to midnight preferred)

**M.** 762 Sanford Blvd., Mt. Vernon, N.Y.—9/78 to 7/80
81 Creek Road, Bogota, N.J.—10/77 to 9/78
21 Enoch Drive, Hackensack, N.J.—4/62 to 10/77

**N.** Diabetic

**O.** If hired, two weeks notice to present employer

**P.** Want ad, *The New York Times*

**Q.** ☒ no (prefer regular hours Monday through Friday)

**D.** employment experience
**E.** spouse
**F.** immediate supervisor
**G.** significant
**H.** personal references
**I.** extracurricular activity
**J.** marital status
**K.** affiliation
**L.** shift work
**M.** previous addresses
**N.** disability
**O.** commitment
**P.** referral
**Q.** rotational work schedule

R. vocational-technical school
S. relevant

**R.** Buck County Vocational School, Carson, Ohio, 1978–80. 1,000 hrs. in Aircraft Maintenance & Servicing program—certificate awarded

**S.** Presently a student pilot; should have license in three months.

# A CASE STUDY

## BETH'S TECHNIQUE

Beth was in her senior year in high school and needed money to insure, run, and take care of her new car. (Actually it was a hand-me-down from her father, but she was glad to get it.) She realized she would have to find a job.

Beth began by asking her guidance counselor, Mr. Quinn, about part-time employment. She was particularly interested in the cooperative program for high school students set up several years ago by a leading employer in the area. She knew about a girl who graduated three years ago and who was now working full-time for the company in a good job.

Mr. Quinn knew about the program. He explained to Beth that the company had cut back on just about all hiring. The program she was interested in had been suspended.

It was two months later when Mr. Quinn called Beth out into the hall from her shorthand class. He had remembered their conversation. He said he had received a call from the local business office of the telephone company. They wanted to hire someone for part-time clerical work. The person hired would have to have shorthand and typing skills.

He told her a little about the job as it had been told to him and asked her if she thought she might like to apply for it. He added quickly that he was obliged to notify four other girls who were qualified for this job and who had also expressed interest in working part-time. Beth said she understood and asked Mr. Quinn to make an appointment for her.

The following Monday Beth reported for her interview. Mr. Quinn had given her two booklets from the state employment services. These booklets told her what to do and what not to do in a job interview.

Beth had been casual in her approach to the material

**Beth's Technique**

The Case Study concerns the theme of the unit. Beth was a senior in high school who needed a part-time job to pay for the car expenses she was incurring. The Case Study describes the steps Beth took to get a job.

Before assigning the Case Study to be read by the class, you may want to ask the students if they think it is easy or difficult to find a job of their choosing. Discuss the steps they might take to find a job.

in the booklets. She just figured she would be herself and use common sense in answering any questions. But she did review the contents of the booklets. She was surprised to find that what they suggested was not very far from her own ideas on this subject. Also there were one or two additional things she had not thought about that made sense to her.

Mr. Justin motioned Beth into the office and told her to sit down. He seemed preoccupied. He asked Beth how fast she could type. She told him. He asked if she could take shorthand. She said she was taking shorthand in school now. He asked what her plans were for the future. Was she going out of town to a four-year college? Beth said she planned to attend the community college in the fall, for secretarial science. Mr. Justin then asked what days and hours she could work now. She told him what time she finished school and what time she was expected home for dinner.

At this point Mr. Justin started talking about the part-time job he had open. The hours would work out fine. Beth said she would be interested. Mr. Justin asked if she had any questions. She asked about the monthly reports Mr. Justin had mentioned. He opened a drawer and pulled out a blank report form. He was painstaking as he showed her how the report was organized and how it was to be filled out. Beth nodded that she understood, and suddenly the interview was over. Mr. Justin thanked Beth for coming in and said he would be in touch with her through Mr. Quinn at the school.

It was a week later when Mr. Quinn called each of the five girls out of class, one at a time. Beth was the last to be called. She was told that she had the job. Afterwards Beth thought about it. She did not know about the other girls' interviews, but she knew she had answered Mr. Justin directly and without hesitation. His questions were what she expected and she was prepared for them. She listened carefully as the job was explained to her, and then she asked a question of her own that seemed important to her since it concerned the job. With that out of the way it was clear she could handle the job and would like to have it. That was all there was to it.

■□■□■

Seeking employment is a job in itself and must be thought of in that way. Effective employment campaigns and job-seeking strategies begin with a basic understanding of the process involved in getting employer and employee together.

The job market consists of many marketplaces of "buyers" and "sellers" of just about any kind of service you could name. Let's say I'm a welder and you have a welding job to be done. We get together in the marketplace for welding work. We discuss the terms of the job and agree on a price, and the transaction is completed.

The question is, How did we learn about each other's needs? If you do not know that I am a good welder, or if I do not know that you will pay well to have a good welding job done, nothing can happen. We both must know how to find each other in the job market.

The task of finding a job must begin by knowing where to look for it. To find the buyer for what you have to sell, you must get to the right marketplace. A welder would be ill-advised to look for work where bricklayers are being sought.

Identifying and cataloging marketplaces is not always as easy as it sounds. We have a tendency to stop our searching once we have found five or six major employers. Actually it is possible that there are many other employers, some larger and some smaller, all comprising what we have called the marketplace.

Also government agencies employ thousands of workers with many different skills. It would be a mistake to rule out this huge part of the marketplace, at least until the terms and conditions of government employment are investigated.

Sizing up the market is the next task in the sequence. At any given time there are strong markets and there are weak markets. If the market is strong, meaning that the demand for the seller's services is up and on the rise, it is a seller's market; the chances for rapidly locating or even selecting a good buyer will be excellent. For example, if the nation enters into a massive shipbuilding program to strengthen the navy, government contracts will be awarded to shipbuilders, large and small, in every major port in the country. The demand for welders will go up. The market for welders will be strong.

But suppose the market is weak for welders. The nation has cut back on its shipbuilding program. The welder will have to work that much harder to find employment—or else find or create new markets. (This echoes Sandburg's words: "Nothing doing today, not a chance!")

Once you have located the marketplace and determined the relative strength of the market for your services, you can go on to the business of advertising. The extent or intensity of an advertising campaign will naturally have to depend directly on the market. A strong market for a particular service will require minimal advertising, while a weak market will require an extensive campaign utilizing every imaginative skill and bit of persistence the seller can generate. In any case the seller of services must reach the marketplace by advertising whatever it is he or she has to sell. This advertisement sets the stage for the buyer and seller to meet.

In the marketplace, the buyer and seller seek one another out. Each knows something about the other before they actually meet: one for having read the advertisement and the other for having known what to write and where to send it. Each will probably prefer to remain uncommitted until an agreement appears to be mutually beneficial.

The buyer, or employer, will be taking a look at other sellers, or applicants. The applicant will also be taking a look at other employers. A kind of bargaining takes place as they talk about the job under consideration. "This is what the job consists of. . . . What I am looking for is someone who can. . . . I see that you have done similar work. . . . Do you think you can handle it?" "It sounds fine, but can you tell me a little more about the work I would be doing? What is the pay? What if I get sick and need medical care . . . ?" The meeting comes to a close when each party has gained all the information necessary to arrive at a decision.

■□■□■

Beth probably got the job because she had a fundamental understanding of the business of finding employment. In this unit you will be introduced to the tools and techniques of marketing your services. You will be taking a critical look at your past experiences in applying for work. You will be getting to know something about the market where you will have to look for work. You will be learning how to advertise yourself and your services. You will be learning how to present yourself to an employer. Finally you will be learning how to bid for the job you need or, better still, *want*.

## Thinking It Through

**Discussion Questions**
After the students have completed the reading, use the discussion questions in Thinking It Through. You may want to have a class discussion or have the students write answers to several of the questions.

1. *Why did Beth want a job?*
2. *Why do you think Mr. Justin gave the job to Beth rather than to one of the other four girls who applied for it?*
3. *Where does the task of looking for a job begin for most people?*
4. *Do you think it is a good idea to let a lot of people know that you are looking for a particular kind of job? Why or why not?*
5. *Is having had a part-time job of any benefit in looking for full-time employment? Explain your answer.*
6. *Would volunteer experience count for anything? If so, in what way?*
7. *Mary, a high school graduate, is preparing to look for a certain kind of job for which she is qualified by education, training, and perhaps a little experience. As she organizes her job-hunting campaign, what almost certainly is the first thing she must know?*
8. *In the event of an overcrowded field (more applicants than job openings), what are the alternatives for beginning job-seekers? Rate each alternative given as good, fair, or poor as you see it, and be prepared to explain your rating.*
9. *A manufacturer has created a product to be marketed; Jim has mastered a skill he wants to market. What must they both do, and how is this usually accomplished? Who will respond in each case, and in what way?*
10. *What is the traditional forum for an employer who is looking for an individual with certain skills, and an applicant who possesses these skills?*

11. *What situation faces every job-seeker who applies for a position that has been advertised? What does this suggest the job-seeker should do before any job interview?*

12. *If you were interviewing an applicant for a job, what things would you* have *to know about the applicant? What things would you* want *to know? What conclusions can you draw from the questions you have formulated here?*

13. *What is indicated when an applicant asks questions about the job at an interview? Is it a good idea to ask the interviewer specific questions about the duties of the job being outlined for you? Be prepared to discuss your answer.*

14. *Why is a job interview like a bargaining session?*

# REPORT PROJECTS

## PERSONAL ESSAY IV

***Introduction*** In this essay you will be asked to describe in detail an experience you have had in looking for a job. The kind of work is not important, but the method or process used to get the job is. You probably found that looking for work is a job in itself and that some ways of going about it are better than others.

As you write of your experience, try to pinpoint the reasons for your success or your failure as it relates to the outcome of the experience. Generalizing about why you did or did not get a job is not especially helpful. It is important to isolate and to understand the factors that determine the result of your job-hunting experience. You can always be confident in the knowledge that you have gained something from the experience, and that this bit of information will aid you in the future.

***Directions*** On a separate sheet of paper write the answers to the following questions in the form of an essay. The lettered and numbered headings of the outline are intended as a guide for paragraph organization. Do not write them in your essay.

### Outline

**A.** What has been the most important job you have applied for?

1. How did you find out about the job?
2. Describe the steps you took to apply for the job.
   a. Telephone conversations
   b. Letters written
   c. Applications or other forms filled out
   d. Pre-employment tests taken

**Personal Essay IV**

This essay deals with the mechanics and the psychology of applying for a job. It is divided into two parts. In the first part the students are asked to record the steps they have taken in seeking work and to report the results.

After recounting their experience, the students are asked to examine the reasons for their being hired or not hired. The second part of the essay calls for the students to generalize about what seems important in looking for work.

In introducing this essay, you might find that some of the students have never worked or even looked for a job. Since the first part of the essay is based on the experience of applying for a job, these students will be unable to respond. They should be directed to go ahead to Section B of the outline to develop in their essay what specific preparations and attitudes they think are important when looking for work.

Finally, the teacher should make clear that this essay deals *only* with the job-hunting procedure. It has nothing to do with how one should conduct oneself while on the job.

e. Interviews with the employer (What kinds of questions were you asked; what were your answers? What were your questions and the employer's answers?)

f. Discussion of salary

3. Were you hired for the job?

   a. How was this accomplished? (What steps were taken to advise you when, how, and where you were to begin work?)

   b. Why do you think you were hired? (If there were others who applied for the same job, why were you the one that was hired?)

4. Were you *not* hired for the job?

   a. How were you notified?

   b. How did you feel about not being hired?

   c. Did the employer explain to you why you were not hired? Did you ask?

   d. As you think about it now, if you had to single out one or two factors that accounted for your not being hired, what would they be?

5. Did you reject or turn down the job before or after it was offered to you?

   a. When did you inform the employer you did not want the job? How did you do this?

   b. What reasons did you give? (Were these the real reasons why you did not take the job?)

   c. What reaction did the employer have when you told him you did not want the job? Do you feel the employer's reaction was justified?

B. Tell what you have gained from this job-hunting experience.

1. What psychological factors seem important to you? (mental attitudes, emotional reactions, feelings)

2. Taking into account the experiences you have had in looking for work, list other things you count as important to keep in mind when applying for a job.

3. Why should you plan before you look for a job?

## PREPARING A RÉSUMÉ

***Introduction*** A résumé is a carefully worded written statement, a specially prepared advertisement of yourself, listing those things you hope will be of interest to a prospective employer. It is a highly regarded business practice to either mail or deliver in person your résumé to a prospective employer. The résumé serves as an introduction to the employer and as the basis for a personal interview.

A résumé should have these general qualities:

1. It should be immediately attractive in terms of neatness, readability, and clarity.
2. It should be organized in such a way that it draws attention quickly to your objective in seeking employment.
3. It should readily offer supportive information that shows the extent to which you can do the work.
4. It should be specific where job-related skills are concerned, but it should not attempt to tell the whole story (which can be developed in an interview).
5. It should be directed to someone who might be interested in your qualifications and who has the power to hire you.

In writing your résumé it will be helpful to refer to your Background and Experience Chart of Unit I. The achievements and accomplishments that relate to your job interests are recorded there along with all names, dates, and addresses you will need. Use the information to develop the details that relate to the job you are seeking. Remember that the best résumés are the ones that tell a unified story, where all the pieces fit together to produce a sharp picture of you as a good prospect for the job.

***Directions*** A sample résumé that follows an accepted format is shown on page 128. Using it as a model, write a rough draft of your résumé on the basis of your present job goal or career interest. Submit it to your teacher for suggestions and corrections, then type a final version for future reference and possible distribution.

**Résumé and Cover Letter**

While the résumé and its covering letter are credited as separate projects, they are to be submitted as one. The teacher should first point out the models in the text and establish the relationship between the two before discussing either separately. It might be helpful to mention that both the résumé and the letter would be sent together to a potential employer.

The teacher will find it effective to work individually with students at the start of the project. The students should be directed to submit rough drafts of both résumé and letter as soon as they are completed. Each covering letter should be checked to see if it states a purpose of writing, refers to the résumé, and suggests an arrangement for an interview. The teacher can then read the résumé to see if it meets the following specifications:

1. Coordination (Do career objectives and job interest tie in with the addressee and the statements included in the body of the letter?)
2. Content (Is the job interest specific and realistically figured at entry level into the field?)
3. Order (Does the career objective develop from an entry position to the student's future plans? Is the order of presentation from most important to least important?)
4. Continuity (Does each entry supplement and support the other entries without detracting from or conflicting with them?)

When both the résumé and the letter have been edited and agreement between teacher

# Model Résumé

MARILYN A. KRAFT
Hibernia Road, Salt Point, New York 12589
(914) 266-8547

<u>Job Interest</u>: Production Assistant, TV/Film--Graphics & Design

<u>Education</u>: Graduated Arlington High School, Poughkeepsie, New York, June 1981

Courses:
Film Appreciation, 12th grade. Critiqued lighting and photographic techniques of 12 full-length Hollywood films.

Social Studies Film Project, "The French Revolution," 11th grade. Participated in all phases of production.

Introduction to Filmmaking, 10th grade. Learned the skills of writing, acting, and directing by producing a 30-minute film, "The Mystery of Hunter's Point."

Award:
Outstanding Student in Home Economics, 12th grade.

<u>Work Experience</u>: Floor Assistant in Toys and Juvenile Furniture departments; Check-out cashier, Calvin's Department Store, 44 Plaza, Poughkeepsie, New York, December 1978 to May 1981.

Babysitting, part-time and full-time, including light housekeeping duties, 1975 to present.

<u>Career Objective</u>: I am interested in obtaining an entry-level position in the graphics and design phases of TV and film production that will offer me the opportunity to utilize my present abilities and advance my knowledge and skills in production phases of the industry, to qualify fully as a producer of educational presentations designed for public airing.

<u>Personal</u>: Born February 12, 1963, Chicago, Illinois. Health excellent.

<u>References</u>: References will be supplied upon request.

Hibernia Road
Salt Point, New York 12589
June 25, 1980

Mr. James Witherspoon
Director of Production
Educational Broadcasting System
2102 Sterling Road
Los Angeles, California 95327

Dear Mr. Witherspoon:

I am enclosing my résumé for your review.

I have learned from reading an article in Mass Media that you are planning to expand your production facilities at your New York location. As a recent high school graduate who is interested in all phases of media production work, I feel there might be a place for me in your organization.

I would be very pleased to meet with the director of your New York office to discuss my interests.

Very truly yours,

Marilyn A. Kraft

Marilyn A. Kraft

enclosure

and student has been reached, the final draft can be typed and turned in for grading.

Some students may wish to mail out one or more résumés with covering letters, if only as trial balloons. They should be encouraged to do so with the instructions that each covering letter has to be personalized for each addressee.

As a final note, the teacher should urge students to keep their résumés. This is a point-of-departure résumé, and all future résumés will grow from it as education and work experience accumulate over the years.

## PREPARING A RÉSUMÉ COVERING LETTER

***Introduction*** When mailing a résumé to a prospective employer a covering letter should accompany it. The letter should do the following:

1. Introduce the applicant to the employer.
2. Refer the employer to the enclosed résumé.
3. Explain why the letter is being sent.
4. Tell the employer of the applicant's interest in the company.
5. Request an interview with the employer.

***Directions*** Using the letter on page 129 as a model, write your own résumé covering letter to an imaginary (or real) employer.

### Job Market Survey

The Job Market Survey can be introduced as an extra grade option for students. While the final product is an individual written report, the project can be adapted easily to a committee orientation. The directions and outline offer students specific suggestions as to how this approach can be managed. When the committee work is completed and the written reports are turned in, the teacher can have the chairperson of the Job Market Survey Committee report the group's findings to the class.

The project can be completed entirely as an individual effort. But because of the scope of the report, results will probably fall short of what can be accomplished by the committee method and will take the student much longer to produce.

## PINPOINTING A JOB MARKET

***Introduction*** Trying to land a job is something like trying to get elected to public office. You conduct a campaign for the job you want and hope you will be elected from among the other candidates.

To begin with, you must know something about the job market and its employers. You canvass the area learning about various possibilities and opportunities for employment. You develop systematically a good approach for each prospective employer. You make notes as you go, keeping track of people, places, and facts to remember. You follow up on any leads you pick up in the field. And you let it be known that you are an enthusiastic job-seeker who will work hard when hired.

This report will help you locate and size up the job market in your area. It will be a starting point for your campaign. You will be recording for future reference all kinds of detailed information about the many sources that can be used later to open doors for you.

***Directions*** Copy each of the headings and subheadings given below, and for each section that can serve your job or career interests fill in the requested information.

To ease the legwork, it is a good idea to arrange to cooperate with other members of your group or class in putting together the common information required in this report—at least up to the point that it becomes necessary for you to get the particulars as they relate to your own special career interest.

Seven "share assignments" have been labeled in the outline that follows. Eight interested students can form a committee and agree on a chairperson. Each member completes a single assignment while the chairperson coordinates the effort and assembles the data. This information can then be shared with each committee member to complete his or her own report.

## Outline

**A.** Free Employment Services and Programs (Federal, State, Community) [Share Assignment 1]

1. Name, address, and telephone number of agency
2. Type of services offered
3. Names of persons to contact

**B.** Commercial Employment Agencies [Share Assignment 2]

1. Name, address, and telephone number of agency
2. Type of job specialization, if any
3. Name and title of person to see

**C.** Classified Telephone Directory Listing of Local Employers

1. Name of firm, address, and telephone number
2. Person to see, if known

**D.** Public Library [Share Assignment 3]

1. Name, address, and telephone number
2. Job- or employment-related information posted on bulletin boards; free leaflets (see librarian)

3. Titles and authors of books that relate to your occupational interest
4. Titles of trade journals, papers, or magazines in your field of interest; name and address of companies where journals can be ordered
5. Reference room sources for information about major public corporations who hire workers in your field of interest

E. Chamber of Commerce [Share Assignment 4]

1. Address and telephone number
2. Person to see about local employment

F. Schools and Colleges [Share Assignment 5]

1. Name of school, address, and telephone number
2. Kinds of services offered to those enrolled
3. Names of any placement, guidance, or vocational counselors

G. Civil Service Centers and Publications [Share Assignment 6]

1. Location of center where announcements and applications may be obtained
2. Title of publications listing civil service jobs

H. Labor Organizations

1. Name of union, local, address, and telephone number
2. Name of secretary or business agent

I. Newspapers and Magazines with Classified Sections [Share Assignment 7]

1. Name of publication; whether it is published daily, weekly, or monthly
2. Place where want ads normally appear in any of these publications

3. Number of jobs listed during a given period of time related to your field of interest
4. Sections in the paper that include stories related to expansion, new industry, growth, or leads to job opportunities

J. Personal Contacts

1. Name, address, and telephone number
2. Occupation and name of employer
3. Relationship to you
4. How person can be of help
5. Is person satisfied with career choice?

## FILLING OUT A JOB APPLICATION FORM

***Introduction*** Filling out an application for a job is the usual procedure for all but the very smallest of business organizations. It is something you will probably have to do many times in the course of your working life. It is a good idea, then, to prepare yourself for the questions most usually asked.

Incomplete and incorrectly filled out application forms are common in the field of business. But applications that contain the information called for in a knowledgeable, straightforward, and readable way create an immediate favorable impression with the employer. To make sure your application makes this good impression, you should have a clear idea about the details of your background and about your employment objectives.

For questions pertaining to your background, you need to know names, addresses, telephone numbers, dates, and facts—a good many of which you can take from your Background and Experience Chart of Unit I. For statements referring to your employment objectives, you need to know what you want and what you can do for this employer.

Your application should be closely related to your résumé and your covering letter. It should also show that you know something about the firm you are applying to and

**Job Application**

This project should be completed by all students and should be personally monitored by the teacher. A model job application form like the one in the text is found on page T16 of the Teacher's Edition. It can be used as a guide for making forms that students can complete. However, copies of job application forms from local companies can be used for this project, if available.

In introducing the project, the teacher should emphasize that the Background and Experience Chart of Unit 1 and the Résumé of this unit are essential reference tools in filling out a complete and unified job application form. In addition, the teacher should review the terms used most often on standard application forms that are likely to be misunderstood. (Most of these are presented in the Useful Terms section of this unit.) For example, many students do not realize that under the entry *previous addresses* it

# Model Job Application Form

SILVER BURDETT COMPANY
250 JAMES STREET
MORRISTOWN, NEW JERSEY 07960

APPLICATION FOR EMPLOYMENT

NAME — LAST / FIRST / MIDDLE

TODAY'S DATE — MO / DAY / YR

PRESENT ADDRESS — NO. / STREET / CITY / STATE / ZIP

HOME TELEPHONE NO.

REFERRED TO SILVER BURDETT BY (PLEASE GIVE NAMES, DATES, ETC.)

Employment Agency ______ Previously Employed ______

Silver Burdett Employee ______ Walk-in ______

Advertisement ______ Other ______

SOCIAL SECURITY NO.

BIRTHDATE IF UNDER 18 OR OVER 65

HAVE YOU EVER BEEN EMPLOYED BY SILVER BURDETT BEFORE?

DO YOU HAVE OR HAVE YOU HAD ANY ILLNESSES, HEALTH PROBLEMS OR PHYSICAL DEFECTS THAT WOULD HINDER YOU IN THE PERFORMANCE OF YOUR DUTIES IN THE POSITION FOR WHICH YOU ARE APPLYING?

☐ NO ☐ YES (PLEASE GIVE DETAILS)

PERSON TO BE CONTACTED IN CASE OF EMERGENCY

NAME / NO. STREET / CITY / STATE / TELEPHONE NO.

POSITION OR TYPE OF WORK DESIRED

☐ FULL TIME ☐ SUMMER
☐ PART TIME ☐ FREE LANCE

WEEKLY SALARY DESIRED

DATE YOU CAN START WORK

WHAT TYPE OF WORK DO YOU EVENTUALLY HOPE TO DO?

EDUCATION (INCLUDE SPECIALIZED AND VOCATIONAL COURSES)

| NAME OF SCHOOL | LOCATION (CITY & STATE) | TYPE OF DEGREE OR CERTIFICATE | MAJOR AND MINOR OR DESCRIPTION OF COURSE(S) | % OF EXPENSES EARNED |
|---|---|---|---|---|
| HIGH SCHOOL | | | | |
| COLLEGE/UNIVERSITY | | | | |
| COLLEGE/UNIVERSITY | | | | |
| GRADUATE SCHOOL | | | | |
| GRADUATE SCHOOL | | | | |
| OTHER | | | | |
| OTHER | | | | |

SKILLS

| TYPE? ☐ YES ☐ NO ______ W.P.M. | OFFICE, BUSINESS, EDP EQUIPMENT AND MACHINES THAT YOU CAN OPERATE | LANGUAGES, DEGREE OF PROFICIENCY (SPEAK, READ, WRITE) |
|---|---|---|
| SHORTHAND? ☐ YES ☐ NO ______ W.P.M. | | |

OTHER SKILLS, PROFESSIONAL DESIGNATIONS, LICENSES, ETC.

FORM 1073T

AN EQUAL OPPORTUNITY EMPLOYER M/F

(PLEASE TURN OVER)

EXPERIENCE (INCLUDE ALL TEMPORARY, PART-TIME, SUMMER AND SELF EMPLOYMENT)

| NAME OF PRESENT OR LAST EMPLOYER | DATES EMPLOYED | | NAME AND TITLE OF IMMEDIATE SUPERVISOR |
|---|---|---|---|
| | STARTED | LEFT | POSITION AND DUTIES AND RESPONSIBILITIES |
| COMPLETE ADDRESS | WEEKLY SALARY | | |
| | START | FINAL | |
| TYPE OF BUSINESS | $ | $ | SPECIFIC REASON(S) FOR LEAVING |

| NAME OF NEXT PREVIOUS EMPLOYER | DATES EMPLOYED | | NAME AND TITLE OF IMMEDIATE SUPERVISOR |
|---|---|---|---|
| | STARTED | LEFT | POSITION AND DUTIES AND RESPONSIBILITIES |
| COMPLETE ADDRESS | WEEKLY SALARY | | |
| | START | FINAL | |
| TYPE OF BUSINESS | $ | $ | SPECIFIC REASON(S) FOR LEAVING |

| NAME OF NEXT PREVIOUS EMPLOYER | DATES EMPLOYED | | NAME AND TITLE OF IMMEDIATE SUPERVISOR |
|---|---|---|---|
| | STARTED | LEFT | POSITION AND DUTIES AND RESPONSIBILITIES |
| COMPLETE ADDRESS | WEEKLY SALARY | | |
| | START | FINAL | |
| TYPE OF BUSINESS | | $ | SPECIFIC REASON(S) FOR LEAVING |

MILITARY

| HAVE YOU EVER SERVED IN THE ARMED FORCES OF THE U.S.? | NO<br>YES (DETAILS BELOW) | | | | LIST DUTIES, SCHOOLS ATTENDED AND ANY SPECIAL TRAINING RECEIVED IN SERVICE |
|---|---|---|---|---|---|
| BRANCH OF SERVICE | DATES | | RANK AT | | |
| | FROM | TO | ENTRY | SEP. | |
| | | | | | |
| | | | | | |

PROFESSIONAL AND CHARACTER REFERENCES (DO NOT INCLUDE RELATIVES OR FORMER EMPLOYERS)

| NAME | HOME ADDRESS | TELEPHONE | OCCUPATION | NO. YEARS KNOWN |
|---|---|---|---|---|
| NAME | HOME ADDRESS | TELEPHONE | OCCUPATION | NO. YEARS KNOWN |
| NAME | HOME ADDRESS | TELEPHONE | OCCUPATION | NO. YEARS KNOWN |

APPLICANT'S SIGNATURE

I certify that to the best of my knowledge, all statements made are complete and correct and I understand that any misrepresentations may result in loss of employment. I agree and understand that I must pass a physical examination and have all references cleared as a condition of employment.

SIGNATURE:

FOR PERSONNEL DEPT. USE ONLY – DO NOT WRITE BELOW

| INTERVIEWED BY | COMMENTS | REFERRAL |
|---|---|---|
| | | |

is not necessary to report moves made five years ago. On the other hand, the teacher should caution students not to leave anything out that ought to be included. If the application calls for all periods of unemployment to be recorded in the work experience section, these should be filled in. Certain kinds of missing data are certain to be queried by an interviewer, and this may pose an awkward problem for the ill-prepared applicant.

As each application is completed, the teacher should review it with the student to see that each section is comprehensively and concisely developed, and that the application is presentable both in appropriate language and in appearance. It may be necessary to have certain students complete a revision before awarding credit when there are inconsistencies or omissions especially if the student is actually applying for a job.

that you could become a useful employee for that company. Most applicants organize their background information so they can present it clearly and coherently enough on the application form. However, relatively few people understand the importance of matching their employment objectives to the company's needs. To illustrate this, suppose a friend has told you that the large company she works for is hiring assemblers. You have the background and training that matches what she has told you about the job, so you decide to apply. On the application form under "Position Objective" you write "Assembler," then in the appropriate sections you describe the training and experience you feel qualifies you for the job you are seeking.

At another company, suppose you just walk into the personnel office "cold" and fill out an application form. You need a job and are willing to do anything. You have heard the company is a good one to work for, so you apply for a job. At which company will the application be well received by the employer? The rule to remember is: *Learn about the company first before filling out the application form.* Find out what the company does, what its present needs are, and how you can best serve the employer. The application form that is completed on the basis of some advance information and that focuses on some clearly defined objective offers you the best chance of getting the job you want.

***Directions*** A sample job application form is found on pages 134–135. Most job application forms are similar in that they all call for the same kinds of basic information. The form in your book is divided into the following categories:

1. Name, address, social security number, and age if you are under 18
2. Position or type of work desired
3. Educational background
4. Special skills
5. Work experience
6. Military training (if any)
7. References
8. Your signature

Your teacher may wish to have this sample form or one similar to it reproduced for distribution to your class. After studying the directions and questions, begin filling out your copy of the job application form. If you have difficulty answering any of the questions, consult your teacher. Remember, good handwriting and neatness are important when filling out such forms.

## PREPARING FOR A JOB INTERVIEW

***Introduction*** The job interview is the turning point between the job campaign and the job itself. It is at this point that the door is cracked open slightly to getting a job that interests you, and possibly to opening the way to a career of your choice. What happens during the course of the interview is all-important as far as your future is concerned.

To begin with, if you have done your homework well up to this point, this is not the only firm to which you have applied or will be applying to for work. With many job possibilities to consider, you will be bargaining on equal terms with each employer. You will be looking the company over as carefully as the employer will be looking you over. This attitude helps you see the job interview in the perspective of one opportunity among many, and it gives you an added measure of ease and confidence in the interview situation.

Your preparation for an interview is as important as your preparation for a thorough job campaign. If you have already submitted a résumé and an application form, the interviewer will probably have them on hand as a reference during your interview. If the employer does not have your résumé or application, you might take these and any appropriate records or letters of recommendation with you to your appointment. You can expect the interviewer to base a few questions on what you have included or perhaps left out of your résumé and job application form. You should anticipate such questions and be prepared to answer them.

In business the impression that counts is often the first one, and this impression is based largely on appearance and personal manner. Make sure your clothes and grooming are in accordance with the best accepted business standards of the area. Go to your interview alone and

**Job Interview**

The Job Interview is the major project of Unit IV and is the culmination of all earlier projects of this unit. The text is lengthy and detailed and should be gone over thoroughly before introducing the activity. The key points of the introduction can be listed on the chalkboard by a student (or the teacher) as they are discussed by the class.

Later, when the directions for the demonstration have been read, the teacher can review each step of the interview including preparation and follow-up. Students can then get together in pairs to plan their interview, write their ideas down on paper, and practice their parts. When they are called on, they will take their place before the class. (The student playing the part of the Applicant might be directed to wait outside the door of the classroom until he or she is invited in by the Interviewer.)

When the interview ends (with a handshake or simulated exit), the pair will remain before the class to respond to questions and comments. Classmates will attempt to pinpoint mistakes—both deliberate and unplanned. Finally, the teacher may wish to summarize the problems exhibited in each interview before calling on the next pair of students.

be on time. Learn the interviewer's name *before* you meet, if possible. Use it when you are introduced and make it sound as if you have been eagerly waiting for this moment, which indeed should be the case.

Let the interviewer guide you to the office, invite you to take a chair, and set the tone for any light conversation designed to put you both at ease. Your attitude should be complementary to the extent that you know both of you have put some time and effort into arranging this meeting. When the conversation shifts to the business at hand, be ready to join the interviewer in discussing your qualifications for the job. The interviewer's questions will usually fall into three general categories that include your background and education, your work experience, and your particular interests in working for the company. Answer the questions as simply and directly as you can, giving a complete explanation for each inquiry.

As you tell about yourself, show some enthusiasm—get interested in what you are saying. Watch for signs that the interviewer is with you—a nod of the head, a smile. Conclude each statement with a smile of your own looking directly at the interviewer, indicating you are ready to go on to the next question.

Sooner or later your turn will come to ask questions. The interviewer will probably begin to tell you something about the company and the job. It is advisable not to interrupt but to listen carefully. When finished, the interviewer might ask if there is anything else you would like to know about the company or the job. Any well thought out question you might ask is a clear sign of your interest in the job and in the company. Remember, you have as much at stake as the company has. It is your future, too.

The best questions are a normal outgrowth of the information that has been exchanged up to this point. These are the questions that will help bring the job into focus for you. Other questions might relate to promotions, advanced education or training plans, raises, life- and health-insurance plans, vacation days, sick days or sick leave, travel pay, lunchroom facilities, and so on. Working conditions are an important aspect of the job.

Many young job applicants assume that they need only present themselves and submit politely and patiently to an interviewer's questions to get a job. That is not so. If you want the job you must make this fact known to the interviewer before you leave the office. Take the initiative when it is offered and ask your questions. Let the interviewer see that you want to learn whether this is a place where you could function productively and happily. Most interviewers and company representatives will bend over backwards to illustrate how their company is just such a place. And your questions will show that you are vitally interested to find this out.

When the factors related to a possible match have been explored—the right person for the job, the right job for the person—the interview will end. Again permit your interviewer to signal that this has happened and to lead you out of the office. If you have not yet reached a mutual agreement about the job, you will probably be told when the company's decision is to be made and how you will be notified. If for some reason you are not told, ask. For example, you might say, "It was good to meet and talk with you, Mrs. Greene. When can I expect to hear from you about the job? The word *when* sets the limits for future negotiations with this company about this job.

While thank-you letters for the interview are not necessary, they can further enhance the impression you have made. If you have not heard from the employer by the time specified at the close of the interview, a phone call to inquire is altogether proper. By reminding the interviewer of your verbal agreement, you are reestablishing your contact with the interviewer and reasserting your interest in the job. There is nothing to be lost here, and possibly much to be gained.

As to the matter of record-keeping, you should summarize each job interview immediately after it has taken place while the details are still fresh in your mind. It is important to write down the name of the company, address and phone number, date and time of interview, interviewer's full name and title, and the date you are to be notified of the company's decision. Include notes on the salary figures and other key issues discussed during the interview. Your records should also state when you submitted a résumé, filled out an application form, and took any preemployment tests. This information, kept in your career file, makes it possible for you to renew your association with this employer and, of course, helps you to make sound decisions about taking this job or any other job you might be considering.

***Directions*** Pair up with another student in your group or class and decide which of you is to be the Applicant and which the Interviewer in a demonstration Job Interview you will present. Consider carefully the principles discussed above and develop a scenario in which there is one, *and only one*, flaw or problem. The flaw may be on the side of the Applicant or on the side of the Interviewer; it may be large or small. It must, however, be readily identifiable and consistent throughout the demonstration. For example, the Applicant might do everything right except for always leaving part of a question unanswered. Or, the Interviewer might continually fail to provide cues to the Applicant and not assume the role of guiding the conversation. Have the class determine what the problem is in each interview and discuss how to correct it.

In preparing your demonstration you may wish to use your own applications, résumés, and covering letters. These should provide a suitably realistic base for the development of the interview. Your teacher can assist you further if you need help with the setting, props, or questions to be used in the interview.

# RELATED READING

## THE MOTHER

*Paddy Chayefsky*

### ACT I

FADE IN: *Film—a quick group of shots showing New York in a real thunderstorm—rain whipping through the streets—real miserable weather.*

DISSOLVE TO: *Close-up of an old woman, aged sixty-six, with a shock of gray-white hair, standing by a window in her apartment, looking out, apparently deeply disturbed by the rain slashing against the pane.*

*We pull back to see that the old woman is wearing an old kimono, under which there is evidence of an old white batiste nightgown. Her gray-white hair hangs loosely down over her shoulders. It is early morning, and she has apparently just gotten out of bed. This is the bedroom of her two-and-a-half-room apartment in a lower-middle-class neighborhood in the Bronx. The bed is still unmade and looks just slept in. The furniture is old and worn. On the chest of drawers there is a galaxy of photographs and portrait pictures, evidently of her various children and grandchildren. She stands looking out the window, troubled, disturbed.*

*Suddenly the alarm, perched on the little bed table, rings. Camera moves in for close-up of the alarm clock. It reads half past six. The old lady's hand comes down and shuts the alarm off.*

CUT TO: *Close-up of another alarm clock, ringing in another apartment. It also reads half past six; but it is obviously a different clock, on a much more modern bed table. This one buzzes instead of clangs. A young woman's hand reaches over and turns it off.*

*Camera pulls back to show that we are in the bedroom of a young couple. The young woman who has turned the*

**Related Reading**

*The Mother* is reprinted here in its entirety. This play tells the story of an old lady who has recently been widowed. Sixty-six years old and fiercely independent, she wants to go back to work, even though she has not had a job in forty years. Work is the measure of Mrs. Fanning's self-respect. She knows that all the cards are stacked against her, but she is determined to find a job.

Assign the Related Reading to the class as homework. The questions at the end of the reading section can then be used as a guide for class discussion.

*clock off is a rather plain girl of thirty. She slowly sits up in bed, assembling herself for the day. On the other half of the bed, her husband turns and tries to go back to sleep.*

SON-IN-LAW: [*From under the blankets*] What time is it?

DAUGHTER: [*Still seated heavily on the edge of the bed*] It's half past six.

SON-IN-LAW: [*From under the blankets*] What did you set it so early for?

DAUGHTER: I wanna call my mother. [*She looks out at the window, the rain driving fiercely against it.*] For heaven's sake, listen to that rain! She's not going down today, I'll tell you that, if I have to go over there and chain her in her bed . . . [*She stands, crosses to the window, studies the rain.*] Boy, look at it rain.

SON-IN-LAW: [*Still under the covers*] What?

DAUGHTER: I said, it's raining

*She makes her way, still heavy with sleep, out of the bedroom into the foyer of the apartment. She pads in her bare feet and pajamas down the foyer to the telephone table, sits on the little chair, trying to clear her head of sleep. A baby's cry is suddenly heard in an off room. The young woman absently goes "Sshh." The baby's cry stops. The young woman picks up the receiver of the phone and dials. She waits. Then . . .*

DAUGHTER: Ma? This is Annie. Did I wake you up? . . . I figured you'd be up by now. . . . Ma, you're not going downtown today, and I don't wanna hear no arguments . . . Ma, have you looked out the window? It's raining like . . . Ma, I'm not gonna let you go downtown today, do you hear me? . . . I don't care, Ma . . . Ma, I don't care . . . Ma, I'm coming over. You stay there till . . . Ma, stay there till I come over. I'm getting dressed right now. I'll drive over in the car. It won't take me ten minutes . . . Ma, you're not going out in this rain. It's not enough that you almost fainted in the subway yesterday . . . Ma, I'm hanging up, and I'm coming over right now. Stay there . . . all right, I'm hanging up . . .

*She hangs up, sits for a minute, then rises and shuffles quickly back up the foyer and back into her bedroom. She disappears into the bathroom, unbuttoning the blouse of her pajamas. She leaves the bathroom door open, and a shaft of light suddenly shoots out into the dark bedroom.*

SON-IN-LAW: [*Awake now, his head visible over the covers*] Did you talk to her?

DAUGHTER: [*Off in bathroom*] Yeah, she was all practically ready to leave.

SON-IN-LAW: Look, Annie, I don't wanna tell you how to treat your own mother, but why don't you leave her alone? It's obviously very important to her to get a job for herself. She wants to support herself. She doesn't want to be a burden on her children. I respect her for that. An old lady, sixty-six years old, going out and looking for work. I think that shows a lot of guts.

*The daughter comes out of the bathroom. She has a blouse on now and a half-slip.*

DAUGHTER: [*Crossing to the closet*] George, please, you don't know what you're talking about, so do me a favor, and don't argue with me. I'm not in a good mood. [*She opens the closet, studies the crowded rack of clothes.*] I'm turning on the light, so get your eyes ready. [*She turns on the light. The room is suddenly bright. She blinks and pokes in the closet for a skirt, which she finally extracts.*] My mother worked like a dog all her life, and she's not gonna spend the rest of her life bent over a sewing machine. [*She slips into the skirt.*] She had one of her attacks in the subway yesterday. I was never so scared in my life when that cop called yesterday. [*She's standing in front of her mirror now, hastily arranging her hair.*] My mother worked like a dog to raise me and my brother and my sister. She worked in my old man's grocery store till twelve o'clock at night. We owe her a little peace of mind, my brother and my sister and me. She sacrificed plenty for us in her time. [*She's back at the closet, fishing for her topcoat.*] And I want her to move out of that apartment. I don't want her living alone. I want her to come live here with us, George, and I don't want any more arguments about that either. We can move Tommy in with the baby, and she can have Tommy's room. And that reminds me—the baby cried for a minute there. If she cries again, give her her milk because she went to sleep without her milk last night. [*She has her topcoat on now and is already at the door to the foyer.*] All right, I'll probably be back in time to make you breakfast. Have you got the keys to the car? . . . [*She nervously pats the pocket of her coat.*] No, I got them. All right, I'll see you. Good-by, George . . .

*She goes out into the foyer.*

SON-IN-LAW: Good-by, Annie . . .

*Off in some other room, the baby begins to cry again, a little more insistently. The husband raises his eyebrows and listens for a moment. When it becomes apparent that the baby isn't going to stop, he sighs and begins to get out of bed.*

DISSOLVE TO: *The old lady standing by the window again. She is fully dressed now, however, even to the black coat and hat. The coat is unbuttoned. For the first time, we may be aware of a black silk mourning band that the old lady has about the sleeve of her coat. Outside, the rain has abated considerably. It is drizzling lightly now. The old lady turns to her daughter, standing at the other end of the bedroom, brushing the rain from her coat. When the old lady speaks, it is with a mild, but distinct, Irish flavor.*

OLD LADY: It's letting up a bit.

DAUGHTER: [*Brushing off her coat*] It isn't letting up at all. It's gonna stop and start all day long.

*The old lady starts out of her bedroom, past her daughter, into her living room.*

OLD LADY: I'm going to make a bit of coffee for myself and some Rice Krispies. Would you like a cup?

*The daughter turns and starts into the living room ahead of her mother.*

DAUGHTER: I'll make it for you.

OLD LADY: You won't make it for me. I'll make it myself.

*She crowds past the daughter and goes to the kitchen. At the kitchen doorway, she turns and surveys her daughter.*

OLD LADY: Annie, you know, you can drive somebody crazy, do you know that?

DAUGHTER: *I* can drive somebody crazy?! *You're* the one who can drive somebody crazy.

OLD LADY: Will you stop hovering over me like I was a cripple in a wheel chair. I can make my own coffee, believe me. Why did you come over here? You've got a husband and two kids to take care of. Go make coffee for them, for heaven's sakes.

*She turns and goes into the kitchen, muttering away. She opens a cupboard and extracts a jar of instant coffee.*

OLD LADY: I've taken to making instant coffee, would you like a cup?

*The daughter is standing on the threshold of the kitchen now, leaning against the doorjamb.*

DAUGHTER: All right, make me a cup, Ma.

*The old lady takes two cups and saucers out and begins carefully to level out a teaspoonful of the instant coffee into each. The daughter moves into the kitchen, reaches up for something in the cupboard.*

DAUGHTER: Where do you keep your saccharin, Ma?

*The old lady wheels and slaps the daughter's outstretched arms down.*

OLD LADY: Annie, I'll get it myself! [*She points a finger into the living room.*] Go in there and sit down, will you?! I'll bring the cup in to you!

*The daughter leans back against the doorjamb, a little exasperated with the old lady's petulant independence. The old lady now takes an old teapot and sets it on the stove and lights a flame under it.*

OLD LADY: You can drive me to the subway if you want to do something for me.

DAUGHTER: Ma, you're not going downtown today.

OLD LADY: I want to get down there extra early today on the off-chance that they haven't given the job to someone else. What did I do with that card from the New York State Employment Service? . . .

*She shuffles out of the kitchen, the daughter moving out of the doorway to give her passage. The old lady goes to the table in the living room on which sits her battered black purse. She opens it and takes out a card.*

OLD LADY: I don't want to lose that. [*She puts the white card back into her purse.*] I'm pretty sure I could have held onto this job, because the chap at the Employment Service called up the boss, you see, over the phone, and he explained to the man that I hadn't worked in quite a number of years . . .

DAUGHTER: [*Muttering*] Quite a number of years . . .

OLD LADY: . . . and that I'd need a day or so to get used to the machines again.

DAUGHTER: Did the chap at the Employment Service explain to the boss that it's forty years that you haven't worked?

OLD LADY: [*Crossing back to the kitchen*] . . . and the boss understood this, you see, so he would have been a little lenient with me. But then, of course, I had to go and faint in the subway, because I was in such a hurry to get down there, you know, I didn't even stop to eat my lunch. I had brought along some sandwiches, you see, cheese and tomatoes. Oh, I hope he hasn't given the job to anyone else . . .

*The old lady reaches into the cupboard again for a bowl of sugar, an opened box of Rice Krispies, and a bowl. The daughter watches her as she turns to the refrigerator to get out a container of milk.*

DAUGHTER: Ma, when are you gonna give up?

*The old lady frowns.*

OLD LADY: Annie, please . . .

*She pours some Rice Krispies into the bowl.*

DAUGHTER: Ma, you been trying for three weeks now. If you get a job, you get fired before the day is over. You're too old, Ma, and they don't want to hire old people . . .

OLD LADY: It's not the age . . .

DAUGHTER: They don't want to hire white-haired old ladies.

OLD LADY: It's not the age at all! I've seen plenty of old people with white hair and all, sitting at those machines. The shop where I almost had that job and he fired me the other day, there was a woman there, eighty years old if she was a day, an old crone of a woman, sitting there all bent over, her machine humming away. The chap at the Employment Service said there's a lot of elderly people working in the needle trades. The young people nowadays don't want to work for thirty-five, forty dollars a week, and there's a lot of old people working in the needle trades.

DAUGHTER: Well, whatever it is, Ma . . .

OLD LADY: [*Leaning to her daughter*] It's my fingers. I'm not sure of them any more. When you get old, y'know, you lose the sureness in your fingers. My eyes are all right, but my fingers tremble a lot. I get very excited, y'know, when I go in for a tryout, y'know. And I'll go in, y'know, and the boss'll say: "Sit down, let's see what you can do." And I get so excited. And my heart begins thumping so that I can hardly see to thread the needle. And they stand right over you, y'know, while you're working. They give you a packet of sleeves or a skirt or something to put a hem on. Or a seam or something, y'know. It's simple work, really. Single-needle machine. Nothing fancy. And it seems to me I do it all right, but they fire me all the time. They say: "You're too slow." And I'm working as fast as I can. I think, perhaps, I've lost the ability in my fingers. And that's what scares me the most. It's not the age. I've seen plenty of old women working in the shops.

*She has begun to pour some milk into her bowl of cereal; but she stops now and just stands, staring bleakly down at the worn oilcloth on her cupboard.*

DAUGHTER: [*Gently*] Ma, you worked all your life. Why don't you take it easy?

OLD LADY: I don't want to take it easy. Now that your

father's dead and in the grave I don't know what to do with myself.

DAUGHTER: Why don't you go out, sit in the park, get a little sun like the other old women?

OLD LADY: I sit around here sometimes, going crazy. We had a lot of fights in our time, your father and I, but I must admit I miss him badly. You can't live with someone forty-one years and not miss him when he's dead. I'm glad that he died for his own sake—it may sound hard of me to say that—but I'm glad. He was in nothing but pain the last few months, and he was a man who could never stand pain. But I do miss him.

DAUGHTER: [*Gently*] Ma, why don't you come live with George and me?

OLD LADY: No, no, Annie, you're a good daughter. . . .

DAUGHTER: We'll move Tommy into the baby's room, and you can have Tommy's room. It's the nicest room in the apartment. It gets all the sun . . .

OLD LADY: I have wonderful children. I thank God every night for that. I . . .

DAUGHTER: Ma, I don't like you living here alone . . .

OLD LADY: Annie, I been living in this house for eight years, and I know all the neighbors and the store people, and if I lived with you, I'd be a stranger.

DAUGHTER: There's plenty of old people in my neighborhood. You'll make friends.

OLD LADY: Annie, you're a good daughter, but I want to keep my own home. I want to pay my own rent. I don't want to be some old lady living with her children. If I can't take care of myself, I just as soon be in the grave with your father. I don't want to be a burden on my children . . .

DAUGHTER: Ma, for heaven's sakes . . .

OLD LADY: More than anything else, I don't want to be a burden on my children. I pray to God every night to let me keep my health and my strength so that I won't have to be a burden on my children . . . [*The teapot suddenly hisses. The old lady looks up.*] Annie, the pot is boiling. Would you pour the water in the cups?

*The daughter moves to the stove. The old lady, much of her ginger seemingly sapped out of her, shuffles into the living room. She perches on the edge of one of the wooden chairs.*

OLD LADY: I been getting some pains in my shoulder the last week or so. I had the electric heating pad on practically the whole night. . . . [*She looks up toward the windows again.*] It's starting to rain a little harder again. Maybe, I won't go downtown today after all. Maybe, if it clears up a bit, I'll go out and sit in the park and get some sun.

*In the kitchen, the daughter pours the boiling water into each cup, stirs.*

DAUGHTER: [*To her mother, off in the living room*] Is this all you're eating for breakfast, Ma? Let me make you something else . . .

DISSOLVE TO: *A park bench. The old lady and two other old ladies are seated, all bundled up in their cheap cloth coats with the worn fur collars. The second old lady is also Irish. Her name is Mrs. Geegan. The third old lady is possibly Jewish, certainly a New Yorker by intonation. Her name is Mrs. Kline. The rain has stopped, it is a clear, bright sunny March morning.*

OLD LADY: . . . Well, it's nice and clear now, isn't it? It was raining something fierce around seven o'clock this morning.

MRS. GEEGAN: [*Grimacing*] It's too ruddy cold for me. I'd go home except my daughter-in-law is cleaning the house, and I don't want to get in her way.

MRS. KLINE: My daughter-in-law should drop dead tomorrow.

MRS. GEEGAN: My daughter-in-law gets into an awful black temper when she's cleaning.

MRS. KLINE: My daughter-in-law should grow rich and own a hotel with a thousand rooms and be found dead in every one of them.

MRS. GEEGAN: [*To the old lady*] I think I'll go over and visit Missus Halley in a little while, would you like to go? She fell down the stairs and broke her hip, and they're suing the owners of the building. I saw her son yesterday, and he says she's awful weak. When you break a hip at that age, you're as good as in the coffin. I don't like to visit Missus Halley. She's always so gloomy about things. But it's a way of killing off an hour or so to lunch. A little later this afternoon, I thought I'd go to confession. It's so warm and solemn in the church. Do you go to Saint John's? I think it's ever so much prettier than Our Lady of Visitation. Why don't you come to Missus Halley's with me, Missus Fanning? Her son's a sweet man, and there's always a bit of fruit they offer you.

OLD LADY: I don't believe I know a Missus Halley.

MRS. GEEGAN: Missus Halley, the one that fell down the stairs last week and dislocated her hip. They're suing the owners of the building for forty thousand dollars.

MRS. KLINE: They'll settle for a hundred, believe me.

MRS. GEEGAN: Oh, it's chilly this morning. I'd go home, but my daughter-in-law is cleaning the house, and she doesn't like me to be about when she's cleaning. I'd like a bottle of beer, that's what I'd like. Oh, my mouth is fairly watering for it. I'm not allowed to have beer, you know. I'm a diabetic. You don't happen to have a quarter on you, Missus Fanning? We could buy a bottle and split it between us. I'd ask my son for it, but they always want to know what I want the money for.

OLD LADY: [*Looking sharply at Mrs. Geegan*] Do you have to ask your children for money?

MRS. GEEGAN: Oh, they're generous. They always give me whenever I ask. But I'm not allowed to have beer, you see, and they wouldn't give me the twenty-five cents for that. What do I need money for anyway? Go to the movies? I haven't been to the movies in more than a year, I think. I just like a dollar every now and then for an offering at mass. Do you go to seven o'clock novena, Missus Fanning? It's a good way to spend an hour, I think.

OLD LADY: Is that what you do with your day, Missus Geegan? Visit dying old ladies and go to confession?

MRS. GEEGAN: Well, I like to stay in the house a lot, watching television. There's ever so much fun on television in the afternoons, with the kiddie shows and a lot of dancing and Kate Smith and shows like that. But my daughter-in-law's cleaning up today, and she doesn't like me around the house when she's cleaning, so I came out a bit early to sit in the park.

*The old lady regards Mrs. Geegan for a long moment.*

MRS. KLINE: My daughter-in-law, she should invest all her money in General Motors stock, and they should go bankrupt.

*A pause settles over the three old ladies. They just sit, huddled, their cheeks pressed into the fur of their collars. After a moment, the old lady shivers noticeably.*

OLD LADY: It's a bit chilly. I think I'll go home. [*She rises.*] Good-by, Missus Geegan ... Good-by, Missus ...

*The other two old ladies nod their good-bys. The old lady moves off screen. We hold for a moment on the remaining two old ladies, sitting, shoulders hunched against the morning chill, faces pressed under their collars, staring bleakly ahead.*

DISSOLVE TO: *Door of the old lady's apartment. It opens, and the old lady comes in. She closes the door behind her, goes up the small foyer to the living room. She unbuttons her coat and walks aimlessly around the room, into the bedroom and out again, across the living room and into the kitchen, and then out of the kitchen. She is frowning as she walks and rubs her hands continually as if she is quite cold. Suddenly she goes to the telephone, picks it up, dials a number, waits.*

OLD LADY: [*Snappishly*] Is this Mister McCleod?! This is Missus Fanning in Apartment 3F! The place is a refrigerator up here! It's freezing! I want some steam! I want it right now! That's all there is to it! I want some steam right now!

*She hangs up sharply, turns—scowling—and sits heavily down on the edge of a soft chair, scowling, nervous, rocking a little back and forth. Then abruptly she rises, crosses the living room to the television set, clicks it on. She stands in front of it, waiting for a picture to show. At last the picture comes on. It is the WPIX station signal, accompanied by the steady high-pitched drone that indicates there are no programs on yet. She turns the set off almost angrily.*

*She is beginning to breathe heavily now. She turns nervously and looks at the large ornamental clock on the sideboard. It reads ten minutes after eleven. She goes to the small dining table and sits down on one of the hard-back chairs. Her black purse is still on the table, as it was during the scene with her daughter. Her eyes rest on it for a moment; then she reaches over, opens the purse, and takes out the white employment card. She looks at it briefly, expressionlessly. Then she returns it to the purse and reclasps the purse. Again she sits for a moment, rigid, expressionless. Then suddenly she stands, grabs the purse, and starts out the living room, down the foyer, to the front door of her apartment—buttoning her coat as she goes. She opens the door, goes out.*

*Camera stays on door as it is closed. There is the noise of a key being inserted into the lock. A moment later the bolts on the lock shift into locked position. Hold.*

FADE OUT.

## ACT II

FADE IN: *Film. Lunchtime in the needle-trade district of New York—a quick montage of shots of the streets, jammed with traffic, trucks, and working people hurrying to the dense little luncheonettes for their lunch.*

DISSOLVE TO: *Interior of the Tiny Tots Sportswear Co., Inc., 137 West Twenty-seventh Street, on the eighth floor. It is lunchtime. We dissolve in on some of the women operators at their lunch. They are seated at their machines, of which there are twenty—in two rows of ten, facing each other Not all of the operators eat their lunch in: about half go downstairs to join the teeming noontime crowds in the oily little restaurants of the vicinity. The ten-or-so women whom we see—munching their sandwiches and sipping their containers of coffee and chattering shrilly to one another—all wear worn house dresses. A good proportion of the operators are Negro and Puerto Rican. Not a few of them are gray-haired, or at least unmistakably middle-aged.*

*The rest of the shop seems to consist of endless rows of pipe racks on which hang finished children's dresses, waiting to be shipped. In the middle of these racks is a pressing machine and sorting table at which two of the three men who work in the shop eat their lunch. At the far end of the loft—in a corner so dark that a light must always be on over it—is an old, battered roll-top desk at which sits the bookkeeper, an angular woman of thirty-five, differentiated from the hand workers in that she wears a clean dress.*

*Nearby is the boss, a man in his thirties. He is bent over a machine, working on it with a screw driver. The boss is really a pleasant man; he works under the illusion, however, that gruffness is a requisite quality of an executive.*

*Somehow, a tortured passageway has been worked out between the racks leading to the elevator doors; it is the only visible exit and entrance to the loft.*

*As we look at these doors, there is a growing whirring and clanging announcing the arrival of the elevator. The doors slide reluctantly open, and the old lady enters the shop. The elevator doors slide closed behind her. She stands surrounded by pipe racks, a little apprehensive. The arrival of the elevator has caused some of the people to look up briefly. The old lady goes to the presser, a Puerto Rican.*

OLD LADY: Excuse me, I'm looking for the boss.

*The presser indicates with his hand the spot where the boss is standing, working on the machine. The old lady picks her way through the cluttered pipe racks to the bookkeeper, who looks up at her approach. The boss also looks up briefly at her approach, but goes back to his work. The old lady opens her purse, takes out the white card, and proffers it to the bookkeeper. She mutters something.*

BOOKKEEPER: Excuse me, I can't hear what you said.

OLD LADY: I said, I was supposed to be here yesterday, but I was sick in the subway—I fainted, you see, and . . .

*The boss now turns to the old lady.*

BOSS: What? . . . What? . . .

OLD LADY: I was sent down from the . . .

BOSS: What?

OLD LADY: [*Louder*] I was sent down from the New York State Employment Service. I was supposed to be here yesterday.

BOSS: Yes, so what happened?

OLD LADY: I was sick. I fainted in the subway.

BOSS: What?

OLD LADY: [*Louder*] I was sick. The subway was so hot there, you see—there was a big crush at a Hundred and forty-ninth Street . . .

BOSS: You was supposed to be here yesterday.

OLD LADY: I had a little trouble. They had my daughter down there and everything. By the time I got down here, it was half past five, and the fellow on the elevator—not the one that was here this morning—another fellow entirely. An old man it was. He said there was nobody up here. So I was going to come down early this morning, but I figured you probably had the job filled anyway. That's why I didn't come down till now.

BOSS: What kind of work do you do?

OLD LADY: Well, I used to do all sections except joining and zippers, but I think the fellow at the Employment Service explained to you that it's been a number of years since I actually worked in a shop.

BOSS: What do you mean, a number of years?

OLD LADY: [*Mumbling*] Well, I did a lot of sewing for the Red Cross during the war, y'know, but I haven't actually worked in a shop since 1916.

BOSS: [*Who didn't quite hear her mumbled words*] What?

OLD LADY: [*Louder*] Nineteen sixteen. October.

BOSS: Nineteen sixteen.

OLD LADY: I'm sure if I could work a little bit, I would be fine. I used to be a very fast worker.

BOSS: Can you thread a machine?

*The old lady nods.*

*He starts off through the maze of pipe racks to the two rows of machines. The old lady follows after him, clutching her purse and the white card, her hat still sitting on her head, her coat still buttoned. As they go up the rows of sewing machines, the other operators look up to catch covert glimpses of the new applicant. The boss indicates one of the open machines.*

BOSS: All right. Siddown. Show me how you thread a machine.

*The old lady sets her purse down nervously and takes the seat behind the machine. The other operators have all paused in their eating to watch the test. The old lady reaches to her side, where there are several spools of thread.*

OLD LADY: What kind of thread, white or black? . . .

BOSS: White! White!

*She fumblingly fetches a spool of white thread and, despite the fact she is obviously trembling, she contrives to thread the machine—a process which takes about half a minute. The boss stands towering over her.*

BOSS: Can you make a sleeve?

*The old lady nods, desperately trying to get the thread through the eye of the needle and over the proper holes.*

BOSS: It's a simple business. One seam.

*He reaches into the bin belonging to the machine next to the one the old lady is working on and extracts a neatly tied bundle of sleeve material. He drops it on the table beside the old lady.*

BOSS: All right, make a sleeve. Let's see how you make a sleeve.

*He breaks the string and gives her a piece of sleeve material. She takes it, but is so nervous it falls to the floor. She hurriedly bends to pick it up, inserts the sleeve into the machine, and hunches into her work—her face screwed tight with intense concentration. She has still not unbuttoned her coat, and beads of sweat begin to appear on her brow. With painstaking laboriousness, she slowly moves the sleeve material into the machine. The boss stands, impatient and scowling.*

BOSS: Mama, what are you weaving there, a carpet? It's a lousy sleeve, for Pete's sake.

OLD LADY: I'm a little unsure. My fingers are a little unsure.

BOSS: You gotta be fast, Mama. This is week work. It's not piecework. I'm paying you by the hour. I got twenny dozen cottons here, gotta be out by six o'clock. The truckman isn't gonna wait, you know . . . Mama, Mama, watch what you're doing there . . . [*He leans quickly forward and reguides the material.*] A straight seam, for heaven's sake! You're making it crooked! . . . Watch it! Watch it! Watch what you're doing there, Mama . . . All right, sew. Don't let me make you nervous. Sew . . . Mama, wadda you sewing there, an appendicitis operation? It's a lousy sleeve. How long you gonna take? I want operators here, not surgeons . . .

*Through all this, the terrified old lady tremblingly pushes the material through the machine. Finally she's finished. She looks up at the boss, her eyes wide with apprehension, ready to pick up her purse and dash out to the street. The boss picks up the sleeve, studies it, then drops it on the table, mutters.*

BOSS: All right, we'll try you out for a while. . .

*He turns abruptly and goes back through the pipe racks to the desk. The old lady sits, trembling, a little slumped, her coat still buttoned to the collar. A middle-aged Negro woman, sitting at the next machine over her lunch, leans over to the old lady.*

NEGRO WOMAN: [*Gently*] Mama, what are you sitting there in your hat and coat for? Hang them up, honey. You go through that door over there.

*She points to a door leading into a built-in room. The old lady looks up slowly at this genuine sympathy.*

NEGRO WOMAN: Don't let him get you nervous, Mama. He likes to yell a lot, but he's okay.

*The tension within the old lady suddenly bursts out in the form of a soft, staccato series of sighs. She quickly masters herself.*

OLD LADY: [*Smiling at the Negro woman*] I'm a little unsure of myself. My fingers are a little unsure.

CUT TO: *The boss, standing by the desk. He leans down to mutter to the bookkeeper.*

BOSS: [*Muttering*] How could I say no, will you tell me? How could I say no? . . .

BOOKKEEPER: Nobody says you should say no.

BOSS: She was so nervous, did you see how nervous she was? I bet you she's seventy years old. How could I say no? [*The telephone suddenly rings.*] Answer . . .

*The bookkeeper picks up the receiver.*

BOOKKEEPER: [*On the phone*] Tiny Tots Sportswear . . .

BOSS: [*In a low voice*] Who is it?

BOOKKEEPER: [*On phone*] He's somewhere on the floor, Mister Raymond. I'll see if I can find him . . .

*She covers the mouthpiece.*

BOSS: [*Frowning*] Which Raymond is it, the younger one or the older one?

BOOKKEEPER: The younger one.

BOSS: You can't find me.

*The bookkeeper starts to relay this message, but the boss changes his mind. He takes the receiver.*

BOSS: Hello, Jerry? This is Sam . . . Jerry, for heaven's sake, the twenty dozen just came at half past nine this morning . . . Jerry, I told you six o'clock; it'll be ready six o'clock . . . [*Suddenly lowers his voice, turns away from the bookkeeper, embarrassed at the pleading he's going to have to go through now*] Jerry, how about that fifty dozen faille sport suits . . . Have a heart, Jerry, I need the work. I haven't got enough work to keep my girls. Two of them left yesterday . . . Jerry, please, what kind of living can I make on these cheap cottons? Give me a fancier garment . . . It's such small lots, Jerry. At least give me big lots . . . [*Lowering his voice even more*] Jerry, I hate to appeal to you on this level, but I'm your brother-in-law, you know. . . . Things are pretty rough with me right now, Jerry. Have a heart. Send me over the fifty dozen failles you got in yesterday. I'll make a rush job for you

. . . please, Jerry, why do you have to make me crawl? All right, I'll have this one for you five o'clock . . . I'll call up the freight man now. How about the failles? . . . Okay, Jerry, thank you, you're a good fellow. . . . All right, five o'clock. I'll call the freight man right now . . . Okay . . .

*He hangs up, stands a moment, sick at his own loss of dignity. He turns to the bookkeeper, head bowed.*

BOSS: My own brother-in-law . . .

*He shuffles away, looks up. The old lady, who had gone into the dressing room to hang up her coat and hat, comes out of the dressing room now. The boss wheels on her.*

BOSS: Watsa matter with you? I left you a bundle of sleeves there! You're not even in the shop five minutes, and you walk around like you own the place! [*He wheels to the other operators.*] All right! Come on! Come on! What are you sitting there?! Rush job! Rush job! Let's go! Five o'clock the freight man's coming! Let's go! Let's go!

CUT TO: *The bedroom of the daughter's and son-in-law's apartment. The bed has been made, the room cleaned up. The blinds have been drawn open, and the room is nice and bright. The son-in-law sits on one of the straight-back chairs, slumped a little, surly, scowling. The daughter sits erectly on the bed, her back to her husband, likewise scowling. Apparently, angry words have passed between them. The doorbell buzzes off. Neither of them move for a moment. Then the daughter rises. At her move, the son-in-law begins to gather himself together.*

SON-IN-LAW: I'll get it.

*The daughter moves—in sullen, quick silence—past him and out into the foyer. The son-in-law, who has started to rise, sits down again.*

*In the hallway, the daughter pads down to the front door of the apartment. She is wearing a house dress now and house slippers. She opens the door. Waiting at the door is an attractive young woman in her early thirties, in coat and hat.*

DAUGHTER: Hello, Marie, what are you doing here?

SISTER: Nothing. I just came by for a couple of minutes, that's all. I just brought the kids back to school, I thought I'd drop in for a minute, that's all. How's George?

*She comes into the apartment. The daughter closes the door after her. The sister starts down the hallway.*

DAUGHTER: You came in right in the middle of an argument.

*The son-in-law is now standing in the bedroom doorway*

SON-IN-LAW: [*To the sister*] Your sister drives me crazy.

SISTER: Watsa matter now?

DAUGHTER: [*Following her sister up the foyer*] Nothing's the matter. How's Jack? The kids?

*The two women go into the bedroom, the son-in-law stepping back to let them in.*

SISTER: They're fine. Jack's got a little cold, nothing important. I just took the kids back to school, and I thought I'd drop in, see if you feel like going up to Fordham Road, do a little shopping for a couple of hours. [*To the son-in-law*] What are you doing home?

SON-IN-LAW: It's my vacation. We were gonna leave the kids with my sister, drive downna Virginia, North Carolina, get some warm climate. But your crazy sister don't wanna go. She don't wanna leave your mother . . . [*Turning to his wife*] Your mother can take care of herself better than we can. She's a tough old woman. . . . How many vacations you think I get a year? I don't wanna sit in New York for two weeks, watching it rain.

SISTER: Go ahead, Annie. Me and Frank will see that Mom's all right.

DAUGHTER: Sure, you and Frank. Look, Marie, I was over to see Mom this morning . . .

SON-IN-LAW: Half past six she got up this morning, go over to see your mother . . .

DAUGHTER: After what happened yesterday, I decided to put my foot down. Because Mom got no business at her age riding up and down in the subways.

You know how packed they are. Anyway, I called Mom on the phone, and she gave me the usual arguments. You know Mom. So anyway, I went over to see her, and she was very depressed. We talked for about an hour, and she told me she's been feeling very depressed lately. It's no good Mom living there alone, and you know it, Marie. Anyway, I think I finally convinced her to move out of there and come and live over here.

SON-IN-LAW: You didn't convince me.

DAUGHTER: George, please . . .

SON-IN-LAW: Look, Annie, I like your mother. We get along fine. We go over visit her once, twice a week, fine. What I like about her is that she doesn't hang all over you like my mother does.

DAUGHTER: This is the only thing I ever asked you in our whole marriage . . .

SON-IN-LAW: This is just begging for trouble. You know that in the bottom of your heart . . .

DAUGHTER: I don't wanna argue any more about it . . .

SISTER: Look, Annie, I think George is right. I think . . .

*The daughter suddenly wheels on her sister, a long-repressed fury trembling out of her.*

DAUGHTER: [*Literally screaming*] You keep outta this! You hear me?! You never cared about Mom in your whole life! How many times you been over there this week? How many times?! I go over every day! Every day! And I go over in the evenings too sometimes!

*The sister turns away, not a little shaken by this fierce onslaught. The daughter sits down on the bed again, her back to both her husband and sister, herself confused by the ferocity of her outburst. The son-in-law looks down, embarrassed, at the floor. A moment of sick silence fills the room. Then without turning, but in a much lower voice, the daughter goes on.*

DAUGHTER: George, I been a good wife to you. Did I ever ask you for mink coats or anything? Anything you want has always been good with me. This is the only thing I ever ask of you. I want my mother to live here with me where I can take care of her.

*The son-in-law looks up briefly at his wife's unrelenting back and then back to the floor again.*

SON-IN-LAW: All right, Annie. I won't argue any more with you about it.

SISTER: I guess I better go because I want to get back in the house before three o'clock when the kids come home from school.

*Nobody says anything, so she starts for the door. The son-in-law, from his sitting position, looks up briefly at her as she passes, but she avoids his eyes. He stands, follows her out into the foyer. They proceed silently down the foyer to the doorway. Here they pause a minute. The scene is conducted in low, intense whispers.*

SON-IN-LAW: She don't mean nothing, Marie. You know that.

SISTER: I know, I know . . .

SON-IN-LAW: She's a wonderful person. She'd get up at three o'clock in the morning for you. There's nothing she wouldn't do for her family.

SISTER: I know, George. I know Annie better than you know her. When she's sweet, she can be the sweetest person in the world. She's my kid sister but many's the time I came to her to do a little crying. But she's gonna kill my mother with all her sacrifices. She's trying to take away my mother's independence. My mother's been on her own all her life. That's the only way she knows how to live. I went over to see my mother yesterday. She was depressed. It broke my heart because I told Jack; I said: "I think my mother's beginning to give up." My mother used to be so sure of herself all the time, and yesterday she was talking there about how maybe she thinks she is getting a little old to work. It depressed me for the rest of the day . . .

SON-IN-LAW: Marie, you know that I really like your mother. If I thought it would work out at all, I would have no objection to her coming to live here. But the walls in this place are made out of paper. You can hear everything that goes on in the next room, and . . .

SISTER: It's a big mistake if she comes here. She'll just dry up into bones inside a year.

SON-IN-LAW: Tell that to Annie. Would you do that for me, please?

SISTER: You can't tell Annie nothing. Annie was born at a wrong time. The doctor told my mother she was gonna die if she had Annie, and my mother has been scared of Annie ever since. And if Annie thinks she's gonna get my mother to love her with all these sacrifices, she's crazy. My mother's favorite was always our big brother Frank, and Annie's been jealous of him as long as I know. I remember one time when we were in Saint John's school on Daly Avenue—I think Annie was about ten years old, and . . . oh, well, look, I better go. I'm not mad at Annie. She's been like this as long as I know her. [*She opens the door.*] She's doing the worst thing for my mother, absolutely the worst thing. I'll see you, George.

SON-IN-LAW: I'll see you.

*The sister goes out, closing the door after her. The son-in-law stands a moment. Then, frowning, he moves back up the foyer to the bedroom. His wife is still seated as we last saw her, her back to the door, her hands in her lap—slumped a little, but with an air of rigid stubbornness about her. The son-in-law regards her for a moment. Then he moves around the bed and sits down beside his wife. He puts his arm around her and pulls her to him. She rests her head on his chest. They sit silently for a moment.*

DISSOLVE TO: *Interior, the shop. The full complement of working operators are there, all hunched over their machines, and the place is a picture of industry. The women chatter shrilly with each other as they work. A radio plays in the background. Occasionally, one of the operators lifts her head and bellows out: "Work! Work! Jessica! Gimme some work!" . . . The Bookkeeper, Jessica, scurries back and forth from her desk to the sorting table—where she picks up small cartons of materials, bringing them to the operators—and back to her desk.*

DISSOLVE TO: *The old lady and her immediate neighbor, the Negro woman, both bent over their machines, sewing away. The motors hum. The two women move their materials under the plunging needles. The old lady hunches, intense and painfully concentrated, over her work. They sew in silent industry for a moment. Then . . .*

OLD LADY: [*Without daring to look up from her work*] I'm getting the feel back, you know?

NEGRO WOMAN: [*Likewise without looking up*] Sure, you're gonna be all right, Mama.

OLD LADY: I used to be considered a very fast operator. I used to work on the lower East side in those sweatshops, y'know. Six dollars a week. But I quit in October 1916, because I got married and, in those days, y'know, it was a terrible disgrace for a married woman to work. So I quit. Not that we had the money. My husband was a house painter when we got married, which is seasonal work at best, and he had to borrow the money to go to Atlantic City for three days. That was our honeymoon.

*They lapse into silence. A woman's shrill voice from farther down the row of machines calls out: "Work! Hey, Jessica! Bring me some work!" The two women sew silently. Then . . .*

OLD LADY: I got a feeling he's going to keep me on here. The boss, I mean. He seems like a nice enough man.

NEGRO WOMAN: He's nervous, but he's all right.

OLD LADY: I've been looking for almost four weeks now, y'know. My husband died a little more than a month ago.

NEGRO WOMAN: My husband died eighteen years ago.

OLD LADY: He was a very sick man all his life—lead poisoning, you know, from the paints. He had to quit the trade after a while, went into the retail grocery business. He was sixty-seven when he died, and I wonder he lived this long. In his last years, the circulation of the blood in his legs was so bad he could hardly walk to the corner.

NEGRO WOMAN: My big trouble is arthritis. I get terrible pains in my arms and in my shoulder sometimes.

OLD LADY: Oh, I been getting a lot of pains in my back, in between my shoulder blades.

NEGRO WOMAN: That's gall bladder.

OLD LADY: Is that what it is?

NEGRO WOMAN: I had that. When you get to our age, Missus Fanning, you gotta expect the bones to rebel.

OLD LADY: Well, now, you're not such an old woman.

NEGRO WOMAN: How old do you think I am?

OLD LADY: I don't know. Maybe forty, fifty.

NEGRO WOMAN: I'm sixty-eight years old.

*For the first time, the old lady looks up. She pauses in her work.*

OLD LADY: I wouldn't believe you were sixty-eight.

NEGRO WOMAN: I'm sixty-eight. I got more white hair than you have. But I dye it. You oughtta dye your hair too. Just go in the five-and ten, pick up some kind of hair dye. Because most people don't like to hire old people with white hair. My children don't want me to work no more, but I'm gonna work until I die. How old do you think that old Greek woman over there is?

OLD LADY: How old?

NEGRO WOMAN: She's sixty-nine. She got a son who's a big doctor. She won't quit working either. I like working here. I come in here in the morning, punch the clock. I'm friends with all these women. You see that little Jewish lady down there? That's the funniest little woman I ever met. You get her to tell you some of her jokes during lunch sometime. She gets me laughing sometimes I can hardly stop. What do I wanna sit around my dirty old room for when I got that little Jewish woman there to tell me jokes all day? That's what I tell my children.

*The old lady turns back to her sewing.*

OLD LADY: Oh, I'd like to hear a couple of jokes.

*At this moment there is a small burst of high-pitched*

*laughter from farther down the rows of machines. Camera cuts to long shot of the rows of operators, singling out a group of three Puerto Rican girls in their twenties. One of them has apparently just said something that made the other two laugh. A fourth Puerto Rican girl, across the table and up from them, calls to them in Spanish: "What happened? What was so funny?" The Puerto Rican girl who made the others laugh answers in a quick patter of high-pitched Spanish. A sudden gust of laughter sweeps all the Puerto Rican girls at the machines. Another woman calls out: "What she say?" One of the Puerto Rican girls answers in broken English.*

PUERTO RICAN GIRL: She say, t'ree week ago, she make a mistake, sewed the belts onna dress backward. Nobody found out. Yesterday, she went in to buy her little girl a dress inna store. They tried to sell her one-a theese dresses . . .

*A wave of laughter rolls up and down the two rows of operators.*

She say, the label onna dress say: "Made in California."

*They absolutely roar at this.*

CLOSE UP. *The old lady joining in the general laughter. She finishes the sleeve she has been working on. It is apparently the last of the bunch. She gathers together in front of her the two dozen other sleeves she has just finished and begins to tie them up with a black ribbon. She lifts her head up and—with magnificent professionalism—calls out.*

OLD LADY: Work! Work! . . .

*Camera closes down on the bundle of sleeves she has tied together with the black ribbon.*

DISSOLVE TO: *The same bundle of sleeves. We pull back and see it is now being held by the boss. He is frowning down at them. At his elbow is standing one of the Puerto Rican girls. She is muttering in broken English.*

PUERTO RICAN GIRL: So what I do? The whole bunch, same way . . .

BOSS: [*Scowling*] All right, all right. Cut them open, resew the whole bunch . . .

PUERTO RICAN GIRL: Cut! I didn't do! I can't cut, sew,

five o'clock the truckman . . . I gotta sew them on the blouse. Take two hours . . .

BOSS: All right, all right, cut them open, sew them up again . . .

*The girl takes the bundle of sleeves and shuffles away. The boss turns, suddenly deeply weary. He goes to the desk.*

BOSS: [*To the bookkeeper*] The old lady come in today, she sewed all the sleeves for the left hand. She didn't make any rights. All lefts . . .

BOOKKEEPER: So what are you gonna do? It's half past four.

BOSS: Call up Raymond for me.

*The bookkeeper picks up the phone receiver, dials. The boss looks up and through the pipe racks at the old lady, sitting hunched and intense over her machine, working with concentrated meticulousness. The boss's attention is called back to the phone by the bookkeeper. He takes the phone from her.*

BOSS: [*In a low voice*] Jerry? This is Sam. Listen, I can't give you the whole twenty dozen at five o'clock. . . . All right, wait a minute, lemme . . . All right, wait a minute. I got fifteen dozen on the racks now . . . Jerry, please. I just got a new operator in today. She sewed five dozen sleeves all left-handed. We're gonna have to cut the seams open, and resew them . . . Look, Jerry, I'm sorry, what do you want from me? I can get it for you by six . . . Jerry, I'll pay the extra freight fee myself . . . Jerry . . . Listen, Jerry, how about those fifty dozen faille sport suits? This doesn't change your mind, does it? . . . Jerry, it's an accident. It could happen to anyone . . . [*A fury begins to take hold of the boss.*] Look, Jerry, you promised me the fifty dozen fai . . . Look, Jerry, you know what you can do with those fifty dozen failles? You think I'm gonna crawl on my knees to you?! [*He's shouting now. Every head in the shop begins to look up.*] You're a miserable human being, you hear that? I'd rather go bankrupt than ask you for another order! And don't come over my house no more! You hear?! I ain't gonna crawl to you! You hear me?! I ain't gonna crawl to you! . . .

*He slams the receiver down, stands, his chest heaving, his face flushed. He looks down at the bookkeeper, his fury still high.*

BOSS: Fire her! Fire her! Fire her!

*He stands, the years of accumulated humiliation and resentment flooding out of him.*

FADE OUT.

## ACT III

FADE IN: *Interior of a subway car heading north to the Bronx during the rush hour—absolutely jam-packed. The camera manages to work its way through the dense crowd to settle on the old lady, seated in her black coat and hat, her hands folded in her lap, her old purse dangling from her wrist. She is staring bleakly straight ahead of herself, as if in another world. The train hurtles on.*

DISSOLVE TO: *Interior of the old lady's apartment—dark—empty. Night has fallen outside. The sound of a key being inserted into the lock. The bolts unlatch, and the door is pushed open. The old lady enters. She closes the door after herself, bolts it. She stands a moment in the dark foyer, then shuffles up the foyer to the living room. She unbuttons her coat, sits down by the table, places her purse on the table. For a moment she sits. Then she rises, goes into the kitchen, turns on the light.*

*It takes her a moment to remember what she came into the kitchen for. Then, collecting herself, she opens the refrigerator door, extracts a carton of milk, sets it on the cupboard shelf. She opens the cupboard door, reaches in, extracts the box of Rice Krispies and a bowl. She sets the bowl down, begins to open the box of cereal. It falls out of her hands to the floor, a number of the pebbles of cereal rolling out to the floor. She starts to bend to pick the box up, then suddenly straightens and stands breathing heavily, nervously wetting her lips. She moves out of the kitchen quickly now, goes to the table, sits down again, picks up the phone, and dials. There is an edge of desperation in her movements. She waits. Then . . .*

OLD LADY: Frank? Who's this, Lillian? Lillian, dear, this is your mother-in-law, and I . . . oh, I'm sorry, what? . . . Oh, I'm sorry . . . Who's this, the baby sitter? . . . This is Missus Fanning, dear—Mister Fanning's mother, is he in? . . . Is Missus Fanning in? . . . Well, do you expect them in? I mean, it's half past six. Did they eat their dinner already? . . . Oh, I see. Well, when do you . . . Oh, I see . . . No, dear, this is Mister Fanning's mother. Just tell him I called. It's not important.

*She hangs up, leaving her hand still on the phone. Then she lifts the receiver again and dials another number. She places a smile on her face and waits. Then . . .*

OLD LADY: Oh, Marie, dear, how are you . . . this is mother . . . Oh, I'm glad to hear your voice . . . Oh, I'm fine . . . fine. How's Jack and the kids? . . . Well, I hope it's nothing serious . . . Oh, that's good . . . [*She is mustering up all the good humor she has in her.*] Oh my, what a day I had. Oh, wait'll I tell you. Listen, I haven't taken you away from your dinner or anything . . . Oh, I went down to look for a job again . . . Yes, that's right, Annie was here this morning . . . how did you know? . . . Oh, is that right? Well, it cleared up, you know, and I didn't want to just sit around, so I went down to this job, and I got fired again . . . The stupidest thing. I sewed all left sleeves . . . Well, you know you have to sew sleeves for the right as well as the left unless your customers are one-armed people . . . [*She is beginning to laugh nervously.*] Yes, it's comical, isn't it? . . . Yes, all left-handed . . .

*She bursts into a short, almost hysterical laugh. Her lip begins to twitch, and she catches her laughter in its middle and breathes deeply to regain control of herself.*

Well, how's Jack and the kids? . . . Well, that's fine. What are you doing with yourself tonight?

*A deep weariness seems to have taken hold of her. She rests her head in the palm of her free hand. Her eyes are closed.*

Oh, do you have a baby sitter? . . . Well, have a nice time, give my regards to your mother-in-law . . . No, no, I'm fine . . . No, I was just asking . . . No, no, listen, dear, I'm absolutely fine. I just come in the house, and I'm going to make myself some Rice Krispies, and I've got some rolls somewhere, and I think I've got a piece of fish in the refrigerator, and I'm going to make myself dinner and take a hot tub, and then I think I'll watch some television. What's tonight, Thursday? . . . Well, Groucho Marx is on tonight . . . No, no, I just called to ask how everything was. How's Jack and the kids? . . . That's fine, have a nice time . . . Good-by, dear . . .

*She hangs up, sits erectly in the chair now. Her face wears an expression of the most profound weariness. She rises now and shuffles with no purpose into the center of the dark room, her coat flapping loosely around her. Then she goes to the television set, turns it on. In a moment a jumble of lines appear, and the sound comes up. The lines clear up into Faye and Skitch Henderson engaging each other in very clever chitchat. The old lady goes back to a television-viewing chair, sits down stiffly—her arms resting on the armrests—and expressionlessly watches the show. Camera comes in for a close-up of the old lady, staring wide-eyed right through the television set, not hearing a word of the chitchat. She is breathing with some difficulty. Suddenly she rises and almost lurches back to the table. She takes the phone, dials with obvious trembling, waits . . .*

OLD LADY: Annie? Annie, I wonder if I could spend the night at your house? I don't want to be alone . . . I'd appreciate that very much . . . All right, I'll wait here . . .

DISSOLVE TO: *Interior of the old lady's bedroom. The son-in-law, in his hat and jacket, is snapping the clasps of an old valise together. Having closed the valise, he picks it off the bed and goes into the living room. The old lady is there. She is seated in one of the straight-back chairs by the table, still in her coat and hat, and she is talking to the daughter—who can be seen through the kitchen doorway, reaching up into the pantry for some of her mother's personal groceries.*

OLD LADY: . . . Well, the truth is, I'm getting old, and there's no point saying it isn't true. [*To her son-in-law as he sets the valise down beside her*] Thank you, dear. I always have so much trouble with the clasp. . . . Did you hear the stupid thing I did today? I sewed all left-handed sleeves. That's a mark of a wandering mind, a sure sign of age. I'm sorry, George, to put you to all this inconvenience . . .

SON-IN-LAW: Don't be silly, Ma. Always glad to have you.

OLD LADY: Annie, dear, what are you looking for?

DAUGHTER: [*In the kitchen*] Your saccharin.

OLD LADY: It's on the lower shelf, dear. . . . This isn't going to be permanent, George. I'll just stay with you a little while till I get a room somewheres with some other old woman . . .

DAUGHTER: [*In the kitchen doorway*] Ma, you're gonna stay with us, so, for heaven's sakes, let's not have no more arguments.

OLD LADY: What'll we do with all my furniture? Annie, don't you want the china closet?

DAUGHTER: No, Ma, we haven't got any room for it . . .

OLD LADY: It's such a good-looking piece. What we have to do is to get Jack and Marie and Frank and Lillian and all of us together, and we'll divide among the three of you whatever you want. I've got that fine set of silver—well, it's not the best, of course, silver plate, y'know—it's older than you are, Annie. [*To her son-in-law*] It was a gift of the girls in my shop when I got married. It's an inexpensive set, but I've shined it every year, and it sparkles. [*To her daughter in the kitchen*] Yes, that's what we'll have to do. We'll have to get all of us together one night and I'll apportion out whatever I've got. And whatever you don't want, well, we'll call a furniture dealer . . . [*To her son-in-law*] . . . although what would he pay me for these old things here? . . . [*To her daughter*] Annie, take the china closet . . . It's such a fine piece . . .

DAUGHTER: Ma, where would we put it?

OLD LADY: Well, take that soft chair there. You always liked that chair . . .

DAUGHTER: Ma . . .

OLD LADY: There's nothing wrong with it. It's not torn or anything. The upholstery's fine. Your father swore by that chair. He said it was the only chair he could sit in.

DAUGHTER: Ma, let's not worry about it now. We'll get together sometime next week with Marie and Lillian . . .

OLD LADY: I want you to have the chair . . .

DAUGHTER: Ma, we got all modern furniture in our house . . .

OLD LADY: It's not an old chair. We just bought it about six years ago. No, seven . . .

DAUGHTER: Ma, what do we need the . . .

OLD LADY: Annie, I don't want to sell it to a dealer! It's my home. I don't want it to go piece by piece into a secondhand shop

DAUGHTER: Ma . . .

SON-IN LAW. Annie! We'll take the chair!

DAUGHTER: All right, Ma, the chair is ours.

OLD LADY: I know that Lillian likes those lace linens I've got in the cedar chest. And the carpets. Now these are good carpets, Annie. There's no sense just throwing them out. They're good broadloom. The first good money your father was making we bought them. When we almost bought that house in Passaic, New Jersey. You ought to remember that, Annie. You were about seven then. But we bought the grocery store instead. Oh, how we scraped in that store. In the heart of the depression. We used to sell bread for six cents a loaf. I remember my husband said: "Let's buy a grocery store. At least we'll always have food in the house." It seems to me my whole life has been hand-to-mouth. Did we ever not worry about the rent? I remember as a girl in Cork, eating boiled potatoes every day. I don't know what it all means, I really don't . . . [*She stares rather abstractedly at her son-*

*in-law.*] I'm sixty-six years old, and I don't know what the purpose of it all was.

SON-IN-LAW: Missus Fanning . . .

OLD LADY: An endless, endless struggle. And for what? For what? [*She is beginning to cry now.*] Is this what it all comes to? An old woman parceling out the old furniture in her house . . . ?

*She bows her head and stands, thirty years of repressed tears torturously working their way through her body in racking shudders.*

DAUGHTER: Ma . . .

*The old lady stands, her shoulders slumped, her head bowed, crying with a violent agony.*

OLD LADY: [*The words stumbling out between her sobs*] Oh, I don't care . . . I don't care . . .

*Hold on the old lady, standing, crying.*

DISSOLVE TO: *Film. Rain whipping through the streets of New York at night—same film we opened the show with—a frightening thunderstorm*

DISSOLVE TO: *The old lady's valise, now open, lying on a narrow single bed. We pull back to see the old lady—in a dress, but with her coat off—rummaging in the valise for something. The room she is in is obviously a little boy's room. There are a child's paintings and drawings and cut-outs Scotch-taped to the wall, and toys and things on the floor. It is dark outside, and the rain whacks against the window panes. The old lady finally extracts from out of the valise a long woolen nightgown and, holding it in both arms, she shuffles to the one chair in the room and sits down. She sets the nightgown in her lap and bends to remove her shoes. This is something of an effort and costs her a few moments of quick breathing. She sits, expressionless, catching her breath, the white nightgown on her lap, her hands folded on it. Even after she regains her breath, she sits this way, now staring fixedly at the floor at her feet. Hold.*

DISSOLVE TO: *The window of the child's bedroom. It is daylight now, and the rain has stopped. The cold morning sun shines thinly through the white chintz curtains. The camera pulls slowly back and finally comes to rest on the old lady sitting just as we saw her last, unmoving, wrapped in thought, the white nightgown on her lap, her hands folded. From some room off, the thin voice of a baby suddenly rises and abruptly falls. The old lady looks slowly up.*

*Then she bends and puts her shoes on. She rises, sets the nightgown on the chair from which she has just risen, moves with a slight edge of purpose down the room to the closet, opens the door, reaches in, and takes out her coat. She puts it on, stands a moment, looking about the room for something. She finds her hat and purse sitting on the chest of drawers. She picks them up. Then she turns to the door of the room and carefully opens it. She looks out onto the hallway. Across from her, the door to her daughter's and son-in-law's bedroom stands slightly ajar. She crosses to the door, looks in. Her daughter and son-in-law make two large bundles under their blankets. For a moment she stands and surveys them. Then the daughter turns in her bed so that she faces her mother. Her eyes are open; she has not been asleep. At the sight of her mother in the doorway, she leans upon one elbow.*

OLD LADY: [*In an intense whisper*] Annie, it just wasn't comfortable, you know? I just can't sleep anywheres but in my own bed, and that's the truth. I'm sorry, Annie, honest. You're a fine daughter, and it warms me to know that I'm welcome here. But what'll I do with myself, Annie, what'll I do? . . .

*The daughter regards her mother for a moment.*

DAUGHTER: Where are you going, Ma, with your coat on?

OLD LADY: I'm going out and look for a job. And, Annie, please don't tell me that everything's against me. I know it. Well, I'll see you, dear. I didn't mean to wake you up. . . .

*She turns and disappears from the doorway. The daughter starts quickly from the bed.*

DAUGHTER: Ma . . .

*She moves quickly across the room to the door of the hallway. She is in her pajamas. She looks down the hallway, which is fairly dark. Her mother is already at the front door, at the other end.*

DAUGHTER: Ma . . .

OLD LADY: I'm leaving the valise with all my things. I'll pick them up tonight. And please don't start an argument with me, Annie, because I won't listen to you. I'm a woman of respect. I can take care of myself. I always have. And don't tell me it's raining because it stopped about an hour ago. And don't say you'll drive me home because I can get the bus two blocks away. Work is the meaning of my life. It's all I know what to do. I can't change my ways at this late time.

*For a long moment the mother and daughter regard each other. Then the daughter pads quietly down to the old lady.*

DAUGHTER: [*Quietly*] When I'm your age, Ma, I hope I'm like you.

*For a moment the two women stand in the dark hallway. Then they quickly embrace and release each other. The old lady unbolts the door and disappears outside, closing the door after her. The daughter bolts it shut with a click. She turns and goes back up the dark foyer to her own bedroom. She goes in, shuffles to the bed, gets back under the covers. For a moment she just lies there. Then she nudges her sleeping husband, who grunts.*

DAUGHTER: George, let's drop the kids at your sister's for a week or ten days and drive down to Virginia. You don't want to spend your one vacation a year sitting in New York, watching it rain.

*The son-in-law, who hasn't heard a word, grunts once or twice more. The daughter pulls the blankets up over her shoulders, turns on her side, and closes her eyes.*

FADE OUT.

THE END

## Discussion Questions

1. *Does the daughter approve of her mother going out to look for a job? What is the daughter's argument? What does she want her mother to do? Does her husband agree with her?*
2. *What recent experience has the Old Lady had in trying to find a job? Does she have any doubts about her ability to hold down a job? Explain. What gives her some encouragement?*
3. *How does the author portray the Old Lady's alternative to*

*working? How does he show what decision the Old Lady has made?*

4. *On what basis does the boss hire the Old Lady? What is the real reason he hires her? Why does he fire her? Would you agree that the reasons for hiring and firing people are not always wholly related to whether they can do the job? List all the unrelated factors you can think of that affect employability.*

5. *Toward the end of the play does it look like the Old Lady has given up on the idea of getting a job? Explain. What restores her determination? All things considered, do you think she will finally land a job and keep it?*

6. *As shown in this play, what single quality would you say is essential in any purposeful job hunting?*

# ADDITIONAL READINGS

**Additional Reading**

In addition to the reading included in each unit, there is an annotated suggested reading list. You may want to assign an additional reading to each member of the class.

The readings in this unit deal with approaches and strategies for finding a job. As you teach this unit you may find other readings to add to the present list.

Each time a student finishes a reading assignment, it is suggested that a Reading Report Form be completed and turned in to the teacher.

Bolles, Richard Nelson, ***What Color Is Your Parachute?***

This book is a practical manual on job hunting. Offbeat in its approach, it covers everything from career planning to landing the job of your choice in a thorough, creative, and highly stimulating way.

Irish, Richard K., ***Go Hire Yourself an Employer***

You must learn to become competent in the job hunt—that is the theme of this book. Using a question-and-answer format, the author gives you an in-depth account of the hiring process and some sound advice on how to approach an employer.

Taylor, Phoebe, ***How to Succeed In the Business of Finding a Job***

Case histories highlight this author's approach to the subject of successful job hunting. Psychologically oriented, the book introduces two career guidance tools: the "Selectascope," a self-help guide for matching the job seeker's requirements with the employer's; and the "Perceptual Résumé," a résumé that emphasizes the similarities between skills offered and positions sought.

Rood, Allan, ***Job Strategy***

Designed mainly for college undergraduates who are planning to enter business and industry as executive trainees, this book cautions against job seeking by trial and error. It relies heavily on the résumé as the center of career planning and job negotiations, and discusses the preparation of an effective résumé at length. It also covers campaigning and interviewing for the job.

Gardiner, Glenn L., ***How You Can Get the Job You Want***

This book features the "Ten-Step Plan" for getting a job. There are helpful and encouraging answers to 230 specific questions related to the business of finding the right job for you. It also tells where to look for additional information on subjects of special interest.

Peskin, Dean B., ***The Art of Job Hunting***

This book, written by a personnel director, offers some excellent inside information to the job hunter. The emphasis is on preparing yourself before you enter the job market. Many people with much to offer simply do not know how to present their talents and abilities to an employer. You can get some good insights here on how to show a positive image for being hired.

Edlund, Sidney, and Mary Edlund, ***Pick Your Job–And Land It***

One of the products of the Great Depression, this often reprinted book is still one of the best manuals for selling yourself to an employer. The book features readable and inspirational case histories of successful job seekers. The sales principles offered are as sound today as they were when the book was written.

Angel, Juvenal L., ***Why and How to Prepare an Effective Job Résumé***

The author of this manual calls a personal résumé an inventory of assets. He sees it as the first step in a job-hunting campaign. Using the device of a "Personal Occupational Worksheet," the author shows you how to construct a résumé that you can adapt to any specific job you want.

Marshall, Austin, ***How to Get a Better Job***

This is the official book of the Job Finding Forum of the Advertising Club of New York. Its contents represent a distillation of twenty-five years experience with thousands of people who have been stalled in their efforts to find rewarding work. Direct and functional in its approach, it is probably one of the best books to read again and again for practical suggestions on how to get started, to determine what you have to offer, and to convincingly present this evidence to an employer.

Larson, Darold E., ***How to Find a Job***

Originally titled *The Job Finder,* this book offers a system that is designed to help the job seeker get an objective view of himself or herself and the market, and to use that view to attain the desired job. Building confidence is the essential ingredient in the system, and the job seeker can pick up some sound information in this book on how to go about doing that.

Splaver, Sarah, ***Your Career–If You're Not Going to College***

As the title implies, this book is concerned with uncovering useful and interesting careers for high school graduates. It also helps you understand what you must do when you begin to think seriously about looking for work.

# What Happens When I Get the Job?

"... every man shall receive his own reward, according to his own labour."

**I Corinthians 3:8**

*What are some of the things I should learn about as I begin work at my first regular job?*

**Unit V Introduction**
Discuss the quote with the class.

**Unit V Theme**
Personal Integrity: values and attitudes on the job

# WORDS IN ACTION

**Words in Action**

Discuss the Useful Terms with your class. These words are commonly used by young people who are either beginning a new job or starting some kind of post-secondary training for a future career.

All unfamiliar words should be checked with the definitions found in the Glossary. When students are ready, assign the Vocabulary Exercise.

## USEFUL TERMS

1. accredited
2. collective bargaining
3. competent
4. correspondence course
5. exemptions
6. exploitation
7. FICA—social security
8. garnishee
9. gross pay
10. hierarchy
11. high school equivalency
12. IRS
13. liable
14. matriculate
15. post-secondary education
16. scholarship
17. take-home pay
18. W-2 form

**Vocabulary Exercise Answers**

A. collective bargaining
B. garnishee
C. high school equivalency
D. social security—FICA
E. exploitation
F. matriculate
G. liable
H. take-home pay
I. W-2 form
J. competent
K. hierarchy
L. exemptions
M. post-secondary education
N. scholarship
O. IRS
P. gross pay
Q. accredited
R. correspondence course

## VOCABULARY EXERCISE

*On a separate sheet of paper write the letters A through R. Now read the sentences below. Write the Useful Term next to the letter of the sentence that best describes it. Blanks have been used in the descriptions to give you clues.*

A. collective bargaining
B. garnishee
C. high school equivalency

**A.** The union pressed its demands, but the company stood firm in an all-night session of ______.

**B.** If you don't pay back what you owe, the company will ______ your wages.

**C.** To enter that program you need either a high school diploma or a ______.

**D.** The federal government withholds this portion of your paycheck for retirement benefits. Most people know this as the ______ contribution, and you can readily identify it on your check stub by the four letters ______.

**E.** You know that these people are in the country illegally. You are taking advantage of their sensitive situation by paying them far less than you would any other worker. You are guilty of a form of ______.

**F.** Once you ______ at the nursing school, you may want to take additional courses so that you can get a B.S. degree as well as an R.N. license.

**G.** If you can prove that the damage was accidental and not the result of neglect, the company will not hold you ______.

**H.** Your employer is required to withhold a percentage of your paycheck for federal, and sometimes state and city income taxes. There are also your contributions for medical and dental insurance, and if applicable, your union dues. With these deductions the remainder becomes your ______.

**I.** Before you can file your federal income tax return you have to wait for your employer to send you your ______.

**J.** As you become more experienced and learn more about your job, you become more ______ in the performance of your duties.

**K.** You will be trained in management and advanced to a responsible post within the organization, taking your place in the ______ of the corporation.

**L.** Your income tax is reduced according to the number of people whom you support financially. For tax purposes, these people (including yourself) are considered ______.

**M.** You have completed high school and taken some accounting courses in college. Have you had any other ______?

**N.** Besides taking out a loan, you could apply for a ______ to

**Correcting Mistakes**

Students should correct their mistakes by checking the terms and definitions in the Glossary.

D. social security—FICA
E. exploitation
F. matriculate
G. liable
H. take-home pay
I. W-2 form
J. competent
K. hierarchy
L. exemptions
M. post-secondary education
N. scholarship

O. IRS
P. gross pay
Q. accredited
R. correspondence course

help support yourself while you are in college. Many are available from many sources.

**O.** If you need assistance in filling out your income tax return, you can always go directly to the ______.

**P.** Before taxes and contributions, your salary is $18,000 a year, or a ______ figure of $692.30 each biweekly pay period.

**Q.** In order for you to receive any loans to further your education, the school you choose will almost always have to be an ______ institution.

**R.** At a time when tuition, room and board, and transportation are substantial expenses in the furtherance of your education, you might want to consider a ______.

# A CASE STUDY

## GARY'S PROBLEM

"Look at it this way," said Ralph. "It's just a job. You can make as much or as little of it as you want."

Gary and Ralph were having their lunch in the section of the warehouse reserved for employees as a kind of lunchroom and lounge. Gary was complaining to the older maintenance man he had made friends with. "I expected things to be different. And they were in the beginning," he said. "It felt good to be out of school—no more homework, tests, or conforming to silly rules. And I was lucky to get this job at the store full-time.

"I didn't have to look for work at all. The job was all right at first, too. It was interesting. I was learning new things, meeting new people all the time. I was finally a part of something that was going on. But now it's the same old thing day in and day out. Boring!"

"You have only been here for eight months," said Ralph. "Relax. I've been here four years and I'm not complaining. It's just the way you look at it."

"Yeah, well, you're married and you have three kids," broke in Gary. "That's the way you look at it."

"Sure I have to work for a living," said Ralph, his patience holding up fairly well. "Most people do. But I'm talking about the job, how you see it and how you go about doing it . . . and what you expect to get from it." Ralph bit into the other half of his sandwich. "Look. We're friends, right? Can I tell you something?"

"Yeah, I guess," said Gary, a little uncertain of what might be coming.

"You're painting yourself into a corner," Ralph began. "You're always waiting for something to happen and when it doesn't, you get impatient, bored. It shows up in the way you do your job. You do less and less and feel you should

**Gary's Problem**

The Case Study is based on the theme of the unit—personal integrity. Gary has been on the job for eight months. At this point he has become dissatisfied with his job. His friend Ralph points out that it is not his job that has changed, but his attitude towards the job.

Assign the Case Study to the class to read for homework.

be getting more and more for it. You're itchy and uncomfortable and you make everybody around you itchy and uncomfortable. Finally you blow it for yourself and maybe lose your job. They see you're unhappy and they let you go."

"And what are you supposed to do when every day is the same as the last and you don't feel as though you are getting anywhere?" interrupted Gary. "I asked for a transfer, and they wouldn't give it to me. They said they needed me here."

"Now, you see, you're talking like a kid who is still in school," said Ralph. "You make it sound like it is their fault you're bored. Hey, they're just running a business! They pay you to do the job you were hired to do. That's all."

"But that's stupid," said Gary. "Wouldn't I be worth more to them if I wasn't bored, if I had a more interesting job? Wouldn't I work harder then?"

"You said your job *was* interesting. What happened?" said Ralph. "And how long would it be before the new job got to be boring and you had to ask for another one? No, you have to be honest with yourself. No employer is going to fool around trying to keep you from getting tired of your job."

Gary opened his carton of chocolate milk. "What do you do then? Quit?"

"What you do is ask yourself some questions and decide what it is you want to do," said Ralph. "Ask yourself, not the person you're working for. Don't expect your employer to figure out what's good for you. If you see that some of your future is here, fine. If not, start the right way someplace else. But as long as you are here, you do what you have agreed to do in the first place, make the most of it, and don't complain."

Gary screwed up his face.

"Now look," said Ralph, softening. "Say you were the boss. What things would you like to see in some guy who was working for you?"

Gary thought for a minute. "Let's see—be on time to work, have a good attitude, be honest, do what you're told to do and don't argue, get along with the people you're working with, dress right for the job, be polite and friendly to the customers. I do all those things," added Gary a little defensively.

"Right. But for whom and for what reason?" said Ralph.

Gary looked confused. "Well, for the boss. That's what is expected, right?"

"Sure," said Ralph. "But can't you turn that around? Can't you do those things for yourself? Can't you be your own boss?"

"Well, yeah," said Gary, not quite ready to understand.

"See," said Ralph. "You really work for yourself if you want to look at it that way. You know the right things to do. Do them and you don't get bored in your work. And you satisfy the real boss—you!"

"That's nice. But what happens if I don't satisfy the other boss who's paying me?" asked Gary only half seriously.

"Right," laughed Ralph, getting up from the rough wooden table they had been seated at. "In that case you had better start looking for a new job." He rolled the remains of his lunch up in the loose papers and heaved the ball into the metal basket in the corner. "I think you'll find, however, that the people who can settle with themselves about the way they do their job generally satisfy those who pay them for it."

They walked off together.

Gary needs to learn that working for a living is not merely a case of reporting to work, putting in your time, and getting paid for it. Under those circumstances, sooner or later someone is bound to grow dissatisfied—if not the employee, the employer.

The work process is quite complex. It is about as complex as human behavior, and it encompasses problems of all kinds—from being bored with your job to being addicted to work; from being too timid to go to your boss to discuss a personal problem to telling someone off who jokes about the length of your hair. It is important to realize that we must provide a good many of our own solutions. We cannot expect our employer to do it all for us.

In this unit you will be taking a look at some job-related and work-related problems. You will also be exploring some avenues of **post-secondary education** with your guidance or vocational counselors. You will be figuring out what it will cost for you to live the life-style of your preference. Throughout the unit you will be considering some of the broader questions associated with work and business, including moral obligations and ethical practices, the role of government and labor, and the responsibility of the business community to the community at large.

**Discussion Questions**

Use the questions in the section Thinking It Through as a guide for a class discussion concerning the Case Study.

Question [illegible] can be worked at the chalkboard as part of a class discussion, or students can individually work on this question as an assignment.

## Thinking It Through

1. *What does Ralph mean when he says you can make as much or as little of your job as you want?*
2. *What is Gary's problem?*
3. *How can he improve his situation if he decides to take Ralph's advice?*
4. *Pretend you took a job as an office manager for a local newspaper. Part of your job was to mail out bills to advertisers and subscribers, and you were told that you could always expect confusion and often unreasonable complaints. How would you deal with this situation as one who plans to make something more of the job than what is expected?*
5. *A worker's attitude toward a job determines to a large measure how well he or she does that job. Make a simple chart consisting of two columns, one headed* Good Attitude *and the other* Poor Attitude. *In the columns write possible responses that show both positive and negative reactions to the following job situations.*
   a. *following accepted procedures for routine tasks*
   b. *taking orders and suggestions from superiors*
   c. *receiving constructive criticism on matters of personal appearance*
   d. *working with others on matters of mutual concern*

**e.** *reporting to work earlier or staying later to complete a job*

**f.** *taking work home on occasions*

**g.** *dealing with difficult clients or customers*

**h.** *accepting a reassignment*

**i.** *improving on general performance*

**j.** *demonstrating loyalty to the employer*

# REPORT PROJECTS

**Personal Essay V and On-the-Job Clinic**

In presenting these two projects the teacher should make sure students understand that they will respond to five problem situations in writing, and later they will read at least one of those responses aloud to the class. It is also important that students understand from the beginning that they are to consider the problem *from the employee's point of view.*

The teacher should ask that the five written paragraphs of Personal Essay V be given priority over all other project work and be handed in immediately upon completion. As the paragraphs are turned in, check to see that all five responses are there and that they are written from the employee's point of view.

As quickly as possible award grades to all essays and return the paragraphs to the students so that they can get ready for the On-the-Job Clinic.

On the day the Clinic is to begin, the teacher should be certain that all students have their written responses in front of them. Students should first read aloud what they have written. They may add extemporaneous remarks later. A student-secretary can be appointed to read aloud each problem from Personal Essay V and call for responses. When several responses to a problem

## PERSONAL ESSAY V

***Introduction*** Below are eleven job-related problem situations. These are typical problems that workers face every day. You will be using these situations as a basis for writing and later discussing possible solutions to the problems.

***Directions*** Select five of the problem situations presented below and write a short paragraph about each *from the employee's point of view.* Give your analysis of the situation and your advice for a solution.

### Job Situations

**A.** Arlene took a job to help pay the bills and then found out that she hated the work. But she felt that it was better to have any job than to be unemployed.

**B.** Chad is worried about keeping his job. There is one important operation he has to perform and he can't seem to get it right. His boss went over the procedure rapidly during Chad's first week on the job and then again later when a large order was held up because of his errors. Chad is still not sure what to do and doesn't know where to turn.

**C.** Denise is bored with her job. As one of the junior managers put it, "Everytime I turn around, she's sitting there, staring into space and twiddling her thumbs." Nevertheless, when Denise is given a specific job to do, she gets right to it and does it quickly and expertly. But when she's finished, she just sits and waits again, bored.

**D.** Two weeks after he got the job, Doug began to notice that many operations were being performed, as he saw it, inefficiently. When he made this observation known to the people he was working with, most just shrugged their shoulders, though some agreed in principle with him. He began to get a reputation as a complainer and a faultfinder, a difficult guy to work with and to be around.

have been read, the problem can be discussed by the class, then summarized by the teacher before examining the next situation.

**E.** It was the third job Belle had had since she graduated from high school a little over a year ago. This last job was the best because it paid the most. It did not matter that the work left her exhausted at the end of the day, or that the slack season was approaching and she could be laid off at any time. Belle just wanted the best-paying job she could find.

**F.** Craig's mother was quite ill, and while everyone in the office knew about it, they never mentioned it when he was around. This was because they knew he was sensitive, and also because he gave the impression that this was his problem to be worked out his way. He resented anyone intruding in his private life, even his boss, who was growing concerned over the situation. Lost in his thoughts and impossible to communicate with, Craig was slipping up on the critical detail work of his job.

**G.** Pam worked with Brian and Carl uncrating small appliances—transistor radios, calculators, digital watches—in the storeroom. For several weeks now Pam had noticed Carl at the end of the day emptying small parcels from his jacket and the pockets of his pants into his locker. These items were accounted for officially as "lost in transit." When Pam, worried, finally took Brian aside and told him what she saw, all he said was, "What do you expect me to do about it?"

**H.** Mark was in over his head and he knew it. It was only a matter of time before they would be calling him at work to demand that he pay some of the unpaid balance of his charge account. He could not pay, yet he could not risk having his employer find out. What could he do?

**I.** It was clear to Tracey that her boss took more than a normal interest in her and it was beginning to unsettle her. She liked her job and took pride in the way she did her work, but lately found herself being interrupted in her duties by her boss more and more. He needed her advice, he said, but Tracey had serious doubts about that.

J. Bill was hurt and angry and didn't mind showing it when he heard that Pedro was promoted to a sales position. Bill had done everything he was told to do. He had learned his job quickly and thoroughly and did it well. He took an adult education course in advertising and sales. He was punctual, cooperative, and always polite to the customers. And he had been with the company longer than Pedro had. Now he was not sure where his future lay.

K. "We're going to have to let you go," was the way the supervisor put it to Margo. "You can pick up your check from the front office any time after one. I'm sorry it didn't work out." Margo, dumbstruck, watched her former supervisor walk away.

## ON-THE-JOB CLINIC

***Introduction*** In Personal Essay V you were exposed to a number of job-related problem situations, each of which suggests that there is a principle or rule that could be applied to each case. As you make your way into the world of full-time employment where workers must support themselves and their families, you will become aware of new sets of rules and standards.

These rules are essentially ones that govern our conduct on the job. Some rules seem to make sense the moment we hear them. Others, however, are more subtle, harder to define until some problem situation comes along and helps to spell them out.

In this report we will be using those situations of Personal Essay V and your response to them as the basis for the On-the-Job Clinic. Your feelings and ideas should help to determine the cause of the problem, provide a solution, and, if appropriate, perhaps suggest some standard of behavior that might prevent such a situation.

***Directions*** A member of the class will be asked to read aloud a problem situation of Personal Essay V. Others will then be invited to read their answers and discuss their own views with the class. In the discussion that follows, perhaps several different interpretations may be presented. The discussions can continue until all the problem situations have been talked over.

## SEMINAR ON LAWS GOVERNING LABOR AND WORKING CONDITIONS

***Introduction*** There was a time, and not too long ago, when the employer could dictate the terms of employment to all the company's employees. A six-day workweek of ten to twelve hours a day, no paid vacations or holidays, unsafe or unsanitary working conditions, no health or life insurance, no pension funds or social security benefits on retirement, children working side by side with heads of families in sweat shops, unfair discrimination in hiring, no wage standards, no pay scales or contracts or agreements to define working conditions—the job was what the employer said it was, take it or leave it. And if you did not take the job, you did not eat. As you probably know from your studies in history, that time is past. Workers of today are protected on and off the job in many ways by laws regulating working conditions and employment practices.

The purpose of this seminar is to consider some of these laws and to see how they can be expected to affect us directly as we prepare to earn a living.

***Directions*** Each of the cases offered below is regulated to some degree by existing laws. Committees of three to five students can investigate each of the cases and report on them, referring to the laws involved and explaining how they apply in such cases. Your school librarian can help each committee locate helpful information.

**Labor Laws Seminar**

The Labor Laws Seminar may be offered as an optional extra-grade report for students interested in labor relations. A committee orientation is proposed in the text due to the complexity of some of the problems presented for investigation. It is suggested that a team of three to five students organize its own research plan on a single problem and prepare a written report of the findings to be read aloud to the class.

After the project is introduced to the class, the teacher should ask students who are interested to sign up for the project. If there is a sufficient number of students, two or more teams can be formed, each with a chairperson and a problem for investigation.

Individual research assignments can be determined by the committees. Each student is responsible for reporting his or her findings to the chairperson who will assemble the data into the final report.

The students can usually find the information they need by using school resources.

Teachers in social studies or business departments may be able to provide information or suggest good source materials.

Beyond the school there is a number of good community resources: the state department of labor, state employment office, or the local branch of a union. Students can also seek information from relatives or family friends who work in law offices.

**A.** Arturo Barton looked at his first paycheck. He was stunned. His salary, he was told, was to be $3.50 an hour. He had worked his full thirty-five hours last week. That meant he should be getting $122.50. The figure on the check read $91.88. He found the $122.50 on the check stub alongside the words **Gross Pay.** Then there was a series of deductions: Federal, State, F.I.C.A., Dues. He never gave his permission for anyone to make these deductions. What right did the employer have to chop off his earnings like that?

**B.** After two weeks on the job, Andrea Fuller climbed up the ladder to reach for a pair of shoes when she slipped on a loose rung and broke her ankle. She was taken straight to the emergency room of the city hospital. It was a serious fracture and she would be on her back for at least a week, then in a cast for six more. The only thing she could think of was how she was going to pay the bills. The doctor did not know when she would be able to go back to work. Her employer would probably let her go. What would she do? What could she do?

**C.** Joanne Washington's brother Seth was fourteen years old. He had a clean-up job with a local contractor and he was earning $1.50 an hour working three hours a day for three days a week after school and six hours on Saturday. Joanne was upset about the arrangement. She felt the contractor was taking advantage of Seth. Wasn't there some law that said an employer could not hire fourteen-year-old students on a regular basis except under certain conditions?

**D.** Eric Andersen was caught in the middle. His supervisor told him to open the crates; his shop steward, who represented Eric's union, told him not to. If he refused to do the job he could be fired for insubordination; if he opened the crates he could find himself very alone and without the union's support if he ran up against a job-related problem in the future. Eric quickly declared himself a neutral until the dispute was resolved, and he asked for another assignment. He also realized he had better find out quickly what was behind all this since it involved him directly.

**E.** The well-tailored representatives of the minority organization were admitted into the office of the president of the company. They settled into the two soft chairs that had been arranged for them.

"Our information," began the large man, "confirmed by your own personnel director, shows that you have not hired one of our number for the past three years. We see this clearly as an example of a discriminatory hiring practice, and we are demanding proportional representation for our people on your payroll—now." The woman representative went on to name the companies in the industry that had begun hiring, even recruiting, from minority quarters. She ended by naming the two people of her particular minority currently in the employ of this company. There was a pause.

"The individuals you refer to," the president spoke slowly and carefully, "have been in our employ, one for over twenty years and the other for nearly twelve. They were hired on no other basis than their ability to perform the duties of the jobs we hired them for."

"Tokenism," interrupted the woman. There was another pause.

"We do not, nor have we ever discriminated in our hiring in the way you are suggesting," continued the president evenly. "Nor is it our policy to create jobs simply to fulfill the needs of the community. We are essentially a company in business to manufacture a line of quality products and to show a fair profit in so doing. And, we will always hire and retain qualified persons regardless of their origins or affiliations as long as we have jobs for them. At the moment there are few jobs of any kind open, as I am sure you are aware. And, as to the other matter, we have not been able to employ any of the seven or eight of your people who applied here in the past three years simply because none could offer the kind of experience we were looking for."

"Sir," said the large man with a sudden new intensity, "do you know why so few of us apply for work here? I will tell you why. It is because we know we have little chance of being hired. And as for your judgment, we cannot accept that any longer. Our people need jobs and we need them *now.*" He leaned forward in his chair. "We are going to suggest that you adjust your hiring procedures, maybe your judgment as well. Our organization is going to see to it that a number of trained, very highly qualified persons apply for jobs with this company in the coming weeks. We will be watching, waiting to see who is hired and who isn't."

Before the president could respond, the man and the woman rose together and left.

**F.** It was now three weeks since Barbara Douglas had been told by the manager, Mr. Cargill, that she was being let go. At that time she said to him that she would be returning to her hometown, and she asked if her last check could be mailed to her there. Mr. Cargill replied that there would be no problem; she would have it by no later than two weeks. After three weeks and no check, she decided she had better phone the company.

"Our books show you were paid your final check when you left," said the bookkeeper. "Mr. Cargill has confirmed that. . . . No, I'm afraid you won't be able to talk to him now, he's busy. You could call back later, of course. But I suggest you review your records first. I don't know that there's anything he or anyone else can do. . . ." Her voice trailed off. There was a sudden sick feeling in the pit of Barbara's stomach as she hung up the phone. Would she ever get her money? She wondered.

**G.** Gale Simpson had come to the state unemployment insurance offices on the advice of a friend who told her she could and should be collecting unemployment insurance. She had filled out and returned the several cards given to her by the receptionist, who told her to have a seat.

Gale had been sitting on the hard wooden bench for a little over an hour when at last she heard her name being called. A small, tired-looking woman motioned to her from the door to a glass-walled cubicle off to one side of the corridor.

"You are not eligible to receive unemployment insurance benefits," said the woman dryly. "You haven't worked long enough to qualify. Let me explain to you how it works." The woman went on to tell Gale under what circumstances she could collect unemployment insurance and how much she would be eligible to receive according to her earnings.

## POST-SECONDARY EDUCATION REPORT

***Introduction*** Advancement in a career or in a company often depends on the mastery of certain job-related skills. This type of learning is sometimes referred to as post secondary education. You can enroll in a college or university as a full-time or part-time student working toward a degree or just improving your basic education. There are also vocational courses at local educational centers that teach or reinforce skills for particular jobs or trades. In any case, once you leave school and begin work, you come to realize that schooling is not over but is actually just beginning.

***Directions*** For this report you will arrange a conference with your vocational or guidance counselor to discuss schools you can attend or courses you can take to prepare yourself for your career. Your written report will record what was discussed at the conference between your counselor and yourself. In its final form, the report should look and read like the minutes of a meeting, so be sure to take careful notes of what was discussed at your conference.

At the conference, tell your counselor about your career plans, your interests, and your ambitions. Ask about programs or schools your counselor would recommend to help you in your career preparation. Perhaps there are school catalogs or brochures that you can borrow to give you more specific information on the suggested courses of study. You may want to discuss with your counselor any questions you have regarding tuition costs or financial assistance, including the availability of loans or **scholarships.** You may also want to discuss the length of time it takes to complete programs, types of degrees, certificates, licensing, or other information concerning your post-secondary educational program. Your counselor may want you to

**Post-Secondary Education Report**

This is an individual report project that all students should complete. Since part of the work in Unit V depends on the students holding a conference with their guidance or vocational counselor, the students should make an appointment with their counselor before beginning work on the unit. The teacher might prepare for each student a simple form to be signed by the counselor verifying the date and time arranged for a conference.

In scheduling the work in Unit V, the teacher should allow time for the students to meet with their counselor, and for them to follow up their conference with some further research on their educational alternatives.

Key questions for a personal interview are suggested in the text. If the students are to use computer printouts as the basis of this project, they should still be expected to organize their information into the body of a formal written report.

come back for a follow-up conference after you have had time to further research the schools and courses of study that were recommended.

**Cost-of-Living Report**

This report is offered as the last project in Unit V. An important adjunct to career planning, the Cost-of-Living Report is extensive and requires considerable time for the class to complete. A suitable schedule for the report should therefore be planned early in the unit.

The teacher can introduce the report by referring to the life-style focus in Unit II. Explain that choosing a way of life for yourself is one thing; being able to afford it is something else again. Money management cannot be accomplished successfully unless all living expenses are considered within the limits of expected income.

The project, as detailed in the text, has three parts: the research assignment of one or more budget items to each student, the individual oral presentations made to the class, and the detailed statement of anticipated expenses submitted by each student.

All students should first examine carefully the Budget Items to familiarize themselves with each of the numbered classifications. Part of a class session can be spent discussing the individual assignments before students sign up for one of the items. (See model of Student Assignment Sheet on page T18 of the Teacher's Edition.)

As soon as the assignments are made, the teacher should provide individual assistance to insure that students understand

## A COST-OF-LIVING REPORT

***Introduction*** In Personal Essay II you worked out a way of life that would be agreeable to you. You wrote about the kind of job situation you wanted, chose a type of home and environment, and stated your ideas on family life. Money, although an important factor determining life-style, was included in the essay only on the basis of how much you wanted to *earn*.

Finding out how much you will have to *pay* to support your chosen life-style is the subject of this report. The information from this research may come as a shock to you, but it is always worthwhile to plan for your expenses. When you know how much you are spending for the necessities of life, you will be able to see what luxuries you can afford.

In this report you will match the cost of your life-style preferences to your income expectations in working out an estimated expense budget for yourself.

***Directions*** This report project is divided into three parts. For the first part each student in the class will be assigned to research one or more of the thirty-two numbered items found in the budget specifications for the Cost-of-Living Report.

To complete this research you will want to use your school library to find information on some of the items. For other items, your parents can provide valuable information. Remember also, the community in which you live has many resource people who can give you accurate information concerning all the numbered items in the budget: insurance agents, real estate brokers, bankers, automobile dealers and mechanics, merchants, and many others.

Do your research carefully and thoroughly. Find out all you can about your assigned budget topic. The budget specifications listed below will help you determine what information and costs you will need to gather. Remember, this assignment is to reflect your personal life-style, the one you described in Personal Essay II. Based on that life-style, you will be building a cost-of-living budget for *yourself.*

Carefully collect your notes and estimated costs as accurately as possible since you will be required to share your findings with the rest of your classmates.

## Budget Items

### *Housing*

1. **Renting a room, apartment, or house**
   a. location (city, town, suburb, or rural area)
   b. number of rooms, baths, garages
   c. furnished or unfurnished
   d. rent per month (with or without utilities included)
2. **Buying a home**
   a. kind of house (ranch, colonial, split level, condominium, trailer)
   b. location (city, town, suburb, or rural area)
   c. number of rooms, baths, garages
   d. asking price
   e. mortgage agreement
   f. required down payment
   g. monthly mortgage payment including taxes

### *Food*

3. **Cost of food per week**
   a. meats, fish, poultry
   b. fruits and vegetables
   c. staples (potatoes, macaroni, spaghetti, bread, flour, cereals)
   d. beverages
   e. snacks
   f. estimated total cost for food per month

what information they are to provide in their reports. The teacher should have the facts and figures relating to living in the locality—real estate, rentals, utilities, transportation, education, and so forth. It is also helpful for the teacher to review his or her own situation and understand all the bills and expenses and the bases for them.

As the presentations are made, students should be instructed to use the Cost-of-Living Worksheets to take notes and enter the facts and figures that they will use in their own individual budget. (Models for these forms are found on pages T20–T22 in the Teacher's Edition.) *It should be made clear that certain expenditure classifications will be of no concern to some students.* If a student plans to rent an apartment, figures on buying a house do not need to be recorded. Similarly, a student who would not keep a pet does not need to record any figures for pet care.

At the conclusion of each presentation, a few minutes should be set aside for discussion by the class. As often happens, a student's presentation might not reflect the variety of individual situations. Therefore, the teacher can serve as a moderator for the discussion, bringing out clearly what is important or useful for all the students to know.

When all the presentations have been made, each student should work out a budget report detailing his or her projected living expenses.

This budget report should be graded independently of the oral presentation.

*Utilities*

4. **Heating expenses**
   a. type of furnace or heating equipment (hot water, forced air, steam, wood or coal stove, solar, baseboard)
   b. size of the area to be heated (number of rooms)
   c. estimated cost to heat water
   d. cost of heating bill per month

5. **Water bill**
   a. list major appliances that use water
   b. amount of water used per month
   c. cost of water per month

6. **Electric bill**
   a. list major appliances that use electricity
   b. unit cost of electricity per kilowatt/hour
   c. electricity cost per month

7. **Telephone**
   a. class of service (private line, party line)
   b. number of telephones in use
   c. standard rate for phone service
   d. toll and long-distance calls
   e. estimated total telephone bill per month

8. **Sewer assessment**
   a. garbage pickup, cost per month
   b. cost of sewer assessment (if annual divide by twelve) per month

*Transportation*

9. **Private transportation**
   a. number and kind of vehicles in use
   b. total mileage per month for each vehicle
   c. average miles per gallon for each vehicle
   d. estimated cost of fuel

e. estimated maintenance cost (oil, lubrication, washes, repairs)

f. estimated cost of tolls, parking, and garage rent per month

g. cost of vehicle registration fee (divide by twelve for monthly average)

h. driver license fee (divide by twelve)

i. estimated total cost of private transportation per month

**10. Public transportation**

a. usual means of transportation (bus, subway, train, ferry, taxi)

b. estimated cost of public transportation per month

*Insurance*

**11. Life insurance**

a. individual or group policy

b. kind of policy (term, straight life, 20-payment life, endowment, annuity)

c. monthly premium

**12. Health insurance**

a. individual or group policy

b. Blue Cross, Blue Shield, major medical, dental, private carrier

c. monthly premium (less employer's contribution, if any)

**13. Auto insurance**

a. number and kind of vehicles

b. type of coverage (liability, collision, property damage, comprehensive including fire and theft)

c. monthly premium

**14. Other insurance**

a. disability coverage—monthly premium

b. homeowner's policy—monthly premium

c. personal property insurance (jewelry, furs, musical instruments, cameras, guns)—monthly premium

*Clothing*

**15. Buying clothes**

a. estimated costs of articles of clothing that must normally be replaced (socks, shoes, stockings, underwear, handkerchiefs)

b. estimated cost of new clothes bought (suits, shirts, blouses, dresses, coats, accessories)

c. total cost of clothing per month

**16. Laundering, cleaning, and pressing**

a. self-service laundry use (estimate number of loads times cost per load)

b. estimated dry cleaning and pressing costs

c. average cost per month

*Health Care*

**17. Professional health care**

a. doctor's visits, physical examination, laboratory tests fees

b. hospital and emergency room charges

c. prescription drugs

d. total estimated cost of health care per year divided by twelve

**18. Personal Health Care**

a. aspirin, cold tablets, chemical disinfectants, cough medicines, other

b. adhesive tape, gauze, bandages, first-aid cream, suntan lotion, other

c. total estimated cost per year divided by twelve

**19. Eyeglasses**

a. eye examination

b. frames and lenses

c. total annual cost divided by twelve

20. **Dental care**
    a. examinations, X rays, cleanings, fillings, orthodontal work, other
    b. total estimated cost per year divided by twelve

*Continuing Education*

21. **Education costs**
    a. tuition
    b. books and supplies
    c. room and board
    d. total estimated annual cost divided by twelve

*Entertainment*

22. **Recreational activities**
    a. expenditures for movies, theater, restaurant, dancing, roller-skating, bowling, tennis, golf, other
    b. estimated total monthly outlay for these activities

*Grooming and Toiletries*

23. **Personal grooming**
    a. haircuts, hairstyling (estimate cost per year and divide by twelve)
    b. soap, toothpaste, shampoos, deodorants, after-shave lotions, cosmetics, other
    c. estimated total cost per month

*Taxes*

24. **Income tax**
    a. gross income from all sources (job, bank interest, gifts, allowances)
    b. exemptions
    c. amount of federal, state, and local taxes paid (divide by twelve to get monthly expenditures)

25. **School and property taxes**
    a. assessed valuation if property is owned
    b. total annual taxes divided by twelve

26. **Sales tax**

a. estimated annual purchases of taxable items

b. annual amount of sales tax paid divided by twelve

*Indebtedness*

27. **Auto and personal loans**

a. amount borrowed

b. annual rate of interest

c. total monthly payment (specify amount paid toward principal and amount paid toward interest)

28. **Charge accounts**

a. type and number of charge accounts

b. estimated amount of indebtedness

c. estimated monthly payment (subtract principal from total debt to find interest charges)

*Subscriptions*

29. **Magazines and newspapers**

a. magazines purchased (if subscriptions, divide the annual rate by twelve)

b. daily newspaper cost per month

c. total cost per month

*Contributions and Donations*

30. **Annual contributions and donations (divide by twelve)**

a. church

b. charities (Heart Fund, March of Dimes, American Cancer Society, other)

c. volunteer organizations (fire, rescue squad, other)

d. political contributions

e. community organizations (child care center, hospital, other)

f. total cost per month

*Dues*

31. **Annual dues (divide by twelve)**

a. union
b. team
c. private club
d. nonprofit organization
e. total cost per month

### *Pet Care*

**32. Annual cost of pet care (divide by twelve)**

a. type of pet
b. food and grooming costs
c. veterinarian fees
d. monthly cost

The second part of the Cost-of-Living is to present to the entire class the budget research data each student has assembled. Each student will present his or her data for one or more of the thirty-two budget items. The rest of the class members, using the Budget Work Sheets provided by the teacher, will record all the information they need to complete their own budget information.

It is important to listen carefully to each presentation. You can then gather the specific information needed for each of the thirty-two items.

The third and last part of the Cost-of-Living Report is to complete your own individual budget report and hand it in to the teacher.

Using your notes from class presentations, estimate your own expenditures for each of the items. Summarize your calculations on a separate sheet of paper following the format shown on page 204. (Caution: For your budget report, the original thirty-two items have been reduced to sixteen categories.)

## Budget Report

| *Budget Categories* | *Cost per Month* | *Cost per Year* |
|---|---|---|
| Housing | ________ | ________ |
| Food | ________ | ________ |
| Utilities | ________ | ________ |
| Transportation | ________ | ________ |
| Insurance | ________ | ________ |
| Clothing | ________ | ________ |
| Health Care | ________ | ________ |
| Continuing Education | ________ | ________ |
| Entertainment | ________ | ________ |
| Grooming and Toiletries | ________ | ________ |
| Taxes | ________ | ________ |
| Indebtedness | ________ | ________ |
| Subscriptions | ________ | ________ |
| Contributions and Donations | ________ | ________ |
| Dues | ________ | ________ |
| Pet Care | ________ | ________ |
| ***Total*** | ________ | ________ |

# RELATED READING

## LEARNING THE RIVER

*Mark Twain*

Related Reading

In the short story "Learning the River," Mark Twain describes his life as an apprenticed riverboat pilot who learned from one of the masters of the trade. The theme of the story exemplifies that of the unit—that attitude largely determines success in a job. Mark Twain's responsibility as a riverboat pilot demanded an exact knowledge of both ship and river. His change in attitude was the most important lesson he learned.

Assign the story to the class to read for homework. The questions at the end of the reading selection can be used as a guide for class discussion.

*Mark Twain began his apprenticeship to a Mississippi pilot in 1857 at the age of twenty-two. He was fairly acquainted with this country, having worked as a type setter for various printers and newspapers in most of the large cities. New adventures awaited him in South America, or so he thought.*

What with lying on the rocks four days at Louisville and some other delays, the poor old *Paul Jones* fooled away about two weeks in making the voyage from Cincinnati to New Orleans. This gave me a chance to get acquainted with one of the pilots, and he taught me how to steer the boat, and thus made the fascination of river life more potent than ever for me.

It also gave me a chance to get acquainted with a youth who had taken deck passage*—more's the pity, for he easily borrowed six dollars of me on a promise to return to the boat and pay it back to me the day after we should arrive. But he probably died or forgot, for he never came. It was doubtless the former, since he had said his parents were wealthy and he only traveled deck passage because it was cooler.

I soon discovered two things. One was that a vessel would not be likely to sail for the mouth of the Amazon under ten or twelve years, and the other was that the nine or ten dollars still left in my pocket would not suffice for so impossible an exploration as I had planned, even if I could afford to wait for a ship. Therefore it followed that I must contrive a new

* *deck passage*, steerage passage

career. The *Paul Jones* was now bound for St. Louis. I planned a siege against my pilot, and at the end of three hard days he surrendered. He agreed to teach me the Mississippi River from New Orleans to St. Louis for five hundred dollars, payable out of the first wages I should receive after graduating. I entered upon the small enterprise of "learning" twelve or thirteen hundred miles of the great Mississippi River with the easy confidence of my time of life. If I had really known what I was about to require of my faculties, I should not have had the courage to begin. I supposed that all a pilot had to do was keep his boat in the river, and I did not consider that that could be much of a trick, since it was so wide.

The boat backed out from New Orleans at four in the afternoon, and it was "our watch" until eight. Mr. Bixby, my chief, "straightened her up," plowed her along past the sterns of the other boats that lay at the Levee, and then said, "Here, take her; shave those steamships as close as you'd peel an apple." I took the wheel and my heart went down into my boots; for it seemed to me that we were about to scrape the side off every ship in the line, we were so close. I held my breath and began to claw the boat away from the danger, and I had my own opinion of the pilot who had known no better than to get us into such peril, but I was too wise to express it. In half a minute I had a wide margin of safety intervening between the *Paul Jones* and the ships, and within ten seconds more I was set aside in disgrace and Mr. Bixby was going into danger again and flaying me alive with abuse of my cowardice. I was stung but I was obliged to admire the easy confidence with which my chief loafed from side to side of his wheel and trimmed the ships so closely that disaster seemed ceaselessly imminent. When he had cooled a little he told me that the easy water was close ashore and the current outside, and therefore we must hug the bank up-stream, to get the benefit of the former, and stay well out down-stream, to take advantage of the latter. In my own mind I resolved to be a down-stream pilot and leave the up-streaming to people dead to prudence.

Now and then Mr. Bixby called my attention to certain things. Said he, "This is Six-Mile Point." I assented. It was pleasant enough information but I could not see the bearing of it. I was not conscious that it was a matter of any interest to me. Another time he said, "This is Nine-Mile Point." Later he said, "This is Twelve-Mile Point." They were all about level with the water's edge; they all looked about alike to me; they were monotonously unpicturesque. I hoped Mr. Bixby would change the subject. But no, he would crowd up around a point, hugging the shore with affection, and then say: "The slack water ends here, abreast this bunch of China trees; now we cross over." So he crossed over. He gave me the wheel once or twice but I had no luck. I either came near chipping off the edge of a sugar-plantation, or I yawed too far from shore and so dropped back into disgrace again and got abused.

The watch was ended at last, and we took supper and went to bed. At midnight the glare of a lantern shone in my eyes, and the night watchman said:

"Come, turn out!"

And then he left. I could not understand this extraordinary procedure; so I presently gave up trying to and dozed off to sleep. Pretty soon the watchman was back again, and this time he was gruff. I was annoyed, I said:

"What do you want to come bothering around here in the middle of the night for? Now, as like as not, I'll not get to sleep again to-night."

The watchman said:

"Well, if this ain't good, I'm blessed."

The "off-watch" was just turning in and I heard some brutal laughter from them, and such remarks as "Hello, watchman! ain't the new cub turned out yet? He's delicate, likely. Give him some sugar in a rag and send for the chambermaid to sing 'Rock-a-by Baby,' to him."

About this time Mr. Bixby appeared on the scene. Something like a minute later I was climbing the pilot-house steps with some of my clothes on and the rest in my arms. Mr. Bixby was close behind, commenting. Here was something fresh—this thing of getting up in the middle of the night to go to work. It was a detail in piloting that had never occurred to me at all. I knew that boats ran all night but somehow I had never happened to reflect that somebody had to get up out of a warm bed to run them. I began to fear that piloting was not quite so romantic as I had imagined it was; there was something very real and worklike about this new phase of it.

It was a rather dingy night, although a fair number of stars were out. The big mate was at the wheel and he had the old tub pointed at a star and was holding her straight up the middle of the river. The shores on either hand were not much more than half a mile apart, but they seemed wonderfully far away and ever so vague and indistinct. The mate said:

"We've got to land at Jones's plantation, sir."

The vengeful spirit in me exulted. I said to myself, "I wish you joy of your job, Mr. Bixby; you'll have a good time finding Mr. Jones's plantation such a night as this, and I hope you never *will* find it as long as you live."

Mr. Bixby said to the mate:

"Upper end of the plantation, or the lower?"

"Upper."

"I can't do it. The stumps there are out of water at this stage. It's no great distance to the lower and you'll have to get along with that."

"All right, sir. If Jones don't like it, he'll have to lump it, I reckon."

And then the mate left. My exultation began to cool and my wonder to come up. Here was a man who not only proposed to find this plantation on such a night but to find either end of it you preferred. I dreadfully wanted to ask a question, but I was carrying about as many short answers as my cargo-room would admit of, so I held my peace. All I desired to ask Mr. Bixby was the simple question whether he was ass enough to really imagine he was going to find that plantation on a night when all plantations were exactly alike and all of the same color. But I held in. I used to have fine inspirations of prudence in those days.

Mr. Bixby made for the shore and soon was scraping it, just the same as if it had been daylight. And not only that but singing:

"Father in heaven, the day is declining," etc.

It seemed to me that I had put my life in the keeping of a peculiarly reckless outcast. Presently he turned on me and said:

"What's the name of the first point above New Orleans?"

I was gratified to be able to answer promptly, and I did. I said I didn't know.

"Don't *know*?"

This manner jolted me. I was down at the foot again, in a moment. But I had to say just what I had said before.

"Well, you're a smart one!" said Mr. Bixby. "What's the name of the *next* point?"

Once more I didn't know.

"Well, this beats anything. Tell me the name of *any* point or place I told you."

I studied awhile and decided that I couldn't.

"Look here! What do you start out from, above Twelve-Mile Point, to cross over?"

"I—I—don't know."

"You—you—don't know?" mimicking my drawling manner of speech. "What *do* you know?"

"I—I—nothing, for certain."

"By the great Caesar's ghost, I believe you! You're the stupidest dunderhead I ever saw or ever heard of, so help me Moses! The idea of you being a pilot—*you*! Why, you don't know enough to pilot a cow down a lane."

Oh, but his wrath was up! He was a nervous man, and he shuffled from one side of his wheel to the other as if the floor was hot. He would boil awhile to himself and then overflow and scald me again.

"Look here! What do you suppose I told you the names of those points for?"

I tremblingly considered a moment and then the devil of temptation provoked me to say:

"Well to—to—be entertaining, I thought."

This was a red rag to the bull. He raged and stormed so (he was crossing the river at the time) that I judged it made him blind, because he ran over the steering-oar of a trading-scow. Of course the traders sent up a volley of red-hot profanity. Never was a man so grateful as Mr. Bixby was, because he was brimful and here were subjects who could *talk back*. He threw open a window, thrust his head out, and such an irruption followed as I never had heard before. The fainter and farther away the scowmen's curses drifted, the higher Mr. Bixby lifted his voice and the weightier his adjectives grew. When he closed the window he was empty. You could have drawn a seine through his system and not caught curses enough to disturb your mother with. Presently he said to me in the gentlest way:

"My boy, you must get a little memorandum-book, and every time I tell you a thing, put it down right away. There's only one way to be a pilot and that is to get this entire river by heart. You have to know it just like ABC."

That was a dismal revelation to me, for my memory was never loaded with anything but blank cartridges. However, I did not feel discouraged long. I judged that it was best to make some allowances, for doubtless Mr. Bixby was "stretching." Presently he pulled a rope and struck a few strokes on the big bell. The stars were all gone now and the night was as black as ink. I could hear the wheels churn along the bank but I was not entirely certain that I could see the shore. The voice of the invisible watchman called up from the hurricane-deck:

"What's this, sir?"

"Jones's plantation."

I said to myself, "I wish I might venture to offer a small bet that it isn't." But I did not chirp. I only waited to see. Mr. Bixby handled the engine-bells and in due time the boat's nose came to the land, a torch glowed from the forecastle, a man skipped ashore, a darky's voice on the bank said: "Gimme de k'yarpet-bag, Mass' Jones," and the next moment we were standing up the river again, all serene. I reflected deeply awhile, and then said—but not aloud—"Well, the finding of that plantation was the luckiest accident that ever happened, but it couldn't happen again in a hundred years." And I fully believed it was an accident, too.

By the time we had gone seven or eight hundred miles up the river, I had learned to be a tolerably plucky up-stream steersman, in daylight, and before we reached St. Louis I had made a trifle of progress in night work, but only a trifle. I had a note-book that fairly bristled with the names of towns, "points," bars, islands, bends, reaches, etc., but the information was to be found only in the note-book—none of it was in my head. It made my heart ache to think I had only got half of the river set down, for as our watch was four hours off and four hours on, day and night, there was a long four-hour gap in my book for every time I had slept since the voyage began.

My chief was presently hired to go on a big New Orleans boat and I packed my satchel and went with him. She was a grand affair. When I stood in her pilot-house I was so far above the water that I seemed perched on a mountain, and her decks stretched so far away, fore and aft, below me, that I wondered how I could ever have considered the little *Paul Jones* a large craft. There were other differences too. The *Paul Jones's* pilot-house was a cheap, dingy, battered rattletrap, cramped for room, but here was a sumptuous glass temple: room enough to have a dance in, showy red and gold windowcurtains, an imposing sofa, leather cushions and a back to the high bench where visiting pilots sit to spin yarns and "look at the river," bright, fanciful "cuspidores" instead of a broad wooden box filled with sawdust, nice new oilcloth on the floor, a hospitable big stove for winter, a wheel as high as my head costly with inlaid work, a wire tiller-rope, bright brass knobs for the bells, and a tidy, white-aproned, black "texas-tender," to bring up tarts and ices and coffee during mid-watch, day and night. Now this was "something like," and so I began to take heart once more to believe that piloting was a romantic sort of occupation after all. The moment we were under way I began to prowl about the great steamer and fill myself with joy. She was as clean and as dainty as a drawing-room; when I looked down her long, gilded saloon, it was like gazing through a splendid tunnel; she had an oil-picture, by some gifted sign-painter, on every stateroom door; she glittered with no end of prism-fringed chandeliers; the clerk's office was elegant, the bar was marvelous, and the bar-keeper had been barbered and upholstered at incredible cost. The boiler-deck (*i.e.*, the second story of the boat, so to speak) was as spacious as a church, it seemed to me, so with the forecastle, and there was no pitiful handful of deck-hands, firemen, and roustabouts down there but a whole battalion of men. The fires were fiercely glaring from a long row of furnaces and over them were eight huge boilers! This was unutterable pomp. The mighty engines—but enough of this. I had never felt so fine before. And when I found that the regiment of natty servants respectfully "sir'd" me, my satisfaction was complete.

When I returned to the pilot-house St. Louis was gone and I was lost. Here was a piece of river which was all down in my book but I could make neither head nor tail of it: you understand, it was turned around. I had seen it when coming up-stream but I had never faced about to see how it looked when it was behind me. My heart broke again, for it was plain that I had got to learn this troublesome river *both ways*.

The pilot-house was full of pilots, going down to "look at the river." What is called the "upper river" (the two hundred miles between St. Louis and Cairo, where the Ohio comes in) was low, and the Mississippi changes its channel so constantly that the pilots used to always find it necessary to run down to Cairo to take a fresh look when their boats were to lie in port a week, that is, when the water was at a low stage. A deal of this "looking at the river" was done by poor fellows who seldom had a berth and whose only hope of getting one lay in their being always freshly posted and therefore ready to drop into the shoes of some reputable pilot for a single trip, on account of such pilot's sudden illness or some other necessity. And a good many of them constantly ran up and down inspecting the river, not because they ever really hoped to get a berth but because (they being guests of the boat) it was cheaper to "look at the river" than stay ashore and pay board. In time these fellows grew dainty in their tastes and only infested boats that had an established reputation for setting good tables. All visiting pilots were useful, for they were always ready and willing, winter or summer, night or day, to go out in the yawl and help buoy the channel or assist the boat's pilots in any way they could. They were likewise welcomed because all pilots are tireless talkers when gathered together, and as they talk only about the river they are always understood and are always interesting. Your true pilot cares nothing about anything on earth but the river, and his pride in his occupation surpasses the pride of kings.

We had a fine company of these river inspectors along this trip. There were eight or ten, and there was abundance of room for them in our great pilot-house. Two or three of them wore polished silk hats, elaborate shirt-fronts, diamond breastpins, kid gloves, and patent-leather boots. They were choice in their English, and bore themselves with a dignity proper to men of solid means and prodigious reputation as pilots. The others were more or less loosely clad, and wore upon their heads tall felt cones that were suggestive of the days of the Commonwealth.

I was a cipher in this august company and felt subdued, not to say torpid. I was not even of sufficient consequence to assist at the wheel when it was necessary to put the tiller hard down in a hurry; the guest that stood nearest did that when occasion required—and this was pretty much all the time, because of the crookedness of the channel and the scant water. I stood in a corner, and the talk I listened to took the hope all out of me. One visitor said to another:

"Jim, how did you run Plum Point, coming up?"

"It was in the night there, and I ran it the way one of the boys on the *Diana* told me: started out about fifty yards above the woodpile on the false point and held on the cabin under Plum Point till I raised the reef—quarter less twain*—then straightened up for the middle bar till I got well abreast the old one-limbed cottonwood in the bend, then got my stern on the cottonwood and head on the low place above the point, and came through a-booming—nine and a half."

"Pretty square crossing, ain't it?"

"Yes, but the upper bar's working down fast."

Another pilot spoke up and said:

"I had better water than that and ran it lower down; started out from the false point—mark twain—raised the second reef abreast the big snag in the bend and had quarter less twain."

One of the gorgeous ones remarked:

"I don't want to find fault with your leadsmen but that's a good deal of water for Plum Point, it seems to me."

There was an approving nod all around as this quiet snub dropped on the boaster and "settled" him. And so they went on talk-talk-talking. Meantime, the thing

---

* *quarter less twain*, the depth of the water at that point. On a sounding, or lead, line, used to measure depth, bits of leather called marks are placed at intervals. The first of these, which indicates two fathoms, is called mark twain.

that was running in my mind was, "Now, if my ears hear right, I have not only to get the names of all the towns and islands and bends, and so on by heart, but I must even get up a warm personal acquaintanceship with every old snag and one-limbed cottonwood and obscure wood-pile that ornaments the banks of this river for twelve hundred miles; and more than that, I must actually know where these things are in the dark, unless these guests are gifted with eyes that can pierce through two miles of solid blackness. I wish the piloting business was in Jericho and I had never thought of it."

At dusk Mr. Bixby tapped the big bell three times (the signal to land) and the captain emerged from his drawing room in the forward end of the "texas," and looked up inquiringly. Mr. Bixby said:

"We will lay up here all night, captain."

"Very well, sir."

That was all. The boat came to shore and was tied up for the night. It seemed to me a fine thing that the pilot could do as he pleased, without asking so grand a captain's permission. I took my supper and went immediately to bed, discouraged by my day's observations and experiences. My late voyage's note-booking was but a confusion of meaningless names. It had tangled me all up in a knot every time I had looked at it in the daytime. I now hoped for respite in sleep, but no, it reveled all through my head till sunrise again, a frantic and tireless nightmare.

Next morning I felt pretty rusty and low-spirited. We went booming along, taking a good many chances, for we were anxious to "get out of the river" (as getting out to Cairo was called) before night should overtake us. But Mr. Bixby's partner, the other pilot, presently grounded the boat and we lost so much time getting her off that it was plain the darkness would overtake us a good long way above the mouth. This was a great misfortune, especially to certain of our visiting pilots, whose boats would have to wait for their return, no matter how long that might be. It sobered the pilot-house talk a good deal. Coming up-stream, pilots did not mind low water or any kind of darkness; nothing stopped them but fog. But down-stream work was different; a boat was too nearly helpless with a stiff current pushing behind her, so it was not customary to run down-stream at night in low water.

There seemed to be one small hope, however: if we could get through the intricate and dangerous Hat Island crossing before night, we could venture the rest, for we would have plainer sailing and better water. But it would be insanity to attempt Hat Island at night. So there was a deal of looking at watches all the rest of the day and a constant ciphering upon the speed we were making; Hat Island was the eternal subject; sometimes hope was high and sometimes we were delayed in a bad crossing and down it went again. For hours all hands lay under the burden of this suppressed excitement; it was even communicated to me and I got to feeling so solicitous about Hat Island, and under such an awful pressure of responsibility, that I wished I might have five minutes on shore to draw a good, full, relieving breath and start again. We were standing no regular watches. Each of our pilots ran such portions of the river as he had run when coming up-stream, because of his greater familiarity with it, but both remained in the pilot-house constantly.

An hour before sunset Mr. Bixby took the wheel and Mr. W. stepped aside. For the next thirty minutes every man held his watch in his hand and was restless, silent, and uneasy. At last somebody said, with a doomful sigh:

"Well, yonder's Hat Island—and we can't make it."

All the watches closed with a snap, everybody sighed and muttered something about its being "too bad, too bad—ah, if we could *only* have got here half an hour sooner!" and the place was thick with the atmosphere of disappointment. Some started to go out but loitered, hearing no bell-tap to land. The sun dipped behind the horizon, the boat went on. Inquiring looks passed from one guest to another, and one who had his hand on the door-knob and had turned it, waited, then presently took away his hand and let the knob turn back again. We bore steadily down the bend. More looks exchanged and nods of surprised admiration—but no words. Insensibly the men drew together behind Mr. Bixby, as the sky darkened and one or two dim stars came out. The dead silence and sense of waiting became oppressive. Mr. Bixby pulled the cord and two deep, mellow notes from the big bell floated off on the night. Then a pause, and one more note was struck. The watchman's voice followed, from the hurricane-deck:

"Labboard lead, there! Stabboard lead!"

The cries of the leadsmen began to rise out of the distance and were gruffly repeated by the word-passers on the hurricane-deck.

"M-a-r-k three! M-a-r-k three! Quarter-less-three! Half twain! Quarter twain! M-a-r-k twain! Quarter-less—"

Mr. Bixby pulled two bell-ropes and was answered by faint jinglings far below in the engine-room, and our speed slackened. The steam began to whistle through the gauge-cocks. The cries of the leadsmen went on—and it is a weird sound, always, in the night. Every pilot in the lot was watching now, with fixed eyes, and talking under his breath. Nobody was calm and easy but Mr. Bixby. He would put his wheel down and stand on a spoke, and as the steamer swung into her (to me) utterly invisible marks—for we seemed to be in the midst of a wide and gloomy sea—he would meet and fasten her there. Out of the murmur of half-audible talk one caught a coherent sentence now and then—such as:

"There; she's over the first reef all right!"

After a pause, another subdued voice:

"Her stern's coming down just *exactly* right, by

*George*! Now she's in the marks; over she goes!"

Someone else muttered:

"Oh, it was done beautiful—*beautiful*!"

Now the engines were stopped altogether and we drifted with the current. Not that I could see the boat drift, for I could not, the stars being all gone by this time. This drifting was the dismalest work; it held one's heart still. Presently I discovered a blacker gloom than that which surrounded us. It was the head of the island. We were closing right down upon it. We entered its deeper shadow, and so imminent seemed the peril that I was likely to suffocate, and I had the strongest impulse to do *something*, anything, to save the vessel. But still Mr. Bixby stood by his wheel, silent, intent as a cat, and all the pilots stood shoulder to shoulder at his back.

"She'll not make it!" somebody whispered.

The water grew shoaler and shoaler by the leadsman's cries, till it was down to:

"Eight-and-a-half! E-i-g-h-t feet! E-i-g-h-t feet! Seven-and—"

Mr. Bixby said warningly through his speaking-tube to the engineer:

"Stand by, now!"

"Ay, ay, sir!"

"Seven-and-a-half! Seven feet! Six-and—"

We touched bottom! Instantly Mr. Bixby set a lot of bells ringing, shouted through the tube, "*Now*, let her have it—every ounce you've got!" then to his partner, "Put her hard down! snatch her! snatch her!" The boat rasped and ground her way through the sand, hung upon the apex of disaster a single tremendous instant, and then over she went! And such a shout as went up at Mr. Bixby's back never loosened the roof of a pilot-house before!

There was no more trouble after that. Mr. Bixby was a hero that night, and it was some little time, too, before his exploit ceased to be talked about by rivermen.

Fully to realize the marvelous precision required in

laying the great steamer in her marks in that murky waste of water, one should know that not only must she pick her intricate way through snags and blind reefs, and then shave the head of the island so closely as to brush the overhanging foliage with her stern, but at one place she must pass almost within arm's reach of a sunken and invisible wreck that would snatch the hull timbers from under her if she should strike it—and destroy a quarter of a million dollars' worth of steamboat and cargo in five minutes, and maybe a hundred and fifty human lives into the bargain.

The last remark I heard that night was a compliment to Mr. Bixby, uttered in soliloquy and with unction by one of our guests. He said:

"By the Shadow of Death, but he's a lightning pilot!"

## Discussion Questions

1. *At first Mark Twain figured that the job of piloting a riverboat was romantic and not very difficult. What made him think this? What soon changed his ideas about the job?*

2. *What common mistake did the young apprentice make as certain things were explained to him by Mr. Bixby? What did Mr. Bixby finally have to tell Mark Twain to do?*

3. *Do you think it was an accident that Mr. Bixby was able to find Jones's plantation at night, as Twain believed? If it was not an accident, how do you think he did it?*

4. *What complication in Mark Twain's advancement took place when he and Mr. Bixby changed boats at St. Louis and headed downstream?*

5. *How could you recognize a "true" riverboat pilot, according to the author? What qualities did they all share?*

6. *As Mark Twain began to understand how much there was to piloting a boat on the Mississippi, how did his attitude change?*

7. *In the end Mark Twain developed a great respect for Mr. Bixby and the job of piloting a riverboat. What incident contributed to this? What outstanding professional qualities did Mr. Bixby reveal in this incident?*

# ADDITIONAL READINGS

**Additional Readings**

In addition to the reading included in this unit, there is an annotated suggested reading list.

You may want to assign an additional reading to each member of your class.

Each time a student finishes a reading assignment, it is suggested that a Reading Report Form be completed and turned in to the teacher.

Masters, Edgar Lee, ***"Judge Selah Lively"***

Consider the reasons we elevate ourselves or work to achieve prominence and power. In this poem a little man aspires to a higher position. But his motives ought to be examined carefully.

Garland, Hamlin, ***"Under the Lion's Paw"***

To own a small plot of land free and clear has been the aim of many humble and hardworking people. In this short story Haskins and his wife, bargaining in simple good faith, take on terrible burdens to make the farm pay for itself. When the time comes to buy the farm, they find that the price has gone up—as a result of their own labors.

Sinclair, Upton, ***The Jungle***

Jurgis Rudkus was a Lithuanian peasant who came to America shortly after the turn of the century. He had heard that one could find freedom and grow rich working in the stockyards near a city called Chicago. What he found was brutal exploitation of the workers, and conditions of filth, poverty, disease, death, and despair. This novel, an exposure of the labor and sanitary conditions in the Chicago stockyards, caused a national furor in 1906, leading swiftly to the passage of pure food laws. But as the disappointed author later wrote, "I aimed at the public's heart and by accident I hit it in the stomach." Nobody cared about "wage slavery," only contaminated meat.

Miller, Arthur, ***All My Sons***

During a war soldiers die, others mourn their loss, and still others make money. This play tells how Joe Keller made lots of money and in the process may have caused the death of his own son, a pilot in the air force, as well as others who depended on the aircraft engine parts he manufactured. The tightly constructed drama tests the limits of the observation that "lying, fraud—and in this case war profiteering—are an essential part of American big business."

Saroyan, William, ***"Where I Come From People Are Polite"***

This short story, written in a lighter vein, tells of a young man who one day quits his job, borrows a motorbike, and goes off on a long ride. His behavior and his attitude are entirely unconventional. The reactions of others in the story raise the question of what it means to conduct oneself in a businesslike manner.

Williams, William Carlos, ***"In Chains"***

What choices or chances do any of us really have in a world dominated by corruption? What must we learn in our state of helplessness before we finally give up hope? This little poem tells about what probably keeps most of us going.

Peter, Laurence J., ***The Peter Prescription***
Peter, Laurence J., and Raymond Hull, ***The Peter Principle: Why Things Always Go Wrong***

"In a hierarchy every employee tends to rise to his or her level of incompetence." This is the Peter Principle. Not to be taken too seriously, the first of these two books explains why so many people do not seem to be able to do their jobs and why so little work is accomplished. The second book with far less tongue-in-cheek aims at putting matters right by fulfilling one's best potential and avoiding the pitfalls of incompetence.

Allen, Frederick Lewis, ***"Horatio Alger, Jr."***

You will be amply rewarded if you will only work hard, save your money, keep yourself straight, and use your head at all times. . . . If you believe this you are still being influenced by a way of thinking generated over a hundred years ago by Alger, a writer of popular boys' books. This biographical essay analyzes the author and his rags-to-riches stories in an attempt to account for the remarkable survival of their oversimplified lessons in business economics and the philosophy of work.

**Unit VI Introduction**
Discuss the Samuel Johnson quote with the class. Ask the students which kind of knowledge is more important. Have them explain their answers.

**Unit VI Theme**
Personal Growth: evaluating progress in career planning

# 6 What Have I Learned About Myself and the Career that Interests Me?

"Knowledge is of two kinds: we know a subject ourselves, or we know where we can find information upon it."
**Samuel Johnson**

*What progress have I made in planning for my future?*

# A CASE STUDY

## POLLY'S REMINISCENCES

**Polly's Reminiscences**

Polly, a recent college graduate in home economics, has been working at her first permanent job for five weeks. Before leaving her office late Friday afternoon, she thinks back into the past to recall the events that led her to her present position.

This story summarizes many of the activities and projects that the students have been assigned to accomplish in this course.

Assign the Case Study for homework.

Polly arranged the scattered papers into separate piles on her desk. It was 5:10 P.M. on a Friday, and everybody else had left the building. The mounds of paper were labeled in her mind as Family Counseling, Financial Advisories, Media Releases, and Meetings. These were matters to be taken up next week, the fifth week of her first permanent full-time job. She was the new county agent in home economics at the Farm and Home Center in the valley.

Polly was pleased with herself because this was the kind of work she had imagined for herself when she was a teenager. It was also the beginning of the career she had mapped out for herself as she went to college. Her thoughts drifted back to the career report she had had to do in ninth grade. The report was part of an English assignment. She had been learning how to research a topic and to organize her findings in a written report. She had chosen the field of zoology to research, mainly because it was her hobby at that time. She had her own microscope and loved to study the small swimming creatures she found in the ponds near her home. She took out school library books that told about these tiny organisms. From other books she learned about careers in microbiology. She sent for pamphlets that described the work of the zoologist. She talked to people in the county health offices who worked in the field of environmental sanitation. She visited a laboratory that conducted experiments in bacteriology related to pest control. Her report earned her a 95, and she had a better understanding of the kinds of jobs open to people who train in the fields of zoology and microbiology.

Later she changed her mind about her first career interest. She had been learning more about herself—about what she would be best qualified to do. In tenth grade she thought she might like to be a child psychologist. She was earning extra money baby-sitting at that time, and some children she was caring for seemed neglected, perhaps even abused. She felt sorry for them and wanted to help them. But further inquiry made her aware that the preparation for this work was long and that the field was overcrowded. She also learned that counseling included parents as well as children. That seemed to be more than she was ready to undertake.

Then one day—she recalled it was when she was in the eleventh grade—she went to her family doctor for a routine physical examination. As she sat down later with him, he casually asked her about her plans after graduation from high school. She told him about her hobbies and the things she was interested in, about her concern with the energy problem, the environment, and family living. She was interested in consumer buying habits as they were affected by advertising. Her doctor suggested that home economics might be a good field for her to look into—perhaps teaching. The more she thought about it, the more it made sense. She was good at budgeting. She thought she would like to work with families. She liked to plan things and to interest other people in her ideas.

Polly remembered that she had had a glorified image of herself as a leading consumer advocate who would tell people everywhere what to buy and what not to buy. Maybe she would even become a television celebrity, the outstanding authority in the field of consumerism. *Consumerism*—the word even had a special magic attached to it! Polly knew she would have to do more than daydream in planning her future career, however. Taking a practical approach, she talked to the home economics teachers at school. They told her about their work as teachers and helped her to understand more about the field in general, including the work involved and the jobs a person might enter after college. That night she decided to begin a career file. The file folders she labeled were Careers in Home Economics, Consumer Protection, Family Health and Safety, Home Management, Interior Decorating, Women in Society, and Job Hunting. She was beginning to formulate some definite career ideas, and the next step was to think about a college.

She remembered the days she had spent browsing through the college bulletins her guidance counselor had given her to look at. It had been a difficult choice to make because, according to the catalogs, so many colleges seemed to offer just what she wanted. But then, by the aid of a machine-scored preference questionnaire, she narrowed her choice of schools to one. It was a small school in New Hampshire—about 2,800 students, mostly women. And the school was recognized for its excellent program in home economics.

Polly recalled how she had arranged for a two-day visit that spring and fell in love with the school as soon as she saw it. The campus was located about two miles from a small New England town, and the buildings were informal and inviting. She met and spoke with the dean and several of the teachers. Students were enthusiastic about the programs and activities they were involved in. Polly knew it would be a good place for her to **matriculate.**

She thought about her sophomore year at college. It had been a year of decision for her. She remembered how hard it was for her to select a major. Her ideas were shifting more and more toward financial counseling. She sat down one afternoon with her adviser and they worked out an individualized degree program for her remaining two years. Her major was to include consumerism, home management and finance, and family relations.

That summer she worked for the credit union of her father's company. She was in the customer service department. Her job was to answer questions about mortgages, car and boat loans, and vacation loans for employees. She spent a good deal of her time on the phone. She also typed letters and occasionally advised employees who came into her office with financial problems and questions. The experience was valuable and reinforced her career objectives, providing a practical base for her college program.

Polly recalled her senior year at college. She had been very busy. She took a course in management because she was interested in the problems of organization; she also took a course in COBOL, computer language, because she felt she might need it. She took additional courses in energy alternatives and public relations. She was elected president of her college's chapter of the American Home Economics Association. It was at this time that she began writing letters to government agencies, service organizations, banks, and large corporations that could help her understand where and how she might become employed. She added many good leads to her job-hunting file and rewrote parts of her résumé.

In March or April when she was home for spring recess, she saw a position announcement posted in the state employment office. The job was for a cooperative extension agent in home economics. The job was in her own county. She read through the duties and responsibilities and checked the qualifications. She took down all the information and wrote that night for an application.

Polly remembered the contents of the letter she had received from the cooperative extension in response to her inquiry. There was a three-page position description and an application blank. The job summary read ". . . to serve as energy and financial management specialist. . . . plan, coordinate, implement, and evaluate educational programs. . . . coordinate these program efforts with county and community agencies and businesses and act as contact person for mass media." The duties of the job were divided roughly into 40 percent for energy programs, 30 percent for home financial management, 20 percent for human development and family planning, and 10 percent for publicity and media. The agent would work under the county administrative director and supervise a secretarial staff. The person hired would be a program leader and would work with other agents.

Polly came to the section on qualifications: ". . . a bachelor's degree in home economics from an accredited institution, a working background in financial management, an understanding of mass media skills, and some experience in planning educational programs related to energy and family resource management." Polly filled out the application carefully and returned it with a résumé and a simple covering letter. It was several weeks before she received an answer. Then one day about a month before she was to graduate, she received a letter addressed to her at her college. The supervising director of the center wanted her to come in for an interview. He suggested that she telephone for an appointment as soon as she was able. Polly phoned the next day.

She vividly recalled the interview. It went well. Within a week she was informed by mail that the job was hers.

Polly smiled as she remembered the excitement of getting that letter. Her planning, hard work, and research had certainly paid off. She was on her way—nothing could stop her now. She was working at a job that she felt suited her best; the future certainly looked bright.

Polly stood up and rolled the chair under her desk. She looked around her office one more time before turning off the lights and locking the door. Although the weekend had hardly begun, Polly was already looking forward to Monday morning when she would be back at her desk meeting the challenges of her still relatively new position.

## Thinking It Through

**Discussion Questions**
Use the questions in the section Thinking It Through as a guide for a class discussion of the Case Study.

1. *How did Polly go about learning about herself?*
2. *Did chance play a part in Polly's final career decision? Explain your answer.*
3. *Discuss the steps Polly took in arriving at her final career choice.*
4. *Do you think Polly is fully satisfied with her career choice? Explain your answer.*
5. *Do you think it is important for a student to plan his or her career? Why?*
6. *What steps have you taken in planning your career?*

# REPORT PROJECT

## PERSONAL ESSAY VI

***Introduction*** This assignment is the culminating activity for the entire course. You are to evaluate and summarize what you have accomplished this year in the course Putting English to Work for Work.

***Directions*** Write out in essay form the answers to the following questions. Respond to all points of the outline in complete sentences without using the letters or numbers. Each letter in the outline should be used to develop a paragraph in your essay.

### Outline

**A.** What printed matter have you consulted to find out about the career you are interested in? (Include books, magazines, newspapers, catalogs, manuals, circulars, notices.) Give exact titles whenever possible.

**B.** What people have you spoken to about the work you are interested in? Give their names and job titles.

1. relatives, friends, acquaintances
2. people who are working in the career field
3. personnel directors or placement officers
4. teachers, professors, admissions or recruitment officers, guidance counselors
5. students taking courses in the field

**C.** What meetings or programs have you attended that relate to the career you are interested in? (Include conventions, conversations, job clinics, lectures, films or television documentaries, employment days.) If

**Personal Essay VI**

This essay asks the students to evaluate the experience they have gained by completing the reports, projects, and activities found in this book. Since the essay is the culminating activity for the program, it could be used as a final examination for the course.

At the completion of the course, the teacher should return the career file folders to the students for their future reference and use. Each folder will now contain an assortment of valuable career insights, along with a sampling of the skills and knowledge it takes to secure a rewarding job and a successful working future.

you attended a conference or convention, give the title, when and where it was held, the sponsor, and the keynote speaker.

**D.** In general what have you learned about yourself and the career that interests you?

1. What is most attractive to you about the field or job?
2. What are some of the things you do not like but feel you can live with?
3. What kinds of sacrifices are you willing to make to get what you want in a career?
4. What alternatives have you considered?

**E.** What definite plans have you made to get into the field of your choice? Give the exact nature of the commitment.

1. What commitments have you secured?
   - **a.** written or verbal statement indicating you will be hired
   - **b.** letter of admission to a formal program of post-secondary studies
   - **c.** enlistment agreement for some branch of the service
2. What commitments will you be seeking in the near future?

**F.** What would you tell others of your experiences in investigating and planning for a career?

1. What mistakes have you made that others could avoid?
2. What has been your most rewarding experience to date?
3. What would your parting advice be?

**G.** How has this course helped you to focus on your career goals? Explain.

■□■□■

# APPENDIX

## ADDITIONAL READINGS

*The Adding Machine*, Elmer Rice · Unit 3

*Ah, Wilderness!*, Eugene O'Neill · Unit 1

*All My Sons*, Arthur Miller · Unit 5

*The Art of Job Hunting*, Dean B. Peskin · Unit 4

*Babbitt*, Sinclair Lewis · Unit 3

*Beyond the Horizon*, Eugene O'Neill · Unit 3

"Cassandra," Edwin Arlington Robinson · Unit 3

*Death of a Salesman*, Arthur Miller · Unit 2

*Demian*, Hermann Hesse · Unit 1

"Dolor," Theodore Roethke · Unit 3

*Go Hire Yourself an Employer*, Richard K. Irish · Unit 4

"Horatio Alger, Jr.," Frederick Lewis Allen · Unit 5

*How to Find a Job*, Darold E. Larson · Unit 4

*How to Get a Better Job*, Austin Marshall · Unit 4

*How to Succeed in the Business of Finding a Job*, Phoebe Taylor · Unit 4

*How You Can Get the Job You Want*, Glenn L. Gardiner · Unit 4

"In Chains," William Carlos Williams · Unit 5

*Job Strategy*, Allan Rood · Unit 4

"Judge Selah Lively," Edgar Lee Masters · Unit 5

## AUTHORS OF RELATED READINGS



## CASE STUDIES

# GLOSSARY

***accredited*** Commissioned, authorized, or certified. A school or college is accredited, usually by the state, as having met all the formal requirements for proper operation. (Unit 5)

***affiliation*** Membership in or connection with an organization. (Unit 4)

***alternatives*** Other possibilities. (Unit 2)

***aptitude*** The capability or capacity for doing something; sometimes an inherent ability (born in you as a special gift or talent), sometimes an acquired one. (Unit 1)

***assets*** As related to employment, the skills, knowledge, and traits you have that demonstrate you can do the job. (Unit 1)

***avocation*** A sideline, not one's regular or principal line of work (vocation). (Unit 2)

***career source*** Any central organization or agency that offers helpful information related to a career in some particular field. For example, information about sales can be obtained from the Sales Executive Club of New York; about the armed forces, from local recruitment offices; about music, from the American Federation of Musicians. (*Note:* Listings of these organizations are often available at high school guidance offices; colleges; libraries; and federal, state, and county offices.) (Unit 3)

***collective bargaining*** The process by which an employer and representatives of employees sit down and discuss a work contract. (Unit 5)

***commitment***[1] A pledge or promise to engage yourself, usually to serve the needs of the community. (Unit 1)

***commitment***[2] A contract or agreement usually with present employer. (Unit 4)

***compensated employment*** Work for which one is paid. (Unit 1)

***competent*** Possessing the necessary skill, knowledge, or experience to do the job. (Unit 5)

***continuing education*** Education sought for its own sake and pursued out of personal interest. (Unit 2)

***correspondence course*** An educational course taken by mail. (Unit 5)

***dependent*** One who depends directly upon you for financial support. (Unit 4)

***disabilities*** Physical limitations or handicaps such as hearing and visual impairments, missing limbs, mental retardation; medical problems such as epilepsy and diabetes. (Units 1 and 4)

***employability rating*** Your standing in the job market at any given time; all the factors that relate to your competing successfully with others for any given job. (Unit 1)

***employment experience*** Jobs for which you were paid and all periods of unemployment. (Unit 4)

***employment risk*** A factor used in evaluating an applicant or candidate for a job. (It costs an employer a considerable amount of money to hire and train someone for a job. If the employee is not satisfactory, it costs the employer still more to hire and train someone else. The employer will try to minimize the risk. Like any investor, the employer is looking for a good return on his or her investment.) (Unit 1)

***exemptions*** Tax deductions for persons who depend upon you for support; also granted for people over 65 years of age and for physical disabilities. (Unit 5)

***exploitation*** An unjust or improper use of another person for one's own profit or advantage. (Unit 5)

***extracurricular activities*** Activities other than school subjects or courses—teams, clubs, volunteer work in or out of school. (Unit 4)

***FICA*** The acronym representing the first letter of each word in the Federal Insurance Contributions Act. It refers to a deduction listed on your paycheck stub, that the employer takes from the wages paid to an employee and sends directly to the federal government to provide a pension fund for retired workers. (Unit 5)

***formal education*** Schooling for which some sort of credit is awarded. (Unit 2)

***fringe benefits*** The extra returns beyond salary—such as medical plans, dental plans, life insurance, and illness allowances—that goes with the job. (Unit 3)

***future demands*** The job openings anticipated for the future in any given category of work; based in part on past and present employment trends and on developments that are likely to affect the labor market of the future. For example, the demand for skilled technicians in the energy resources field is expected to increase steadily into the final decade of this century. (Unit 3)

***garnishee*** To withhold money from one's salary to pay off an existing debt. (Unit 5)

***gross pay*** Full salary before any deductions have been taken. (Unit 5)

***hierarchy*** The ranking of positions within an organization. (Unit 5)

***high school equivalency*** A high school diploma attained by passing a special examination. (Unit 5)

***immediate supervisor*** The person to whom you report while on the job. (Unit 4)

***IRS*** Initials of the Internal Revenue Service; the Federal Income Tax Bureau to which you pay your federal taxes. (Unit 5)

***job security*** Freedom from fear of losing your job. (Unit 1)

***liable*** Legally responsible. (Unit 5)

***life-style*** The life one leads from day to day, often built around one's work situation. (Unit 2)

***marital status*** Whether you are single, married, separated, divorced, or widowed. (Unit 4)

***matriculate*** To enroll in a program of studies leading to a degree. (Unit 5)

***outbuildings*** Buildings such as barns, garages, or sheds that are not connected to the main dwelling. (Unit 2)

***pecuniary gain*** Financial gain; money in the sense of realizing a profit or amassing wealth. (Unit 2)

***personal reference*** People who know you well and will speak for your talents, abilities, or character. (Usually close personal friends of the family; doctors, ministers, teachers, but *not* relatives.) (Unit 4)

***post-secondary education*** Education or training beyond high school. (Unit 5)

***previous address*** The place where you lived before moving to your present or permanent address. (Unit 4)

***profile*** A biographical sketch or cross-section of a person's way of life. (Unit 2)

***referral*** How or through whom you found out about the job. (Unit 4)

***relevant*** Appropriate, applicable, pertinent; being directly related to your application for employment. (Unit 4)

***relocate*** Move elsewhere, often for or with the job. (Unit 2)

***résumé*** A concise profile or written record of what a job-seeker has to offer an employer. The résumé is used as an introduction and later to provide a focus for a personal interview. (Units 1 and 4)

***rotational work schedule*** Working hours that could vary by the day, the week, or the month. (Unit 4)

***rural*** Country, not suburban or city. (Unit 2)

***scholarship*** A sum of money available to qualified persons upon proper application to help pay for their education or research. (Unit 5)

***security data*** Any record of arrests or convictions. (*Note:* Information of this kind does not necessarily keep you from getting the job. It should be reported accurately and objectively whenever and wherever called for.) (Unit 4)

***shiftwork*** Working hours ranging around the clock, for example: 8 to 4, 4 to 12, or 12 to 8. (Unit 4)

***significant*** Having meaning, important. (Unit 4)

***Social Security*** A system set up by the federal government to provide a pension fund for retired workers or dependents. The employer deducts a percentage of the employee's wages and sends it directly to this pension fund. (Unit 5)

***spouse*** A husband or wife. (Unit 4)

***stop-gap job*** Any fill-in position taken only to remain employed while preparing or waiting for an opening in the field of your primary career interest. (Unit 3)

***subsistence*** Existence; the minimum (as of food and shelter) necessary to support one's self or family. (Unit 2)

***surname*** Last name; family name. (Unit 4)

***take-home pay*** Net pay after all deductions have been taken out. (Unit 5)

***vocational skill*** A specialized, work-related skill in demand and marketable and usable in connection with some particular job; usually acquired through specialized training. Examples are typing, welding, hairdressing, carpentry. (Unit 1)

***vocational-technical school*** Any school where some specialized skill or trade is taught. (Unit 4)

***W-2 Form*** An employer's statement of how much tax was withheld from an employee's annual salary. This statement is sent to the employee in January; it includes the amount of tax withheld during the preceding year. (Unit 5

***work environment*** The surroundings and conditions that accompany the job. (Unit 3)

# INDEX

1 2 3 4 5 6 7 8 9 10-RRD-85 84 83 82 81